WHERE YOUR
HAPPINESS
HIDES

WHERE YOUR
HAPPINESS
HIDES

22 Beliefs and **1** simple code
that will transform your life

Mark Worthington

BALBOA.PRESS
A DIVISION OF HAY HOUSE

Balboa Press books may be ordered through booksellers or by contacting:

Balboa Press
A Division of Hay House
1663 Liberty Drive
Bloomington, IN 47403
www.balboapress.com.au
AU TFN: 1 800 844 925 (Toll Free inside Australia)
AU Local: (02) 8310 7086 (+61 2 8310 7086 from outside Australia)

Cover and Illustrations by Azari da Roza | Diagrams and Pictures by Bill Shapter
Edited by Zena Shapter

Prepared for publication by Andrea Gussy.

ISBN: 978-1-9822-9410-6 (sc)
ISBN: 978-1-9822-9411-3 (e)

Print information available on the last page.

Balboa Press rev. date: 12/14/2022

CONTENTS

This book is dedicated to those who have taught me much about life and myself and helped me escape the unhappy trance in which I once languished. They include:

- *Charles Kovess, Australia's passion provocateur, who taught me the power of beliefs and how to be a stronger man.*
- *Paul Joseph, a Sydney-based teacher, who challenged my mind to understand the truths of the universe that I was ready to hear.*
- *Ava Leonard, a Sydney-based holistic wellness specialist, who helped me see, and release, hundreds of personal limiting beliefs through her amazing intuition.*
- *Lucy Phillips, an extraordinary woman, who showed me the power of feelings and forgiveness, and how to ground them into everyday life.*
- *Mark Hunter, a coach and communications specialist, who taught me the power of authentic self-expression and self-belief.*
- *Sue Thompson, who brought me access to new ideas, beyond my consciousness at the time, allowing me to apply these to my life to great effect.*

In all this, the greatest teachers in my life were my parents. Their loving kindness, devotion and imperfections, which we all possess, allowed me to see mine and, at the same time, witness the perfection of love and the power of knowing that I was always enough, regardless of what I achieved or owned.

Mark Worthington

INTRODUCTION: HAPPINESS IS YOUR CHOICE

If anyone ever asked me what I wanted in life, for me or my family, I always responded with 'to be happy'. Isn't that what life's all about?

At least this is what I told myself, but for most of my life I was pretty unhappy. At best my life was mediocre, until a few years ago. To the outside world I was regarded as a success on many measures – I had two properties, five wonderful children, a good income, a professional profile, a 21-year relationship and, from the outside, what appeared to be a fit, healthy body. So why did I feel so unfulfilled and dull?

In my 50s, I worked out the answer and it was simple: I had chosen a life that in many ways I didn't want, but felt I needed to endure to satisfy others. It took me a long time to see that there was a better way to exist, one that would bring me joy and fun, one I now find blissful every waking hour of the day.

My life has gone from awful to awesome, and all it took was a choice – a choice to no longer suffer, to no longer settle for mediocrity, and to no longer live my life for the sake of others. I also allow others to live their lives without my judgement or control, because I have learnt that there is no love in controlling or judging another's life. I now live for me, and it is so exciting and relaxing at the same time. I'm not selfish, just self-centred – in a good way! Whereas life once felt like I was stuck in a field of prickles and weeds, it now feels like I'm skipping through a field of sunflowers under a big, beautiful blue sky.

I wonder if you can relate to any of these situations in your life?

- I had a string of busy jobs that always seemed to demand more and more from me. I worked long hours out of obligation.
- I had mortgages that kept me awake at night in a state of worry.
- I felt time poor and never seemed to have time for myself, unless I got up early and sacrificed sleep to exercise. I was fit but not fun.
- I was consistently busy looking after my house in Sydney and driving kids to their activities, such as dance lessons and sports.
- I cared about my job title and how big my house was, yet I said money didn't matter to me. I was in a weird state of denial about my priorities.

- I limited my life to safe activities with people I trusted because I didn't fully trust people until I got to know them well.
- I had two messy divorces, and my wives and I lost significant wealth as a result.
- I experienced multiple ailments, including a significant muscle disorder and a bad back for over 30 years, which saw me constantly visiting doctors. These expensive visits helped but never solved my pain, because at the end of the day they were caused by stress – yes, by me. I learned to disown my pain, and as a result I kind of disembodied myself. So I felt fit but fatigued and unwell.
- I didn't see enough of my friends, and they complained that I was somewhat antisocial. They were right, because I believed I was too busy to have fun, and that I had to be serious to be successful.
- I lived for weekends and holidays, spending far too much money on expensive holidays each year to try and escape my life.
- I became a needy partner. With few friendships, I relied too much on my respective partners for company.
- I had no dreams because I was in survival mode: stressed and trying to play it safe so that I lost nothing. I protected what I had out of fear, even though it brought me great stress and ultimately led me to lose exactly what I thought I needed to protect.
- I looked forward to having enough money to stop work and retire. Doing nothing one day, sadly, had become a key goal in life.
- I enjoyed few hobbies of my own, because my life was dedicated to making sure my other family members were happy.
- I juggled my responsibilities as a father, worker, and homeowner, determined to be perfect but never measuring up to this need in me. This was tough to say the least.
- I spent too much money thinking it would give me happiness and buy me love. I hadn't bargained on the debt I accumulated being such a burden.
- I saw my role as a provider to others, so most of the money I earned went to paying for their lifestyles while I flogged myself in the office, often deep into the night.
- I rarely expressed how I felt. I feared my own emotions and bottled them up inside my tight, stressed body, refusing to admit that they existed.
- I rarely saw my family of origin, because both my brothers were in the same rat race as me. The badge of honour of 'being busy' sat squarely on my chest.
- I was so obsessed with time that I had a clock in every room of my house and at least eight watches. They measured the life that was ticking away, like a time bomb with a shortening fuse.
- I thought it must be my fault if those I loved or served were unhappy, such was my conditioned desire to keep the peace at all costs.
- I found it hard to meet new people because I feared I wasn't worthy of their attention.

Looking back, I was not happy. Some keywords that describe my old life capture the extent of the unhappiness and emptiness I felt:

Obligated	Heavy
Stressed	Competitive
Caged	Tired
Constricted	Unloved
Serious	Inauthentic
Worried	Self-loathing
Self-sacrificing	Not-enough
Disconnected	Controlled

All these feelings swelled inside me daily, but I suppressed them because I thought I was living the life I was meant to live. I was a great success, I kept telling myself, one of the lucky ones in this world. Right?

After my second divorce in 2016, however, I quite frankly imploded with pain. I felt like a massive failure. I couldn't seem to forgive myself, or others, for the pain I was going through. My life wasn't supposed to turn out this way. How could it? I had done everything I had been taught to do. I had always won. How could a perfect person like me lose? I was shattered and I cracked, even visiting a psychologist for six months in the hope of escaping the pain and finding answers.

I cried myself to sleep at night, even though my upbringing told me I wasn't supposed to do that. I steeled myself each day and pretended to be 'over it' and in a good place. As I entered my office, I would take on a totally different persona, like an actor on a set playing a part. I couldn't be seen as a loser after all; that would cost me my reputation and my job.

The price of authenticity in this world can be very high.

But the intensity of my pain eventually proved to be my friend not my foe. I reached a point where I said to myself, 'enough is enough, this pain has to end! I'm done with it'.

My roller coaster of a 'successful' life had given me great opportunities and advantages, but also great disappointments and anguish. Many of the things I thought I had achieved were ultimately taken away from me. Many of the things I was attached to and feared losing, I lost.

Eventually I knew that I needed to understand why my life was a train wreck, especially when I had followed the script like a 'good boy' all my life. I decided to investigate, and what I have found has filled my heart with joy and led me to a new and wonderful life that I truly love. I can't get enough of it, and now I want to live forever!

What I discovered was how much of my life was preprogrammed. My subconscious thinking, that I wasn't even aware of, made me do things I really didn't like or mean to do, but I was like someone who was hypnotised. I did some dumb things to satisfy my crazy inner voice. If there had been an Olympics for this, I would have made the finals!

I had never taken the time to consider who I was and what I wanted out of life. I was on a treadmill. I was a cookie that had been cut to satisfy the desires of others. How could I express the qualities of the real me, when it was locked away in a dungeon and ignored? I had the key to the dungeon in my hand, but I never understood what lock it fitted.

The real Mark was a mystery, even to me.

Now, obviously I'm a man, not a woman, and I observe that the expectations placed on women can be very different to men. Whereas men can often feel an obligation to provide, to suppress their emotions and be strong, women can traditionally feel pressured to be attractive, nurturing and supportive, and many men and women now carry the burden of both paradigms. All these things are frankly not fair, and have left many, particularly those of my generation, distorted and constrained. Don't we all deserve real change, from a world of perceived obligation to a world of freedom of choice?

Determined to find the answers, I took on my pain. I faced it and its many emotions. Instinctively I knew my pain contained the answers. It was time to listen to feelings and not suppress them. And every time I faced the pain and went through it, not around it, I felt lighter the next day. Sometimes these investigations were difficult, but I loved every step because it made me lighter and brighter, and every day more sunflowers burst into my life. Once I came to see that I was always enough, my life ceased to be not enough and exploded instead with a fulfilling lightness that fills me still. This triggered a joy in my heart that I had never previously allowed myself to experience. Whereas before my life had felt like a boring movie that I hoped would hurry up and end, now my heart felt as if it were directing and acting an adventure movie! I didn't want it to end!

There is a common expression that we all need to take time out to 'smell the roses'. In the life I used to live I rarely gave myself any such opportunities or even let myself have much fun. I openly admit I had lost my ability to truly play. But now I could play in a field of sunflowers and smell them each and every day.

My self-investigations also revealed to me people who could help me know myself better and get lighter. This accelerated my growth. As I began to know more, so I began to grow more. I owe those people a great deal, for their wisdom has changed my life.

Every step reinforced the possibilities that lay ahead. I was getting to know myself better each day and release the chains that my choices had locked around my legs. I found the keys to freedom, self-awareness and feeling the truth in my heart.

The closer I got to the real me, and the more family and societal expectations I dispelled, the more I began to feel free. I started to like myself, and eventually this friendship turned into love.

The more aware I became, the more fulfilled I became. Every day I got happier as I introduced myself to my-real-SELF, and the more intimately I got to know myself the less I needed from outside myself to feel contented and at peace.

Frankly, I was once obsessed by making money and being important. Wow, the liberation that came with letting those things go was incredible. The size of my house no longer worried me, I didn't care about my job title, and I didn't need to be important as long as the things I did mattered to me and were enjoyable. I know now that I matter, that love matters, that relationships matter, and that being happy in life really is the only correct answer to that age-old question.

Over the last five years I have changed my life completely. I'm still called Mark but now Mark truly is a different person. I have learned to manage my time and not let it manage me. I have learned the importance of fun in my life, and living from a place of wonder, not worry. This has become my catch-cry and it's so awesome!

I trust my feelings and I express them. I don't need to win if I have fun in the contest. The list goes on and, if you read-on, you will discover so much more, and perhaps it will shed light on your own path.

I rarely used to smell the roses, but these days I give myself the luxury of more sleep, and I go to the beach regularly because I have worked out that I love it. Sitting on a beach with the breeze in my face, watching the turquoise patterns of the ocean and the power of the waves, it gives me so much pleasure and so much peace. I love spending time in nature, sitting in the sun, watching the birds, or walking in the bush. I am so different, and it is so liberating to finally be me. No need to achieve every minute of the day. Even alone, I am content.

I have written this book because I wanted to, and it feels so much better to me than being an accountant. That's not a dig at accountants! They do a very significant job; it just wasn't for me any longer.

I haven't been sick for years. Stress has become a thing of the past. These days I have learned to trust my intuition, to think for myself and to do what I want to do in my life. Every morning when I throw open the curtains I can't wait to see what the day brings. Life is sunny and light because, no matter what happens, I will choose to be happy and learn from what takes place. I have learnt the power of choice and the fact that I own my own life, nobody else!

Happiness is a habit as well as a choice. Finding it can take a bit of effort, but it's worth it. Your heart will sing once you let it play its own tune!

If you can relate to any aspect of my life, or the painful feelings and experiences I endured, I urge you to read on because what this book has to share may well change your life for the better too. What do you have to lose, other than some unhappiness?

Ask yourself: why you are living? If being happy is important to you then reconsider the life you are currently choosing. This will involve reconsidering the beliefs you hold, the words you speak, the things you do and the feelings you may be ignoring. A lighter, brighter way of feeling is within reach for anyone who dares to look for it! It may have been hiding from you, but it is closer than you think, and you'll be surprised where it's hiding.

With so many people looking for happiness and unable to find it, is it any wonder our world is so full of turmoil and pain? But that doesn't stop you from taking this journey of self-discovery for your own benefit. How you feel is your experience of life day-by-day, moment by moment. So, the more people who feel joy and happiness, the more those feelings will spread around the societies in which we all live. Happiness is a habit and, as it spreads, so it will change the habitats we all live in and hopefully enjoy.

Once you've read this book, I believe you'll know where to find happiness. The journey to turn over the rock weighing down your happiness can get interesting, even addictive. But as you begin to experience the happiness that was previously hiding, you will know how to be in a state of joy every day, and you will develop new beliefs to sustain your euphoria. You'll be like a light globe that's been turned on by life and is impossible to turn off, no matter what happens.

Once attained, self-awareness cannot normally be lost; so, as you start to know who you are, the real you will continue to grow, then glow.

The process to happiness is de-light-ful and is often referred to as becoming enlightened. It's not hocus-pocus. It does not involve monks in caves. It only needs you and the bravery to turn over the rock under which happiness is hiding. When you choose to be happy, you can bring the light that you naturally are into your life and into your body.

After years of getting to know myself, I was catapulted into a real sense of happiness when I realised that no achievement – past, present, or future – could ever enhance me; and any past, present, or future loss or perceived failure could never diminish me. This was liberation on a grand scale from the tricks of my mind. These days, my happiness is the only true measure of the quality of my life. Once you engage your heart in directing your life, you will feel enjoyment pulsating in every cell of your being.

Don't miss this movie, it's a blockbuster in which you get to star!

That rock that hides your happiness may be heavy at first, but inside you lives the strength to not only turn over the rock, but to see how precious the happiness waiting underneath is to be found.

Ultimately you own your own life, and you can decide how much happiness you experience. You can decide how you feel. No one else gets to do that for you. How awesome is that? The answer may well be unimaginable. It was for me.

When you change your thinking and leave your normal trance behind, you can transform yourself into a more natural you.

If you are unhappy to any extent, this book provides alternatives that may well change your life for the better. Let me take you on this journey of discovery. It will blow your mind… if you let it!

CHAPTER

1

We Are What We Think We Are

For centuries now, people have walked upon the Earth, making choices and adopting beliefs, because, unlike other life forms on this planet, we have the ability to do so. We have created marvellous structures, institutions and buildings, and many beautiful people bring happiness to each other every day.

This level of intelligence is a great privilege. However, with this gift of choice, or free will, we directly influence the quality of the lives that we lead. Put simply, we all choose our own lives, although many of us prefer to be victims and martyrs, as this is easier to do and relieves us of the responsibility for how we feel. In this way, our ability to choose our way of thinking can be a double-edged sword, with us failing to use it in a way that is aligned with our natural loving way of being.

When we speak of how people have developed over the centuries, we refer to our evolution, or how we have evolved. Both these words contain the word 'love' backwards within them as a mirror image. Love truly is the power through which we will grow and advance as a race. Without it we are lost.

We also have the capacity to create a light, bright happy world, for it inevitably becomes what we believe or think it will be. Our dreams are the seeds of our future, and now is the time to grow them.

Intelligence resides within our hearts and our minds, but for the most part we have chosen to live from our logical, egoic minds and not our hearts. Our minds keep us safe and secure, and this, for many of us, is our definition of happiness.

At least this is what we tell ourselves.

If our hearts and minds are not in alignment, we cease to be our real SELVES and we become trapped in a paradigm of inherited, subconscious beliefs and behaviours. This is known as conditioning, and unfortunately it is our normal way of being.

Our conditioning is largely driven by fear, for we have forgotten what is possible and have become content to copy others around us, which prevents us from being who, and what, we really are. We have become lost in a world where we define everything as good or bad, rather than seeing the richness in everything we experience. This has largely been a subconscious choice handed down through centuries of habit. Our limiting belief structures are consequently restricting our joy and happiness, replacing them with much pain and suffering on many fronts.

There is a great upside here, and it would be wrong to beat ourselves up for the mistakes we may have made. What is done is done! The present is what matters, and it arrives fresh and new in every new moment we experience.

In every new moment we are alive, we can create a fresh start that moves us to a better place, a place where we can know ourselves and express our full potency. This path lies in front of each of us. You just need to open the gate that has previously locked you in your comfort zone and take bold new steps towards a better, brighter life.

We can all start this adventure individually. We don't need to wait for others. We can create our own reality, regardless of what others think or do.

This journey is likely to take us all to unchartered waters, but it is a wonderful adventure. We can choose to embrace the unknown as much as we embrace the known in our lives. Our structures and interactions with others, and across our societies, can be shifted quickly if we could all become, and redefine the meaning of one thing: happiness.

Happy people, societies and countries don't start fights or feel the need to compete. They are content. Happiness is in short supply in our world and has been replaced by seriousness. We can break this cycle of despair and allow joy to be our default way of being.

If you have ever watched a child play you will see how they learn and express for fun. They are less conditioned than we adults and more attuned to the energy of joy. Eventually our world knocks this out of us as we grow into a less pure way of living. In a sense we move from the paradigm best described as 'I'm-pure' to the impure way of living that we as adults have created for ourselves.

We describe children as innocent. Some see this as a stage of life before we become sexual, but I look upon it as being a place of inner sense. Children are not yet conditioned by society (much), and they express this with freedom in the sandpit. Their senses are open and ready to learn and have fun. They express themselves 'naturally' until they learn a different 'normal'. As adults we no longer even enter the sandpit, let alone build sandcastles anymore. This book explains what is blocking happiness in our lives, and what is possible if we choose wonder over worry, adventure over security, and enjoyment over money. Our lives are outside-in rather than inside-out. We need to invert our lives to find joy.

Think about it. We care more about what we own, about how important we are and what people think of us, than what we know to be true about ourselves and what we feel. Our inner sense is lost in all this. It's been left in the sandpit.

These views may spark much debate and criticism, probably because they are quite simple. However, if it helps even a few people open their hearts and minds, it will have been worth every minute invested in the creation of this book.

The critical views of others are in fact welcome, for real change can still come with the right exchange of views and truths.

The bottom line is that our fearful minds have chosen a set of beliefs that our loving hearts would reverse if they were given a say. Our hearts are screaming out to have this say now before it's too late! Shouldn't we listen?

Our minds compel us to compete when our hearts would have us collaborate. We put money ahead of love and worry, when we could be in a state of wonder.

We crave importance when all that does is block our ability to be potent.

We resist change when change can help us grow, and we believe we must suffer and enslave ourselves to time and obligation when freedom and bliss is our natural way of being. Happiness swings between love and freedom, and it's possible to give ourselves a better balance of both.

Our world is full of judgement in every waking moment, when acceptance would fill our lives with fun and joy and help us to relax. This judgement has created a world of inequality and self-promotion. We have become humans doing, not humans being, as we immerse ourselves in obligations, commitments and an obsession with time. We have created this, not the watch on our wrist or the phone in our hand. No one can give you the gift of time, for you already have this gift if you choose to open it and be grateful.

What matters is not just matter, so we can choose to walk our talk and give love and happiness the prominence they deserve in our lives. Let's embrace the opportunity to thrive, not our obsession with trying to survive. We have become obsessed with information and knowledge. We are constantly assessed by our ability to remember facts and figures. We need to embrace the age of transformation and do something worthwhile with all the information we have at hand. We need wisdom and knowing to enhance knowledge. We know so much about our planet, but has that stopped us wrecking it?

Our material world has become unnatural, and our way of living threatens our very existence on this planet. It is unsustainable, and often irresponsible on many fronts. We can't seem to see that we are a part of nature, not separate from or above it. If only we could see that, we would surely respect our home on Earth and each other so much more. We shouldn't have to constantly protect ourselves from the self-interest of others. The world is awash with security systems and distrust. We have allowed complexity to overwhelm simplicity in so many ways. We rely too much on lawyers, and our economies are beyond the comprehension of most of us. We are surrounded by illusions and, if we stop to face it all, we will see it. Deep down, don't you crave more simplicity in your life?

We can switch our beliefs from the dark to a lighter path with no more than a new way of thinking. From this path a new freshness will descend, and a brand-new adventure will unfold for us all. We will be de-light-ed as we grow into full and vibrant lives.

This is the adventure we all crave in our hearts. It's called enjoyment (the energy of joy). We just need to be brave and trust, because our hearts have no shortage of courage to take us down a far less stressful path.

What if we used our collective energies to be in a state of joy, not pain? Don't we owe it to ourselves and our children, before it's all too late? If life is just a holiday from heaven, why not make it fun and full of adventure?

I urge you to read this book with your hearts, not your minds. Don't think the wisdom in this book… feel it!

Happiness is a habit and ultimately our level of happiness defines our habitat. We can only choose it for ourselves, not for others. They will have to choose it for themselves in the same way you will. You have no power to determine the level of happiness of another person, even though you might think you have.

In this book, you will discover the two-step code to finding happiness. However, what blocks most of us from being able to find the happiness in our hearts is a core set of beliefs that keeps us mired in a life of conditioned obligation and despair. These conditioned beliefs vary to some extent from person to person, but for the most part they are commonly shared and inherited from generation to generation. The fact is: your happiness is being hidden under a rock. Now for the big reveal… Without any further ado or fanfare, let me reveal the rock under which your happiness is hiding… yes, it's you! You are the rock.

The rock is created by your lack of self-awareness and limiting beliefs. When you lift away the rock of obligation, fear, oppression, competition, conditioning, insecurity and worry, you will dis-cover a life full of freedom, wisdom, love, intuition, and wonder. Here, there is wonder, not worry; and happiness can escape from its hiding place to fill your life with joy. It will engulf your senses. Just like a child who has won a game of hide-and-seek, who steps into the open with a smile on their face, your happiness will fill you with the energy and vibrancy to live the life you've always wanted.

Let's choose to dream, then plant the seeds that arise, for they will grow into a majestic forest of fun and joy.

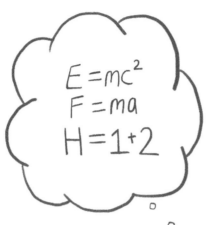
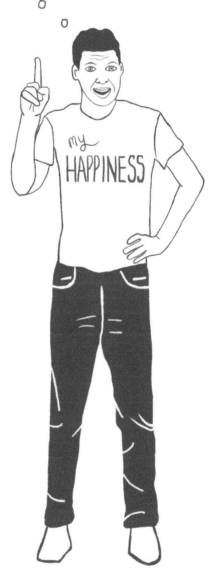

CHAPTER

2

The Code of Happiness

2.1: Happiness is a habit and a choice

In this book, I share what I have learned in my life about achieving real happiness. I mean real happiness, not the illusion I used to think was happiness. My intention is to provoke your thinking only. What you do with it is your choice. You can think about the steps to happiness as being like a computer code or formula. This allows our minds to follow a structured path, which is what they are good at doing.

The code or formula for happiness is one that is easily solved. You won't need a computer or Google to access it. Once you feel your way into it, you will know if it resonates with your own heart, and you can turn over the rock holding you in a state of worry.

This book may challenge your beliefs, if you allow it to; and if you consider the principles it offers, it could transform your life for the better. I encourage you to be bold and open your heart to what you read. Let it be the judge as it works through the formula and belief structures that this book shines light upon. Once you see them, be ready for your mind to challenge them, for it will no doubt resist the seeds of change that this book seeks to grow.

You've got nothing to lose, except perhaps a great deal of stress and unhappiness!

In our natural state we are loving, fun, fearless, caring, collaborative and full of joy. Yet we live in a conditioned trance that blocks us from finding our natural way of being. It keeps us locked up as slaves in a 'normal' place, chained to our perceived obligations. If you have ever seen the movie called *The Matrix*, you will see this trance depicted in a way that's not far wrong. I have finally broken free of my self-imposed matrix.

To allow our true happy selves to surface, we need to allow the stifling conditioned beliefs of society in which we are immersed to soften and dissolve, setting our hearts free to show us what is possible.

In my favourite Christmas carol called My Grown-Up Christmas List, the following words always intrigued me till the penny finally dropped:

> "What is this called the innocence of youth,
> maybe only in our blind belief can we ever find the truth."

As we age and lose our fresh, open minds that are ready to explore the world, we adopt the beliefs we think we need to hold. These distorted but normal beliefs hold us back from knowing our truths in life.

We already know in our hearts what we want our lives to look and feel like. There is a blueprint hiding under that rock holding us down. Self-awareness will lead us to higher self-esteem, and from there we all have the courage to express to the world the truth of ourselves. Self-love and freedom are waiting for you, and all you need to do is listen to your heart. It has all the knowing you need. It's knocking on your inner door, and you alone have the key to let its wisdom in. All you need to do is listen and move that rock aside. It's only in this way your happiness can come forth.

2.2: The current illusion of happiness

Let me show you the code or formula that once defined my life – see if you can associate with it. You may even see it in the society in which you live, and perhaps the world. I certainly did.

Let's call this the 'code of unhappiness':

$$\textbf{Unhappiness} = \begin{array}{c}\textbf{Being out of alignment} \\ \textbf{with your true self}\end{array} + \begin{array}{c}\textbf{Needing to fit} \\ \textbf{in but win}\end{array}$$

Unhappiness comes from our belief that we need to be what others want us to be, but in this place, we feel compelled to compete and win. We want to be important because deep down many of us fear that we are not enough.

Fitting in, and competing so we win, are our normal ways of living, and most of us are caught up in this collective pattern. We believe life is a big struggle we must survive. Everyone and everything is ranked, and this only fuels unhappiness for most people. We don't question this way of life, as we are conditioned to copy it day after day. We want to win but we also crave acceptance. Unfortunately, many of us feel we get neither.

Human beings need each other to survive, thrive and be our full expressions of self. Life on your own can be somewhat lonely and unfulfilling at times. Our current mindsets, unfortunately, lead us to a place of separation.

Yet when we collaborate rather than compete with others there is so much more potential in our lives. When we really care about each other, and reach out to work and play together, life can become a wonderful experience.

Many people have gone through the process called 'soul searching' in their lives to find out who and what they really are, then align with that truth. This is a key step on the journey to happiness, and it's much easier than you think. Knowing yourself is the platform for so many wonderful changes to enter your life. Once self-awareness is switched on, the lights go on inside you. And self-awareness can *only* be found inside you. No one else can find it for you, although others can guide you through this journey.

It's far more important to know yourself than to understand things outside ourselves. Our society mistakenly values our knowledge over our self-knowing. This is the root of many of our problems and stops the seeds of possibility from springing forth.

The 'code of happiness' is therefore very simple, and can be expressed as follows:

$$\text{Happiness (3)} = \text{(1)} \frac{\text{Acknowledging}}{\text{your true self}} + \text{(2)} \frac{\text{Expressing that real you}}{\text{in a collaborative world}}$$

Once we acknowledge ourselves, we have the power to take our life down the path we want it to follow. The bottom line is that the more aware you become of yourself, the more fulfilled you will feel and become. It's impossible not to feel this way!

Acknowledgement of your true self is the experience of life lived by true choice. If you don't know yourself, you make yourself vulnerable to making life choices to satisfy others. From my experience this is a bad place to be and plays havoc with your mental and physical wellbeing.

But when you attain deep self-awareness, you can't help but feel the desire to own your own life. From there you can express your inner desires to the world, irrespective of acceptance and judgement, for in this place you will fall in love with yourself. This is where happiness is fuelled by the love in your heart.

Once we acknowledge who we are, we can find and unite with our true tribe and express our truth with joy. That could be through a job, hobby, or relationship. It is a liberating place to inhabit and will allow happiness to shape your life. No matter where you live or what you own, you will find you can be happy because you are 'home'. As is said, home is where the heart is.

The more you find and get close to the real you, the less you will need anyone or anything else to be happy. Once you know what you want out of life, you are likely to need to make decisions that may at first be uncomfortable. However, from my experience, once you make the change you will feel the freedom that it gives you and the relief that freedom brings. From there you can express your true gifts and love with others who support you as you support them.

As this book will show you, wisdom, self-awareness and collaboration, rather than conditioning, self-denial and competition, are the core components to opening your heart to the fulfilment you deeply desire. This simple formula, once solved, can ripple out to solve the problems and feelings of despair you may well be tolerating day-by-day.

The answer to happiness in mathematic terms is three (3). When you know and acknowledge your true self (1), add that to your true self-expression in unity with others (2), you can be truly happy (3).

There are also three key components of you: your heart (life force/spirit), body, and mind – happiness is to have them all in sync.

Once you are whole, your life can be divine, because you have found where you are meant to be. Some call this enlightenment, for in this place you can't help but light up your heart, and the hearts of those around you.

You can choose to stop tolerating despair and fear, and come on a journey of happiness and love! Let wonder replace worry in your life. Trust me, it's magical!

CHAPTER

3

Is This the Normal We Really Want?

This book is written with love and shines a light on what is possible for you and the world if we change our way of thinking. It is not written in judgement because I know that I, Mark, was part of the 'normal' way of being for many long years. I have stared this down within myself and challenged all I once was.

The world we have created collectively is full of pain and suffering for many, and privileged only for a lucky few. But even those we consider to be fortunate are not without their own demons. Even so-called royals have their disasters, as we often witness in the media. Our world is besieged by complexity, wars, obsession with power, money and sex, financial complexity and volatility, sickness, crime, inequality, lies and stress, just to name a few. Billions of people are living a nightmare they would prefer to end, because the nightmare is too painful. The planet is suffering from our unsustainable ways of life and our insatiable desire to consume at all costs. Our lifestyles are unsustainable, and real change is needed. Why not consider a fresh way of being?

The source of our pain is self-inflicted. It comes from our ignorance, mistaken core beliefs and thoughts. Luckily, everything in our outer reality can be changed if we alter our own inner reality or thoughts. Happiness is available to all of us, but first we need to be brave enough to face how we feel. Unfortunately, many of us have forgotten what it means to feel.

Our beliefs drive our thoughts, which drive our feelings, which ultimately result in our actions. Many of our beliefs are subconscious and not easy to find, but our feelings should be easy to access, if only we didn't suppress and deny them.

Most of us don't understand the cornerstone of our existence that is our beliefs. Beliefs drive every outcome in this world, and if we don't understand our deepest beliefs, because we just absorbed them from those around us, what chance do we have of experiencing outcomes that make us truly happy?

The world is like a playground full of selfish children, scrapping over the toys on offer and, unfortunately, we often pick leaders who are not only the same, but excel in this way of being. How many leaders have let you or your family down?

We can change our thinking after thousands of years of living on this planet, and accept the need for individuality with cooperation, not judgement with disunity. Why do we all want to be the same and condemn those who are not like us?

If we could all reassess our thoughts and beliefs through a greater self-awareness, we would change the way we interact with each other and, more importantly, the way we see ourselves. This would help us return to a more natural way of living.

Transformation is what is needed, and this book is designed not only to point out the problems we all face and their root causes, but to shine a light on the possibilities that have been sitting in the shadows, waiting to be illuminated. Like a field of sunflowers bursting forth for all to see, so is widespread happiness waiting to be set free.

The reality is that we are already pure, potent love, presenting in the world as a person. Isn't it time we lived our truth?

The fastest way to get to this pure place is through happiness. Choose to be happy, because when you are in alignment with joy and happiness, it allows you to more quickly align with the deep wisdom in your heart. This wisdom knows much, including the best way for you to live your life.

It may sound obvious, but when you become happier you can't help but have more fun, no matter what you are doing. One follows the other like night follows day. How would you like to have more fun in your life?

3.1: The pathway to pain

Life can be very demanding and, if you are like me, you may have stumbled or fallen many times along the way. This may have led you through periods of great challenge and pain. Most of this is normally self-inflicted, resulting from our own lack of self-awareness and self-worth. It took me half a century to see this and to put an end to it. I had to change my thinking to make it end, not ignore it any longer. I reached a point where I didn't want to tolerate my unhappiness anymore. I wanted it to end so I faced it head-on.

Isaac Newton proved in his third law of physics that every action has an equal and opposite reaction. In other words, we get what we put out into the world. Ultimately, what we believe will become reality, because we apply our inner thoughts to the creation of the world we live in. In other words, we are what we think.

The solution to our problems lies not in blaming others or demanding that others change, but within our own thoughts and beliefs. When we change ourselves, we change the world around us. You need to start with you and take responsibility for your own life. The blame game we all play needs to end now. It's full time and the siren is sounding on a score line, which sees most of us losing.

Mahatma Ghandi is attributed with the following wisdom:

"Be the change you want to see in the world."
and
"As a man changes his own nature,
so does the attitude of the world change towards him?"

Likewise, Michael Jackson's famous song 'Man in the Mirror' has always touched me with the principle that, if you want to make the world a better place, you need to take a good look at yourself in the mirror and make a change within yourself, first and foremost.

It takes great courage to face your own pain and say no more! You can choose the end of your suffering. It's no one else's responsibility. Every time you do, you light a fire in your heart that can never be extinguished. In fact, that fire can only grow brighter and brighter once you set it alight. Your heart has unlimited fuel for your fire to burn.

We tend to see ourselves as separate from nature. We see the instincts driving other animals to behave in the way they do. They can't change and they don't need to because they are being what they are meant to be. They do not question their part in nature or spend their energy trying to understand it.

We are also a part of nature but, unlike the other animals, we have the intelligence to choose to be what we want to be. We are privileged to have choices. The problem is that our herd or species often makes poor choices. We are not being natural in our way of living. We can choose to look in the mirror, before we as a herd run ourselves over a cliff, possibly already looming in the distance.

Make no mistake: we are a herd. We are all thinking and behaving like each other, conditioned in the same way, with cultural differences of course, but ultimately failing to see that we are all united.

At the same time, it is said that it takes all kinds to make a world. We all have different abilities, characteristics and dreams. We are each unique in our own way of being. There is no other person who is identical to you, not even a twin if you have one. We can express who we really are and access each other as we journey down a new pathway hand-in-hand. Why do we all want to be the same and fit in, when we are all unique, and our herd might be going the wrong way?

3.2: The maze of misery

Our lives can be so wonderful, but most of us are caught in a maze of misery. It's hard to get out of, but it is possible.

The illustration below shows you this maze:

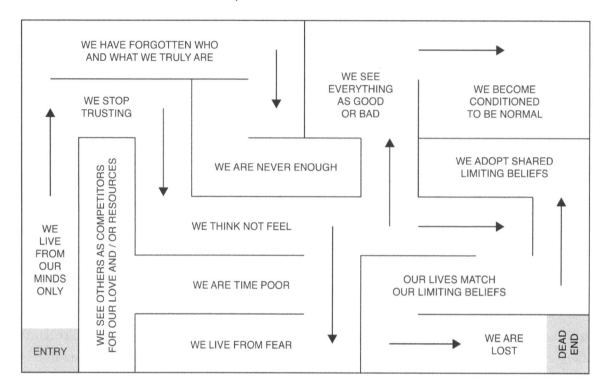

Figure 1: The Maze of Misery

I have used a maze to depict our current world because it's easy to get lost and confused in a maze. You can try to enter a maze in different places, but you can get lost and frustrated as you get caught up in dead-ends. It can also be quite hard to get out of.

My life used to feel like this some days, and I felt trapped and constricted, unable to find freedom and joy. If you have ever witnessed a colony of ants blindly scurrying around, busy and intent on finding the next fragment to justify their existence, then perhaps you can see the parallel to the lives many of us lead. Many of us get caught in lives of obligation and despair, intermittently disrupted with moments of joy. I think you will agree that this is the opposite of what we really want in our lives.

The cause of this is that we have learned to ignore one of our core operating systems: our hearts.

We can, however, escape our maze and create a lighter brighter way of life for us all. Every maze has a way out to freedom and ours can be found in the way we operate. For many of us there is a more natural way, but first we must face our situation through a labyrinth of love, not a maze of misery.

3.3: Our choice of operating systems

As human beings we can operate from two different systems of being: our minds or our hearts. Science has proven that each has its own form of intelligence. To be whole is to live with *both* operating systems in unison, and we are easily capable of this true 'wholeness'.

Our hearts allow us to feel what course of action is best for us. They operate from a place of love and are linked to the desires of our souls. This link is rarely explored. When we decide from our hearts it generally feels right in our stomachs or guts. We all know this. Some refer to it as our gut feeling or intuitive intelligence. This is because our hearts and our bodies are so closely linked.

Our minds are wonderful thinking membranes or systems, but they are linked to our egos, and are therefore susceptible to our conscious and subconscious fears. Our minds are incredible and logical in many ways, but they are highly susceptible to the subconscious programming that takes place through our experiences and preconditioning, which can have us making bad choices. My understanding is that the vast majority of decisions we make are influenced or determined by our subconscious beliefs. Yet it is in our subconscious beliefs that our deepest, suppressed fears lurk, often unnoticed, and they take their toll on our lives by influencing our choices. Like logical computers, if we put garbage into our minds, we will get garbage out. Preconditioned beliefs can operate like a cancer in our lives, or they can be hugely positive. This is influenced by many factors including the environment we grew up in and how sensitive we were to what we experienced. Two people growing up in the same environment could emerge with quite different subconscious beliefs. This shows you the complexity of the human condition.

On the other hand, when both our hearts and minds are in sync we will flourish. We will understand our heart's desire and can give and receive the love our hearts are capable of; while we can also use the powerful, practical and logical intelligence of the mind, or ego, to bring this desire into reality. The mind is a great implementer and has a key role to play. However, it need not be in complete control of our decision-making.

Our minds contain our egos, which can distort reality and alter our behaviours in an attempt to protect and promote us. We need our egos to survive and help us create our personalities, but if left unchecked and misunderstood our egos can cause great damage to our lives. Too many unchecked egos can create a painful world and communities bereft of happiness.

This is what we are currently experiencing on a collective scale, and perhaps you are experiencing it in your own life.

We need to reach the point where the love that our hearts possess can be implemented by our minds, such that it is able to spring forth into our outer realities. This is just a choice. That's all it takes. A simple choice.

In this magical place, great joy and happiness is possible, as we can live the life we are meant to live. Did we really come to Earth to compete and fight over money? Did you really come here to fit in and become what others wanted you to be? We can choose a different operating system. Let's call it an upgrade!

I know in my heart that I came here to be happy, and happiness is a feeling I now choose every day. Can you relate to this, or sense the wonder in it?

3.4: We think not feel

Our whole society is largely based on the concept of thinking not feeling. Thinking gets things done. Feelings are best ignored because they are soft and fluffy and not logical. At least this is what most of us are taught.

Many of us have lost touch with our feelings. I know I did for many years. Feelings are seen as burdensome and irrational.

Whereas the truth is that feelings are a great gift, and when they are trusted and accessed, they bring forth a power beyond that of our logical minds, because feelings are a signpost to our truth. Our hearts bring forth feelings, and our bodies amplify them. Yet many of us suppress our feelings because they can send our lives in a different direction to the one we are following, which we may believe we are expected to follow. We believe feelings challenge us, whereas they actually guide us. Without acknowledging our feelings, it's like driving blindfolded. It will always end in tears.

Most of us fail to listen to our intuition or gut feeling as a guide. Even though it is often free of our biased mindsets, we simply don't trust it. Yet our intuition knows from deep in our hearts where we want our lives to go. It knows the real you.

But most of us don't know it, despite it coming from deep inside ourselves.

From a young age we are taught to think through life. We reward logic. At school we teach subjects that require logical thinking, such as mathematics, science, technology and so on. Creative subjects like the arts and music are taught too, but only the minority participate because many see them as vague, less important and less valuable. Only the truly gifted actively pursue them.

We are obsessed with knowledge in the form of information, and we rarely act on something until we believe we are certain about how it will work out. We are bombarded by the age of information and data. Our brains are jammed with facts and life is a grand memory test.

We need to live with greater knowing, not the gigabytes of knowledge we so crave. This knowing comes from our intuition, the teacher within us, not the information or opinions outside us.

We need to stop fearing our intuition, because it will lead us to the path we really desire. The most powerful combination we can choose is to access our hearts and understand our feelings, then use our logical minds to implement what we discover and decide. This is a holistic way to live.

But it takes great courage. Too many of us do what we are taught to do by others, without knowing what we want or believe. This sends us on the wrong path, which is often dim and painful, and ultimately leads us to unhappiness.

If we are too much in our hearts or too much in our minds, we become imbalanced one way or the other. We need to be in both to be our true selves. At the end of the day the universe gave us both for a reason and it knows better than our much smaller brains.

3.5: We live from fear not love

Marianne Williamson is quoted as saying:

"Love is what we were born with. Fear is what we learned here."

Our general propensity to live from our minds and not our hearts, leaves us open to a life of fear, not love. That our world has become full of fear shows up in the multiple conflicts between human beings, and the general inequality that exists in so many walks of life. Judgement and condemnation of each other is rife. Competition thrives at the expense of collaboration.

When our minds fear for our own wellbeing, they will protect us at all costs. In this state of fear, self-interest rules and we become selfish and competitive, often in unpleasant ways. In its worst form this lack of compassion shows up as violent crime and wars. Neither would ever be tolerated or pursued in this world if love was the driving force in our lives, rather than fear.

Most of us are unknowingly programmed to choose fear. We fear a lack of money, love, sex, power, freedom, time, and control – just to name a few. We live with the fear of missing out. This drives us to treat all these things as commodities we must possess and fight for, because they are, in our minds, in short supply and there is not enough to go around.

We fear that we are unlovable, and so we go on a quest in our lives to prove that we are. This causes us to focus on things outside ourselves that will boost our egos and make others think more highly of us. We often care more about what others think of our lives than we do of living and loving our own lives.

When we fear, we pull back from life and protect ourselves. We live life in a shell. We hide. We are content to survive not thrive. We worry about life rather than wonder what's possible. Fear is our ruler!

Our general lack of self-love is a curse, and it prevents us from opening to the possibility of loving and being loved unconditionally. Unfortunately, most people don't even know what unconditional love is. Read on and its magic is explored.

You get what you put out into the world. So, if we can't love ourselves fully, we can never fully allow love into our own lives. We think another can complete us, but they really can't.

John Lennon said:

> "Evolution and all hope for a better world rest in the
> fearlessness and open-hearted visions of people who embrace life."

The only way to be fearless is to open your heart and become your true self. From here we can collectively change the world, for love is the greatest force we have, and it will always allow us to approach life with inspiration not fear.

So how did we end up in a conditioned way of living?

3.6: The reason we become conditioned

When we are born into this world, we are all born into a particular family, society and country. This is our herd within the bigger worldwide herd. Each of these herds has its own specific way of thinking or being. We commonly call this a culture. It is defined by its mindset or set of beliefs.

As young children we start life as a clean slate. We are innocent but fragile, and dependent on those around us for our very survival. Accordingly, we believe we must adapt and fit in, or we could die or suffer.

As we grow, we interact constantly with our families, particularly our parents and siblings. We witness the way people in our community live, we observe the life we are exposed to in the media, and we become inculcated by the structures around us, and by the interactions with others we experience.

Our personal experiences are all unique and determined largely by our parents, but in many ways they are similar, because collective mindsets prevail in communities and across populations. Our parents do their best to bring us up, but they are conditioned and imperfect as well. Thus generation after generation conditions the thinking of the next. Our mindsets are effectively inherited, without being in a will!

There are exceptions to the rule, but many of us grow up becoming what we think others expect us to be. We are not taught to be who we really are, or to even explore that. This would require us to search inside our own hearts, rather than copy others. Subconsciously we trend towards the norm. We don't question this because fitting in and surviving is our focus, not on being bold enough to be our natural selves.

In my early 50s, I recognised this in me. By all measures, in society, I was successful. So why was I fundamentally unhappy? It was because I had become something that, deep down, I didn't want to be. I was smart enough to fit in and, in the eyes of others, excel; but I was not wise enough to find my own pathway to happiness. I had become very good at things that I really didn't enjoy. This pathway had become shrouded by my lack of self-awareness. It was a dark path with little light and an uneven surface that constantly tripped me up.

We can become obsessed with understanding the world we live in, when what we need is greater self-knowing. It can all change if we learn to know ourselves, for that is where true freedom lies. This means finding our own sovereignty and not just blindly fitting in.

Many of us are like computers, running on the wrong software, and someone else is writing our programmes – not us. We can choose to take control of that code.

Two determinants of our ability to rewrite our codes are: our egos and our levels of self-esteem.

3.7: What is our ego and why is it important?

A traditional understanding of our ego includes acknowledging that our egos reside within our minds and that their role is to protect us and implement thoughts and actions to make us successful and keep us safe. They are important in determining our personalities and keeping us alive.

The human ego is, however, broadly misunderstood. We often picture an egoic person as someone who thinks overly highly of themselves and beyond our assessment of them. When I was growing up, if you spoke positively about yourself, you were called an 'egomaniac' or a 'poser', and you were criticised, even if what you said was true. In effect, self-love was admonished or rejected. Modesty was a preferred trait.

But can't modesty co-exist with a strong sense of self? Can't our egos help us maintain a positive level of self-esteem?

A person in an unhealthy egoic state typically needs to repeatedly tell or show others their qualities or achievements. They are compelled to impress others. Deep down they suffer from insecurity or a need for recognition. The keyword here is 'need'. Their need is created by an inherent insecurity, and it is not a sign of strength.

When we don't 'need' to receive praise or recognition for something we have done or said, we are instead acting from a place of wholeness. We are self-centred. We may still receive praise, but if we don't receive it, it doesn't matter to our sense of self.

As a young boy growing up, I was strongly influenced by the way my parents interacted with each other, and it shaped my thoughts about myself and shaped my ego. For example, my mother constantly criticised my father for not earning enough money and referred to him openly, in front of me, as hopeless. My subconscious mind interpreted this as: a man who does not provide well enough for his family is not worthy of love. The result of this was that my ego propelled me forward in life with a strong focus on making money and needing to give money to others in order to feel loved. Financial success made me feel validated and worthy. However, this set me on an unfulfilling path to misery.

Perhaps you can relate to this? Did the way your parents interact, or things they said, send your subconscious mind a particular message, which then propelled you forward in life with an over-focus on your career, money, success, or achievements?

3.8: What is self-esteem and why is it important?

Our self-esteem plays a critical part in our success and happiness as a person. As young children growing up, we can be highly influenced by our parents and our environment. We learn to adapt to the emotions and events we witness, because we are intelligent beings.

However, deep inside us, we can feel a sense of betrayal at ceasing to live in alignment with who we are. Each time we give into the conditioning we experience, our self-esteem can be diminished and we gradually start to lose our sense of self.

If you could draw the self-esteem of a person who is not whole within themselves, it would look like this:

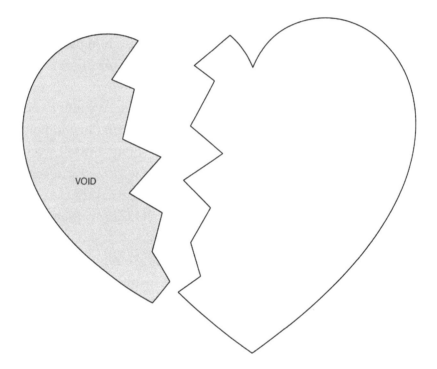

VOID

Figure 2: Our Self-Esteem is not Whole but Has a Hole

The void represents the piece of our self-esteem that we have lost or distorted. It can become a missing part of our self-esteem that we can spend years and great levels of energy trying to fill with things like sex, money, or relationships. Inevitably we may one day realise that these things can never fill the void, because once we do the work to search inside ourselves, we will see that we were always whole and there was no void to fill. We just need a change of beliefs, and a curiosity to explore our own selves.

Throughout 2018 and 2019, I did an intensive mentoring course to identify the limiting conscious and subconscious beliefs that were causing me to perceive a void in my life. On my own I could see the obvious ones, but with help I was able to identify hundreds, yes hundreds, of subconscious fears and misconceptions that had no basis in truth, and which were diminishing my sense of self.

Generally, the more secure the people we are exposed to, the less damage that will most likely be done to our sense of self as we grow up. If your parents were significantly lacking in self-esteem, and therefore had strong egos to protect them, you were more likely to suffer from unhealthy egoistic patterns and a dented self-esteem. Unfortunately, we become what we are exposed to in many ways.

The truth is, however, that regardless of our self-perception we are all enough. It's just the lives that we are living that have become not enough. All we need to do is go inward to find our whole selves. This can be confronting, but it is worth it.

We may disappoint others or make mistakes, but that does not mean we are not enough. Truly we are all enough!

3.9: How does our conditioning show itself?

The main limiting belief structures, or forms of conditioning, that haunt our modern society are outlined in the following chapters. There are so many I am sure I have missed some! However, they have led me to paint a picture of the main collective fears and behaviours that we exhibit in our lives.

Most of them have applied to me at some point or another, so I do not sit in judgement and preach. The world has been full of preachers for hundreds of years, and I doubt much good has come from it. I open my heart to you and bare my soul in the hope it will help others who wish to reconsider their lives.

Why should you reconsider? Because what we call normal is often not *natural*. It may have *become* normal because it is what we are accustomed to, and we are immersed in it. However, an unnatural comfort zone is full of pain and often despair; it is 'the devil we know'. We are like the proverbial frog in hot water: the water is getting hotter and hotter, and we are so deep in the boiling pond we cannot see the way out, yet our lives are getting less and less satisfying.

So let's measure the temperature and act, before we get badly burnt! We have an opportunity here to know ourselves more fully, but first we need to shed the skin we have inherited, riddled with conditioning; then each of us can decide if we want to change.

The more of us who change, however, the more our collective society will advance to a happier place. I am now in the second half of my life. However, I have five children, and I hope they get to experience a better world than the one I have witnessed, and in some cases endured. To create this new world, all we need to do is break the ongoing cycle of conditioning we have been exposed to and be ourselves. It is a simple shift into a new way of thinking.

Happiness is just a choice; but it must start with a dose of self-awareness and honesty. Why not get real and feel?

The world has many wonderful people, but even the most wonderful are most likely carrying limiting subconscious beliefs they simply cannot see, or perhaps don't want to see.

CHAPTER

4

Decoding Our Unhappiness

As mentioned earlier, there are two core components of the code of happiness that dictate our level of happiness. These can be explored in depth once we are aware and substantially free of our preconditioned beliefs and habits. They are:

1. How well do we really know ourselves?
2. Once we find the truth within us, how do we express ourselves within a collaborative society?

The strength of both these inputs into our code of happiness is very important. It's the doorway to joy and love. When we go inward to find out who we really are, and then project that truth onto the world we inhabit, we can't help but improve our life experiences and expressions, as well as the experiences and expressions of those around us.

As night follows day, once you align with your inner self, it will influence the way you interact with everything around you, including other people, animals, and even nature. I urge you to consider this deeply and summon the courage to investigate it. It's actually fun!

Let's consider both aspects of the formula.

4.1: Acknowledging our true selves

Many of us have forgotten who and what we really are, and this has prevented us from becoming the person that deep down we know we want to be. As a result, our self-awareness is very low. Mine was for many years. Of course, only you can assess your own understanding of what makes you happy as a person. The greatest gift we can give ourselves in life is to know ourselves and acknowledge that with absolute honesty, and not take the conditioned way out.

Without self-awareness, our lives are shaped by our unknown subconscious beliefs. This puts us at the mercy of our own ignorance, and we become dictated to by the lack of understanding of our own feelings and beliefs. We become beholden to the programming or 'codes' that are operating our minds and suppressing our true desires.

If we are what we think, and if we live in ignorance, what we draw to us may well be what we don't want. It's like rolling a dice every day. Life has a way of giving us what we fear because we attract it to us through our resistance to it. This is counter-intuitive but true. Murphy's Law says, 'what can go wrong, normally does.' Our fearful way of thinking brings this paradigm into reality.

But when we not only know but openly acknowledge what we are and what we want to experience, we can attract it into our lives with the power of intention. Remember: we are what we think! Without conscious intentions, we may not like what life gives us, and resentment can arise to erode our happiness.

When we go inward, we can access the power that resides within our hearts. We can find our intuition, our insights, our inspiration and our integrity. Once we have been inward to find these wonderful sources of wisdom, we can take what they teach us to the world to make a difference, or perhaps just for fun, because we are no longer grasping externally for things to fill us up. Our self-esteem becomes complete.

If you want to be happy, you therefore need to go inward first before you go outward. Go within or go without the joy that is your birthright. Your inner sense holds the key to your happiness!

To be authentic means to be genuine or real. Many people say they are authentic but are they really? We can only be real if we know who we truly are, and we accept that true identity into our lives. We all know when we meet someone who is genuine, who has acknowledged their true selves, we intuitively sense it.

Deep down, every one of us already knows who we truly are. Acknowledging it can set off a ripple effect in the world felt by all around us, because we each yearn to become authentic. If my experience is any guide, you can be assured that people will admire your move to greater authenticity, because deep inside them they too have a burning desire to do the same. They are often too scared to step outside their cage of conditioning, which keeps them trapped in mediocrity.

Isn't it time you became the real you? After all, every other person and personality in this world is taken!

4.2: Expressing your truth with others

Human beings need each other to survive and thrive. We all have different gifts and skills that come together to create families, businesses, economies, societies, and countries. It takes all kinds of people to make a world.

At its very core, we need each other to keep our species going through reproduction. The recent Covid-19 lockdowns showed us how much we need each other to be connected and happy. If nothing else, our economy relies on the ability of people to trade with each other.

When we believe we are separate, collaboration is often replaced by competition as many of us strive to win. Our fearful minds lead us to constantly hide or lock ourselves away from others, who we fear will manipulate, hurt or steal from us. There is good reason for this, because society is full of unfair and illegal behaviour designed to maximise the position of the perpetrator. Even large wealthy companies have been known to manipulate their market power at the expense of their customers.

Ask yourself this: have you ever been ripped off, robbed, threatened, or harmed by another person without good cause? I have been robbed seven times in my life, so I know how it feels. No wonder we don't trust people till we get to know them and know we are safe to transact or interact with them.

Is this the kind of world we really want?

When we learn to operate more in our hearts and become our true selves, love becomes the basis of how we live. In this place we will naturally care for others, want to connect with them to have fun and express the gifts we have to offer our community. It doesn't mean we won't seek money or compete with others, but we will do it fairly, with the right spirit, and in the interests of pleasure and fun. We will care about the interests of others and give them genuine support if they fall. Imagine a whole society that operates this way!

Once we find our own happiness, our lives will be dominated by our loving intentions. Going inward can bring us home, because home is where the heart is. We don't need a lockdown to be home.

The expression to be 'enlightened' conjures up images of gurus sitting in caves or monasteries for years on end and being detached from society. But enlightenment simply refers to becoming happier or lighter because we are living the life that aligns with the radiance in our hearts. We can all be enlightened; we don't need a cave or to become a monk. All we need is the desire to find our true selves inside us. This is the only place it can be found. You won't find it next door, or in a monastery.

When we connect to ourselves, and turn ourselves on like a light bulb, then fun and how we feel become the priorities in our lives. And if every action has an equal and opposite reaction, guess what you will receive back if you approach life in a more light-hearted way?

In a society where everyone knows who they really are and what they want to be, where they express this knowing openly, the barriers we have erected to happiness will fall away. Imagine a world where fulfilment replaced materialism as our key goal in life. In this place our core needs will be met because our real gifts and talents will be on show for the world to see and, most likely, buy. When simplicity replaces complexity, we can happily live with less because we need less. It's possible that many of us will see that the true purpose of life is to have fun and express ourselves fully without fear every day. We truly need to care-less!

With our new way of thinking, we will achieve a better life balance; and it all starts by allowing your heart to open the door inside you, by seeing who you really are and what makes you happy. Your heart has most likely been knocking on this door for years but may not have been allowed to express itself. Why not embrace new habits that may lead us to happiness not despair? Once we go 'home' we can really create the life of our dreams.

Happiness is a habit, and it's something we can all get used to.

Can you really resist that opportunity of your lifetime?

CAGE OF CONDITIONING

CHAPTER

5

Our Shared Limiting Beliefs

After deep observation of the world and looking into the mirror of my own life, I believe there are several core belief structures casting shadows on our path to happiness. Twenty-two of them, to be precise. By shining a light on these beliefs, I hope we can find a better way forward.

Each of these core beliefs can lead to multiple associated belief structures that could fill many books. In addition, each of us will have different core beliefs depending on our individual experiences, and because each of us (even twins) is unique in our own way. We are also all influenced by these beliefs in different ways, depending on our level of awareness and conditioning. Only you can assess your own situation.

Let your heart make this assessment as you read, because your ego will most likely distort the outcome to protect you. It will resist, like mine did for years. It will probably try to stop you reading on, for it will be confronted by what it hears and sees. My advice is to give your mind compassion, for it knows no better... yet!

The core limiting beliefs I believe we need to reconsider are set out in Figure 3 below. These beliefs bring much worry and pain to our lives.

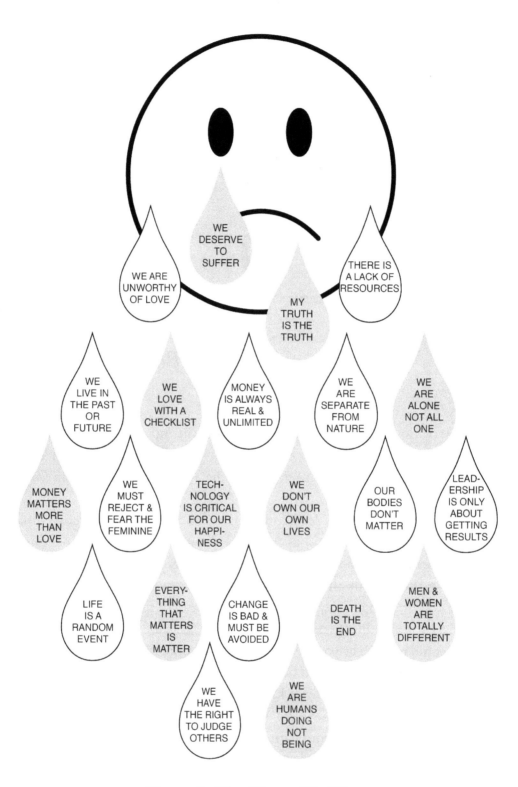

Figure 3: The Worry We Weep

Each of these core limiting beliefs has a ripple effect into our lives and the world we have created. The good news is each one can be reversed. It's just a thought away!

Let's consider each of these limiting beliefs and the associated belief structures that are harming our world and perhaps your life. There are many behaviours and structural problems that flow from the myriad of these mindsets.

5.1: We are unworthy of love

Fundamentally, we are all worthy and capable of giving and receiving unconditional love.

However, as we grow and develop, we are exposed to a constant flow of events and feedback in our lives that often convinces us otherwise. We interpret our interactions with the world, on a conscious and subconscious level, and our level of self-love – and thus our ability to love others – can be boosted or diminished by these interactions.

It's common for all of us to diminish our own sense of self in some way during our lives. We could lack confidence in our looks, our physicality, our financial status, our job status, our relationship situations, and so on. Even the best-looking people can find fault in their physical attributes. Have you ever noticed how few people can take a compliment about how they look? We are programmed for perfection!

As we develop, we often adopt the characteristics of our parents, given that they are our key role models in life. We can also be brought down by our sense of failure to meet our own expectations in specific events or activities. Our expectations or plans can be a futile source of pain, as expectation is the enemy of fun and the creator of the fear of failure.

I grew up with parents who were lacking in self-worth. My father was nervous and withdrawn. My mother felt diminished by a lack of money, her low levels of education and the fact that she was raised in a broken family. I lived the first twenty-five years of my life in their home, and I believe I initially lacked confidence as a result of this. I lacked any direction on how to be in healthy relationships. Perhaps you have your own history that has left you bruised?

Our lack of self-worth can be isolated in one part of our lives, or alive and well in different areas. For instance, many of us lack worthiness with money and love. This lack of worthiness can have diverse impacts. We can either give up on ever receiving what we want, or it can make us determined to receive that very thing and send us into a strong state of overdrive.

When we feel unworthy of something, such as love, we will often look to fill our void with other things to take away our pain and, in other words, complete us. This can lead to addictions to things such as money, drugs, sex and conflict to compensate for our lack of self-esteem.

Lack of self-love pervades all aspects of our lives. It is extremely common and leads us into much unhappiness and detrimental behaviours. When we feel unworthy of something we tend to limit our ability to attract it into our lives. We will consciously or subconsciously block it because, at the end of the day, we are what we think we are. If we feel unworthy of something, it's unlikely to enter our lives. If you don't feel worthy of a promotion at work, you are not likely to apply for that next promotion. As a result, you are not likely to receive that job.

It's those people who feel worthy of money or an equal and balanced relationship, for example, who will most likely receive that into their lives, because they emit the confidence to attract it. You get what you put out! People in relationships typically attract and enter relationships with people with similar levels of self-esteem. The confidence they possess brings forth what they feel worthy of and want. Has this played out in your life?

Many people become rich in life while others limit themselves. The mega-rich may be born into fortunate financial positions, but they also seem to have the confidence to take significant risks and chase their dreams. This idea of worthiness impacts on individuals, businesses, and countries. It's a principle that applies at all levels of life.

If you are not happy with something in your life, a key first step is to consider whether you are blocking what you want from coming into your life. It may not be repelled by you but by external forces; however, if you are blocking its attraction, changing your belief around it will make it much more likely to enter your life.

The truth is that we are all naturally worthy of abundance in every part of our lives. We just need to see this and welcome it in. We are all as good as each other, so the mindset of unworthiness within ourselves, and the self-judgement it brings forth, is normally the big separator. It separates you from what you want and deserve.

There is only one true place to find our worthiness and that is within us, not outside of ourselves. Not everyone will think highly of us, so forget about them! The things we acquire will never fill us up completely, so forget about them! Self-love can only come from our own self-appreciation and sense of worthiness. We need to 'go home' to find who we truly are, and to be appreciated consistently and without conditions.

We need to be our own be-love-d, for it is only there we can be loved forever.

Set out below are the key limiting beliefs that spin off from our belief that we are flawed and unworthy of love. They are extensive because this is a core issue.

5.1.1: We are obsessed with who we are

You might relate to this: you are at a function or event, and you meet someone new. One of the first things they will ask you is what you do for a living. This is how we identify with others. First, we find out their name and if they are well, then we find out how they make money. We may not even hear their answers to the first two questions because our minds are focussed on the third answer. Rarely do we ask what someone's key passions are or what their heart desires out of life. Why? Because we identify too much with the roles we play in society. This is the 'who' or egoic personality that we project.

What do we do? Where do we live? In a house or a unit? Where did you go to school? Where do your children go to school? Are you married? These types of factors define us because our minds can comprehend and assess them. We are conditioned to seek them out so we can put another person onto a scale and rank them against ourselves, and others. We compare ourselves to the other person as our logical minds strive to work out how other people compare to us. This can then set off feelings of inequality, superiority, or inferiority as we strive to consider whether or how we should relate to them.

Single people often subconsciously undertake this assessment process when they meet someone new, to determine whether they're an appropriate match.

Our propensity to meet people with our minds, and not our hearts, means that we are allowing our egos to assess people. We don't seek to find out what a person dreams about or cares about until we have put them in the pecking order and assessed whether they are worthy of our time or are too important for us to know.

If we looked to get to know the real person we are meeting, we would surely seek to discover the factors unique to that person's true self. How do they feel about life? What do they most want to change in their lives? What have they learned from life? What makes them come alive? What do they believe?

When I was a leader in business, I found that people were obsessed with what title their job carried, what level they were at, who they reported to and what they got paid. These are all constructs of the mind. Some people cared more about whether they enjoyed their job or had fun, but most people were conditioned to forego their happiness for extra status or money. Like it or not, their job title or the money it pays gives people a sense of who they are, because they probably are not in touch with their true selves. It's also something that others may be impressed by, and we so deeply crave that. Absolute self-awareness is a rare commodity in our conditioned world. Therefore, if you walked up to a new person and asked them what they stood for in life, what their core beliefs are, most people could not answer.

The first time anyone asked me this question I admit I had no idea how to respond!

There is only one place to find out what and who you are, and that's to look inward into your heart. Most of us are obsessed with how society defines us, but the truth is that this does not matter.

When we ask others who we are or should be, we will get a biased view based on that other person's conditioning or values, and in most cases, they will not want you to be better than them. In Australia we have a phrase for this called the 'tall poppy syndrome'. It leads us to shrink so we don't stand out.

A deep purpose in life is something many people will try to discover at some point in their lives. But unless they access their hearts, this is unlikely to be obvious from their current jobs or life circumstances. Their minds will create for them what their egos want to hear, a successful story of their lives that defines who they are. But the truth of what they are, or could be, can never be clear from the story of their life. It may give indications, but only your heart knows the answer. Is it time you wrote some new chapters in your life?

Once you find out what you truly are, and not who you are seen to be, you can fall in love with yourself. This requires your heart to be your main operating system. Perhaps it needs a reboot because it's been ignored for quite a while? Mine certainly was for many years!

We can choose to see every opportunity to meet with and interact with another human being as an absolute privilege. To do this, we need to consciously drop our habit of rating every person we meet as better, equal, or worse than us. Every one of us is a beautiful representation of the spirit within us, and every one of us is doing our best to live the most meaningful life we can. None of us are perfect and we are all equal, yet at the same time we are all unique.

Allowing our inspiration to guide us home to self-love is the key, because only the spirit within us knows the true depths of our self-worth.

5.1.2: Giving to others makes me more valuable

Many people do good work to help others, including providing them with money and giving them their time. This form of giving is to be encouraged because we can only thrive when we all do so together.

However, many people either give too much, to their own detriment, or give for the sake of recognition, because they want to feel more valuable. Some say that generosity and guilt are often inverse in their energies.

When we love ourselves, we can give to others authentically, without the need for recognition. From this place of love, we can give purely out of love and, even if the other person denies the authenticity of your gift, you will know in your heart that you gave your money or service for the good of someone else, not yourself.

Our tendency to self-sacrifice for others can show up in different ways. I would often work incredibly long hours for employers, sacrificing time I could have spent on my own hobbies or with my loved ones, because deep down this sacrifice made me feel important and safe. My ego was at play and my sacrifice made me a martyr, giving me validation, but very little freedom.

How many people give their time and money to charities or employers to be recognised, rather than out of love?

Few of us are good at receiving from others because of our inherent sense of unworthiness. For most it's easier to give to feel worthy.

In early 2020, Australia's southeast was ravaged by the worst bushfires in living memory. A few celebrities came out and gave money to help those affected. This was a great gesture. However, why did they need to make it known on social media or on television that they had done this? Was it self-promotion? Was it to inspire others to give? Only their hearts will know the answer to this.

Self-compassion ranks just as highly as compassion to others. So, the next time you go to give to others, just check in on why you are giving it. Is it attention seeking? Can you afford it? Are you giving out of love or guilt, or a need to be accepted and belong?

5.1.3: I must be perfect

Perfectionism is widespread in our society. I was once a perfectionist who struggled to cope with failure of any kind. Our need for perfection flies in the face of the fact that, as human beings, we learn from our mistakes. Yet we do everything to make sure we don't expose ourselves to the possibility of failure. This limits our ability to learn. It's a total contradiction.

Since our self-esteem is closely linked to how successful we believe we have been, every time we 'fail' we tend to feel lesser as a person. When we tally all these so-called failures, we can use it as further evidence in our own 'courts' that we are guilty of being unworthy.

During the first 18 years of my life, I pretty much excelled at everything I did, whether it was in academia or sports. However, over the years that followed, I fell short of my expectations in marriage, work, friendships, and even as a parent. You may have your own stories of woe when it comes to failure. However, the simple fact is that sometimes you will get the outcome you desire in life, and other times you won't. There is no 'failure'. Everything in life is either a source of joy or a learning experience and, unfortunately, there is no better way to learn than to make a mistake. And in these mistakes lies joy, if we rejoice in what we have come to understand about ourselves.

It is said that you need light to see in darkness, and darkness to see light. This also applies to us. If you refuse to see life as bad, then the darkness ceases to exist, and everything is just different shades of light.

If you ask a person when they have grown most in their life, they will almost always cite the circumstances of a difficult time they endured (excepting perhaps situations of abuse). They will then tell you what they learnt during that time. Try it for yourself, before you read on, and rejoice in what you learnt because of the difficulties you endured. Then the next time you experience a dark period in your life, embrace the fact that there will be teachings to learn because, almost without doubt, there will be a silver lining to the clouds that have formed.

When you are complete and know who you are, a lesser outcome than you hoped for will not diminish you or enhance your sense of self. Nothing can or ever will. It just enables you to grow and expand. Life is an adventure, not a competition or spectator sport, and what others think of you is truly none of your business. Try instead to focus on measures of happiness to define how you assess your life. Most people tend to assess their lives based on societal barometers, such as levels of wealth or beauty, or events we have won or lost. In truth, our reason for living is to be happy, and when we reach our deathbed nothing else will matter. You can't take your big house or fast car with you, and ultimately your good looks will fade.

Consider measuring success against your feelings of love, fun and fulfilment, and not your bank balance.

New doors will open for you that will be highly rewarding!

5.1.4: I can't put myself first

When I was brought up, I was taught to put others first. To do otherwise was to be selfish, or so I was told.

However, it is possible to give most of our love to others, and not love ourselves enough. It's a balancing act. Those with high levels of compassion, and a tendency to want to nurture others, are more likely to do this, and at great expense to their sense of self.

Many people believe that being self-centred is egotistical and holds us back from sharing love with others. However, the true meaning of someone who is self-centred is not one who is selfish, but one who is deeply known to themselves, because they have accessed their heart. When we love ourselves in this way and are deeply aligned with who we are, we have so much more to share with or offer others. We are lighter and brighter and can spread our happiness to all whom we meet.

As you become more fulfilled as a person, you can offer yourself the contentment and compassion you may have traditionally given to others. You can feel and know your sovereignty and your right to be respected by others, in the same way you respect them. When your self-worth is high you won't allow others to manipulate or take advantage of you, unless you know, in your seat of integrity, that it is fair. You will stand up for what you know is right in an unwavering way and, even if you are persecuted as a result of this, it will not sway you from your belief or course of action because you know you matter and you are not a doormat to be walked over.

Happy people don't start fights. If more people in this world knew who they were and were more content, the world would be a happier place. Happy countries don't start wars; however, they will defend themselves if an attacker cannot be persuaded to be fair.

In 2019, I took a career break. I had devoted 38 years of continual employment to my family and my job. I had given up most of my hobbies and, once I become a parent, focussed primarily on being a provider for my children. During this career break, it took me months to find out who I truly was. I had to learn again what I loved to do, and I embarked on a plethora of new activities that I had secretly admired and wanted to try.

As I aligned myself to my true self, I discovered I had so much more to offer everyone I knew or met, because I was, and am now, more vibrant and lighter.

The greatest beneficiary of this change has been my children, and they have commented on how much more present I am now. In nourishing myself, I put myself in a better position to give to them and nourish them as a result.

Likewise, the recent Covid-19 lockdowns forced many people homewards. It caused many of us great pain, but for those not directly harmed by the virus, it allowed us to slow down and re-evaluate our lives. After all, this is our life we are living, and not the life of others. As a sovereign being we matter, and we all have the right to choose the life we want, not just fit in with what everyone else is doing.

Are you investing too much energy into others, leaving little space for yourself? You deserve to receive some of your own time and attention. This is a natural and happy way of being. We need to forget the conditioned belief that this is a selfish way to live.

Balance is the key to a wonderful life!

5.1.5: I need to be in a relationship

Many people enter and stay in romantic relationships because they need them. They need another person to make them feel whole or complete them. So, if a relationship ends, they will quickly seek another to fill the void that has been exposed in their self-esteem. It's like the tide going out on a beach and exposing the rocks. They can't wait for the next high tide to cover them up.

Sometimes it's easier to find someone else to love us, than it is to fill the empty void that dwells inside us with our own love. But it's unfair on the person we have coupled with to expect them to make us feel complete. It's exhausting for them. Many relationships fail based on this pressure, because love needs to come from our own hearts before we can expect to receive it from another. We can only really expect someone to want to be intimate with us if we have learnt to be intimate, or in love with, ourselves.

When we understand that we generally get out of life what we put into it, we can realise that we only receive intimacy when we become into-my-self. This is not ego-based but a means to getting to know that we are love at our centre or core. Most people say confidence is attractive. I wonder why? When we exude the love we have for ourselves, that authentic self-love brings forth authentic love connections.

Authenticity here is key; it cannot be faked. While it is possible to mould yourself to a partner under the illusion that the relationship is happy, after about two years people cannot help but revert to their true selves and the pretence ends, even if it's not immediately expressed. In the long run, there is no substitute for absolute authenticity in relationships, and the first step in authenticity is acknowledging your true self.

I learned this lesson the hard way, as I know many readers will have also experienced. After my second divorce in 2016, I was devastated and felt like a failure. I tried internet dating, but no permanent relationship eventuated; though those who I did date were very loving and beautiful. The problem was I didn't yet know my authentic self. So, for five years, I committed myself to discovering who I was as a priority. I chose to be alone to discover my truth and not make the same relationship mistakes again and again.

Indeed, it's very common for relationship mistakes to repeat, because we are often attracted to the same type of person, with particular qualities and mannerisms. There is a good chance that, in searching for that type of personality or physicality, mistakes will repeat. For this reason alone, it's better first to go within and discover what is our authentic self, before the lack of this acknowledgement causes continual heartache.

It will also stop you from blaming other people for the demise of your relationship, as tends to happen when a relationship ends.

After much soul searching, I'm pleased to report I am now immeasurably happy. I would like but no longer *need* a romantic partner. This lack of needing is very liberating. Anyone who has been in a relationship based on need will have felt the control that it exerts on both parties.

Deep down as human beings, we all seek to be in a romantic relationship that has at its core unconditional love. We do want to be loved, warts and all, and not be resented for being the person we really are. Unfortunately, it's virtually impossible for two people, who have been conditioned in the way society currently conditions us, to love each other unconditionally.

However, when love can be received and given without condition or demand, an undeniable magic can descend upon two lovers.

Freedom is a core component of this unconditional love. Control is totally contrary to our inbuilt desire for the freedom to express our true selves in life. So being vibrant, because you are able to express who you really are, is the greatest gift you can give yourself, give a partner and give to a relationship.

We often confuse the two concepts of commitment and need in a relationship. They are different!

We can be committed to another because we love someone, and want them in our lives, without having to carry the energy of neediness in that relationship.

Freedom comes when our commitment to each other creates trust but does not preclude each party from being free in their lives. Great relationships that I observe work this way.

I once had a repeating pattern in my romantic relationships that saw me take the blame whenever my partner got sad or upset. If they got sad, I feared they might replace me, so I readily took the blame for any problem in the relationship and tried to change myself rather than sharing the problem and its solution. This was a symptom of my need to be loved by another.

Imagine a relationship in which two partners are giving and receiving love in equal measure and love themselves to the point that there is no need. This is what is possible when you know and love the real you. Deep trust can descend between lovers if they are both capable of this. The truth is that unconditional love cannot be fully present until we shake off the conditioning corrupting our own self-love. True love can only exist where there is desire and want, but not need. Need is the silent enemy of romantic relationships.

Our society though, through its subliminal messages, has taught us to prioritise romance over love. The fairy tale is baked into our mindset at an early age and creates in many people an image of what a relationship should be like. Many of us go through life in search of that prince or princess who will complete us and make us 'happily ever after'. We need to learn how to feel love to give and receive love, rather than obsess over romance. True romance arises off the back of love, not the other way around.

Many people, like the younger me, tend to believe romance can create love. But love can't be created by our minds, only our hearts. It's a vibration inside our hearts and is unlikely to be created by an evening out in an expensive restaurant.

New relationships often offer romance, but not love; and the desire for romance can cause real loving relationships to be discarded. Real love takes acceptance, understanding and self-love, yet many of us don't comprehend the true power of love.

What kind of romantic relationship do you have? Is it based on want or need? Do you focus on romance or love? It might be time to explore this more deeply!

5.1.6: I must compete and win

Our lack of self-worth has also created an insatiable need to win that shows up in all aspects of our society and brings out the very worst in us. We are programmed to fight, not unite; to compete, not to collaborate. We have made life into a battle between individuality and unity. We need each other, but we can't stand losing to others. Our egos allow us to feel validated and superior to others when we win. But when we lose, we feel less worthy. We tend to focus solely on the result, and never whether we have enjoyed the contest or challenge of an event.

In a world where unity is in short supply, our obsession with winning creates a sense of separation or disharmony. At its worst our need to win – to be worthy – can lead to physical violence. Consider the violent scenes of the 1980s English soccer matches. People were regularly harmed over the result of a game of football. Can you see the madness in this?

This need to win can also be addictive. When I was growing up, I was determined to win at everything I did, whether it was sports or academic pursuits. I had to win, or to put it another way, not lose, or I became extremely unhappy. My parents never gave me any recognition for anything I accomplished in my life through participation, particularly my father. He would make fun of me for losing and would not even comment when I won! I was quite accomplished at schoolwork and sports, so I came to believe that I had to be the very best in order to be worthy of recognition. In hindsight this was just an assumption. Still, this lack of recognition set me on a course driven by a never-ending urge to win, to be the best. It also made me reluctant to enter competitions or events where I felt I might not win. My desire to win was equally matched by my fear of failure, which was a debilitating place to inhabit.

Our language around winning supports the perceived importance of winning in our society. Consider these common expressions:

- *Winners are grinners, and losers can suit themselves*
- *Win at all costs*
- *We play to win*
- *That winning feeling*

Expressions such as these highlight the importance of winning to our egos, and the desire to feel important and happy through that win. Many structures have been created in our world to align with this egoic need to win. Most sporting competitions have a final match, and a winner is crowned at the end. Winners usually get the bulk of the financial advantages and praise from media and audiences. At school we rank students and give out awards to those who get the highest marks. Magazines and organisations produce regular lists of the richest people in the world, the sexiest people in the world, and so on. Our professional tennis players all have a ranking, and the top ranked players are highly paid. Success at the Olympics, which is ostensibly all about the spirit of competing, is measured by the medal count at the end, and many countries use this to justify the financial cost of sending teams to the games. The media give all their attention to the competitors that win medals. The rest are dismissed.

Some industries even create their own award structures to satisfy their egos. The acting profession is a prime offender here. Actors get all dressed up and walk down a red carpet so they can bask in their own egoic glory. How upsetting for all those excellent and worthy actors not invited!

Interestingly, we don't lay down red carpets for the best teachers, nurses or aged-care workers; yet Covid-19 showed us how much these people really contribute to life.

We have sayings about the spirit of competition and taking part for fun, but at the end of the day it's the winners who usually get the recognition and money.

There is nothing wrong with success or having sovereignty as a person or nation, but we also don't need to achieve this by having power over another.

The worst example of this need to win, or have power over another, is of course war.

The history of our human world is stained by war. War can never be justified as a way to settle differences and is the worst demonstration of the damaging influence of ego. Wars should never be waged. They are atrocious. The devastation done to a country or city by war is immense. But the damage done by war to a human soul is beyond measure. Even those who win a war ultimately lose, because the act of killing and hurting other human beings goes against our deep ingrained values of love and unity.

War would never happen if we were more readily able to access this sense of unity and know that we are all one big family. Would you kill your brother or sister over land or resources?

Yet we glorify the soldiers who take part in war, whether they win or lose, because their sacrifices are so great.

In 2017, I marched in the annual ANZAC march through the streets of Sydney to honour the fact that my grandfather, George Park, took part in World War II for six years as an infantry soldier. I honoured his bravery in volunteering and fighting, though I also detested the world leaders who had created that horrible war. Adolf Hitler wanted other countries to pay for the brutal reparations imposed on the German people by the victorious allies after World War I. He was not a man with inner peace, and he convinced his whole nation that war rather than forgiveness was the best way to restore Germany's previous loss of face. How many millions of people died because he, and his people, were in so much internal pain?

In 2018 and 2019, I visited Pearl Harbour in Hawaii, to see where World War II began between the United States of America and Japan; and I visited Hiroshima in Japan, the site of the first nuclear bomb unleashed in World War II, to end that same conflict. Hundreds of thousands of Japanese people were killed by that bomb in the most hideous way possible. The temperature at the point of impact of the atomic bomb in Hiroshima was around one million degrees. Imagine the impact of that on the human body – people just disintegrated and died with no warning. I can only imagine the depth of pain and guilt on both sides that has lingered for many years.

The entire conflict was pointless and achieved nothing other than suffering, and great fear.

We need more care and compassion in our world, not competition and conflict. We have become desensitised to the very essence of war.

The only solution that will serve us is to finally see that we are all one big family, regardless of where we live; and that violence, in the shocking form of war, is never ever, ever, ever, ever an option.

Wise leaders, who can access their hearts as well as their minds, are needed by this world before it's too late and humanity destroys itself. Throughout history, insecure and ignorant leaders have destroyed the souls of millions, through forcing them to take part in or witness a war. How many people have been murdered, disfigured, raped or tortured? When making the hideous decision to start a war, leaders must know this will happen. If they can't get this, they need to be replaced or overthrown. Yet our need to win, or our need for revenge when we feel we have lost or been betrayed by another, takes control.

Self-love will, of course, demand we defend ourselves on some occasions from an unprovoked or unfair attack, but that is different to revenge or aggression. Self-defence comes from our hearts and a place of fairness and self-love. Revenge is an egoic reaction to remedy the diminution of our self-esteem that has arisen from a perceived loss.

This relates to personal as well as national issues. After my second divorce, I thought I had lost everything. I didn't realise this was because much of my self-esteem had been based on my marriage, family and wealth, and the divorce had seemingly cost me all three. Ultimately, I found my way to forgiving myself for that mistake, accept that I had been taught to see losing as wrong – rather than a source of learning – and embrace the valuable self-awareness that brought. Forgiveness requires more courage than revenge, because it relies on us accepting the conditioning we may have been taught and letting it go in the interests of peace.

There is a point where you become so strong within yourself that even forgiveness becomes irrelevant. Forgiveness is often for your own happiness, not the other person's happiness, so it's possible to go beyond needing it when you reach a point of gratitude for all you have experienced, whether it felt good or bad at the time. When you reach a point where you are so full of self-love that no one can hurt you – no matter what they do to you – forgiveness becomes unnecessary. There is nothing to forgive.

This is likely how great leaders throughout history have been able to forgive those who harm them, so high is their enlightenment that they can accept the actions of all, and in fact pity them for their lack of enlightenment and compassion.

Indeed, compassion is the key. Compassion would have our societies collaborating for fun, not competing to be the absolute winner and in the process inciting a sense of revenge in those losing. A more natural way to live is to accept that not everyone can win, but everyone can learn. Every loss offers us an opportunity to learn and be in our hearts. Some people are more talented at certain things we compete in, but surely that's okay if we enjoy the experience of the interaction.

What if we devote ourselves to what we enjoy, to what adds value to our lives and what we are interested in, rather than what gives us the most prestige or wealth? Simply change your beliefs and the freedom to enjoy life more will be yours!

Our need for importance stifles our opportunity to be potent, for it holds us back from living a full, free, and fun life. Competing with each other is a flawed strategy. If only we were able to step back and see the world in a giant mirror, we would see that we are a small speck in a giant tapestry. Where do we therefore get this need to be important, beat everyone around us, and only worry about ourselves? Perhaps it starts in our conditioning.

You could start by challenge yourself. Ask yourself how much you need to win, and how you genuinely feel when you don't. Is your happiness overly impacted when a sporting team or political party loses? Are you addicted to winning, or shaken by the fear of losing?

5.1.7: Money makes me more important

A lack of worthiness leads us to seek money and material possessions to make us feel valuable.

Much of life is dedicated to the pursuit of money. In money we find great security, and so to some extent we have become ruled by our desire for money. Money has been described as the 'source of all evil'. It is not, but our egos' lust for it is a major source of pain and leads to much unhappiness.

I have dedicated further discussion to money in later chapters because of its massive influence, although we often overstate its importance. It gives us energy, but it's not love.

Money is easily valued because there are many different markets to assess what things are worth. We wrongly ascribe the value of our money to ourselves and use it to determine our own value, when the reality is we are already precious regardless of our level of wealth. Money is the wrong currency to use for our valuation of ourselves. Truly we are all priceless because you cannot put a monetary value on the life force that is inside us. We are a miracle, money or not!

There is in fact nothing wrong with money, unless we need it to validate our lives. There is nothing wrong with wanting it either. It gives us the energy to thrive. Although rich people can perhaps make money easier because they have the money to invest and security to offset risks; if we give up trying or even dreaming altogether, we can find ourselves in a cycle of mediocrity or poverty, from which we may struggle to escape. We can get caught in the normal nine-to-five work life, contributing primarily to the wealth of others. We may survive pay cheque to pay cheque, but money will be a constant source of stress in our lives.

Money has its uses as a motivator. People can make great wealth if they have a dream and the confidence to follow it through. Walt Disney is a great example. He went broke multiple times before he created Disneyland and brought his dream into reality and then made a fortune.

Like him, we all have natural talents and gifts; though most of us never take the time to discover what our greatest gifts are, or the time to step into that gift to create a living.

I grew up in a modest family with a mother who resented those with more money. My parents spent most of their lives paying off a meagre mortgage and were in a mindset of lack that kept them financially mediocre. I witnessed this mindset of lack, hated it, so grew up determined to not be poor like my parents. I adopted their security conscious mindset and came to overvalue the power of money to give me security. I also wanted to appear wealthy and to have the biggest house I could get, so that I could be admired by others, maybe even resented. I didn't want to be unsuccessful, as I perceived my father to be, at least to my young eyes. Without a doubt, this led me to borrow too much money and live beyond my means.

Yet this is normal for our society, with many people constantly living in debt. We believe it is more important to create an illusion of wealth than to follow our heart's desires, and it leads us to follow the herd for fear of missing out.

What if we worked together to ensure we all have more? What if money and wealth didn't define us or our worth, they only gave us the energy to attain the life of our dreams? We don't need to collect more, to become more.

What is your relationship to money and how do you feel about its impact on your life so far? Do you crave it for validation, to the extent that it overshadows other more important aspects of your life?

5.1.8: Beautiful people are more worthy

We all want to be considered attractive and sexually desirable. When we are complimented about how we look, we feel good about ourselves. It validates our egoic minds, even if our immediate response is to reject the compliment. Do you ever do this?

We even idolise people in our community who are more physically attractive than the average. Those of us who consider ourselves average can be intimidated by beautiful people, because we hold them in such high regard. Top actors and actresses, models and fit sports personalities are key recipients of this type of adoration. Beautiful people can even be perceived to receive greater opportunities in life, though there is no actual grounding for such a belief – it's just that we have been so conditioned to believe that good looks make you more lovable, and this is reinforced by what we see around us each day.

There is a commonly used phrase that 'beauty is only skin-deep'. We have all heard and tried to believe in this, and deep within our hearts we know everyone is equal. Yet it flies in the face of all the beautiful models, royals, or actors who sell the movies, calendars, and television shows. Despite our knowing that beauty does not provide substance to a person's personality, we are conditioned to think beautiful people are better than us.

Sexual attraction is also a powerful force, so much so we can sometimes end up in relationships based on lust rather than love, mistaking one for the other.

At the start of a relationship, lust can provide great potency between two people, and without a doubt it is important to many of us. However, there is a need to distinguish between love and sexual attraction because the latter can have a use-by date, whereas real love never dies. It just gets covered up by debris from our egos.

I am not criticising or downplaying the importance of lust or physical attraction in our lives. Being intimate with someone who we find attractive is a great gift and a natural first base in bringing lovers together. But, by itself, it doesn't often bring us enduring connections with others. Love comes from within us, not from external factors such as the looks of our partner.

Even those who are beautiful still stand in front of the mirror every day and see fault in the way they look. This reflects our natural predisposition to want to be perfect.

During the Covid-19 pandemic, the demand for plastic surgery to make people more attractive tripled in Australia. Why? Is it because people had more time to get the surgery done and to internet date? Or were their fears leading them to want to be better looking, to make themselves more attractive to partners?

Whatever the reason, we have the opportunity to rethink our unnatural obsession with looks because looks are temporary and do not change the essence of who we are.

Do we really want a society that judges people so much on their looks, forcing us to devote time and money to making ourselves look better? Perhaps you can relate to this?

Next time you are on Facebook or Instagram, look closely at the photos people put up of themselves. Do they really need to be in swimwear or looking sexy to be acceptable as a friend?

When you go inward and feel the precious life force inside you, you can let this need to be validated by others go. We are all beautiful at the core. Some people will find you physically attractive and others will not. This is just nature at play, but it can never really change the truth: that we are all beautiful.

Next time you look in the mirror, look not at your shape but stare deeply into your eyes, for here you will sense the true beauty that comes from being alive, happy, and full of love. The eyes are truly the window to your soul, and it's here where another's light shines through!

5.1.9: Sex is about the outcome

Lovemaking is one of life's greatest pleasures, yet our conditioned minds have made sex about the outcome, and not the connection that results from intimacy, resulting in a source of great pain for many people.

We are biologically programmed to reproduce, and so our bodies are primed to seek sexual experiences and orgasms as a result. We have primal urges that we find hard to resist.

At the same time, the beautiful interactions that arise from physical intimacy with another of our choosing, have much more value than a mere orgasm. Deep down, we all know this – we want to love and be loved and to express this love. Our hearts and bodies crave the connection that lovemaking can bring forth. Sex is a powerful uniting force in a relationship, though we often downplay it to make sure that we are not seen as sexual deviants!

We can make the choice to become more natural and make love with equality, focussing on the pleasure of the journey. Lovemaking is a powerful creative force in our world and can provide a great source of happiness in relationships, when approached without conditioning. We are like light globes: unless we are regularly turned on, we will not be a beacon of light in our lives and achieve true happiness!

Yet society has us conditioned to focus on the end orgasm, not the intimacy we can achieve before we get there.

What is the solution?

We rarely tell our sexual partners what we want from our intimate encounters, how we want to feel afterwards – connected and united in love. We are more focussed on giving them what we *assume* they want. We know what has worked for that person previously, or others we had sex with, and we try and reproduce that response. Our egos are very much in charge. In effect we are trying to limit our risk of failure in the bedroom, because that is our worst nightmare come true, so we focus on the orgasm as a sign of success.

But the keyword here is 'assume'. We typically assume we know what our partners want, and we want to believe we are good at sex (just like we believe we are all good drivers!) because that is what the media and movies say we need to be.

How often do we ask what our partner wants, so we can improve the overall experience and enhance our relationship? Only you know the answer to that, but it's likely a rare exchange between most lovers. We bask in our own version of ignorance and assumption.

In 2019 and 2020 I had the opportunity to study tantric sex. This gave me a vastly different perspective on sex. Tantric sex is about slow, intimate lovemaking. It is not about friction and the achievement of an outcome. It's about the transfer of sexual energy between two lovers and the pleasure of the journey or experience. Google it and find out more if you are interested.

The one thing most participants in the course had in common was a general sense of unworthiness to sexual pleasure. They were all more comfortable giving sexual pleasure rather than receiving it, as a rule. To receive pleasure can create a sense of guilt inside us, even though our bodies crave it. We are conditioned to ignore our sexual desires, and we prefer to give so we feel better about ourselves.

But ultimately, we all lose from a tendency to self-sacrifice in this way. The truth is we make love to satisfy our desire to connect with another human being. To persuade ourselves of anything else is delusional.

Can you relate to this obsession with giving in the bedroom and guilt at receiving? Do you suppress your own bodily needs and only tend to them once you believe you have given your partner what you think they desire, an orgasm? In doing this, we disembody ourselves and self-sacrifice our true desires. We matter more than we realise.

Ultimately, if you are in a romantic relationship, the solution is to discuss sex with your partner, with a view to enhancing your connection and valuing the journey. It's never too late to make a fresh start.

If you are single, perhaps contemplate what you want to experience in your next relationship.

And why not Google tantric sex? Who knows, you might open the door to a wonderful new wave of passion in your life!

5.1.10: I can't love someone unless they love me too

When we reach a point in our lives where we can truly love ourselves, with the potency and compassion we deserve, we can then love unconditionally and express our love of others, even if they don't love us or treat us in a loving way.

It's quite normal for our minds to resist admitting our love or desire for another person until they first admit to loving or desiring us. Over and over we therefore suppress our love for others until we are sure they love us and won't reject us in our moment of truth or vulnerability. Our egos can't stand to be crushed by rejection, so we keep our feelings secret and may even deny them to ourselves. In the process, our fear of rejection can stifle us, preventing us from opening up to the infinite possibilities that await our truths.

If, however, we can overcome our fear of rejection and admit our true feelings, a whole new world of fantastic experiences and connections can await us. It may be daunting at first, with both parties making timid concessions to the other, testing the waters, perhaps a little scared but willing to take a chance anyway. We might barely know the other person yet feel compelled to connect anyway. Perhaps you can remember that feeling of tentative yet blossoming connection? When that connection blooms, the thrill of being able to express your feelings freely is such a delight, your heart can finally take centre stage, and a wonderful path of possibilities can open up. It's well worth any risk!

A similar process happens with betrayal. Many of us have loved others who we then believe have betrayed us. The conventional thinking in our minds tells us that, in these circumstances, we should stop loving that other person, after all that is an accepted 'equal and opposite reaction' to the action of betrayal. We think this is necessary as our egos strive to protect us from pain.

However, love can still exist and persist, because it emanates from our hearts and not our minds. It is blocked by the pollution of our minds. But when we allow the truth inside our hearts to be fully felt, regardless of the circumstances, we will see that it is possible to love another irrespective of their feelings or responses to us. Love truly never dies, and can be expressed from outside of a relationship; we just need to broaden our thinking here!

This doesn't mean we need interact with a person who treats us badly or betrays us. Self-love may see us cut off or diminish our connection to that person as we learn to fully value ourselves. Nevertheless, love persists, and we can still acknowledge that love in our selves.

This 'unconditional' love allows us to love others without the need for a payback, or even an ongoing interaction with that person. It exists and that is all it needs to do. After all, don't we do this when a loved one passes on?

5.2: We deserve to suffer

Commensurate with our propensity to lack worthiness in our lives, human society has witnessed a general acceptance of suffering. Deep down, we believe that suffering is virtuous.

In a famous statement to Australia in 1971, Malcolm Fraser, the then Prime Minister, said:

> "Life is not meant to be easy."

Many readily accepted this, as it reinforced their existing preconditioned mindsets. It reflected an unnatural acceptance of unhappiness and stress in life.

Throughout history, human societies have witnessed great suffering through wars, poverty, economic collapses, death, sickness, and so on. We have been somewhat accepting of these events, and to some extent our belief structures have supported them. We haven't stopped often enough to question why they need to take place, because they most likely didn't. We tolerated them. We are mentally programmed to survive, and as a general rule to not expect to thrive, because our minds – and not our hearts – are in command. We live in a place of fear and the need to protect ourselves from misfortune.

The popular reality television show called 'Survivor' films volunteers in an isolated tropical setting, as they compete to survive in teams and win a series of 'eliminations'. The show is somewhat of a metaphor for our lives, because of its over-focus on survival. I look forward to the day when the studios make a show called 'Thriver'!

During my career in business, there was an obvious cultural acceptance of a mild form of slavery. Workers would basically subject themselves to any conditions inflicted on them by their employer, because their basic instinct was to keep their jobs and take home their pay packet at all costs. We spend most of our working lives sacrificing our personal time for an employer, or a series of employers, who at the end of the day may not care too much about our wellbeing. They want profit, and the workers are a key way to get it.

Each year, people give more and more of themselves to stay employed in an increasingly competitive business world. They work more and more unpaid overtime, possibly working weekends and late nights, at the expense of their time with family. They sacrifice their hobbies and end up fundamentally unhappy. I was an expert at this for many years and wore it as a badge of honour. Can you relate to this, or see it in one of your friends or relatives? Are you a proud slave like I once was?

Many people work in jobs they don't like. They live for weekends and annual holidays. Their main plan seems to be to survive to retirement age, so they can then do nothing or very little. In effect, they fail to see that they are giving up their happiness in the present, in the hope they will find it in their future. This is based on their fundamental instinct to survive, not thrive, even if that involves misery and suffering. In this place, life can become very mediocre.

I was a martyr in my working life. I was brought up by a generation that had experienced two world wars and several economic depressions. They were accustomed to suffering, and I was taught as a child not to complain about life's limitations. It was our lot. I was forced to go to school when I was sick, and I entered the workforce prepared to be loyal to an employer regardless of how they treated me. I worked ridiculously long hours in jobs I never really loved, and I never complained. I was conditioned to self-sacrifice myself for my career and money. I was taught to keep a 'stiff upper lip' and put up with things, no matter how bad they got. I wasn't to show emotions unless they were positive. Emotions were for the weak. Many people, like me, learned to push through pain and poor health even if it didn't serve them.

During the Covid-19 pandemic, however, people became more aware of how much they had previously pushed themselves to their limits – as revealed by how often they went to work when sick, and the lack of time they spent at home with family and relaxing. Covid-19 stopped people going into work when sick and encouraged people to work from home. This gave many the opportunity to realise how much our health and relationships matter, not just our bank balances.

All throughout history people have incited war, whereas no political event can ever warrant the bloodshed of another human being. We have blindly followed our egoist leaders into such wars, without challenging this hard enough. Why? Because we accept that hardship is a part of life, when in fact it's just a screwed-up belief structure adopted by our minds that are hell-bent on helping us to fit in and survive. War is the ultimate competition, riddled with suffering and the need to survive, and so we glorify it. It's madness! The day we stop so readily accepting hardship and suffering, that is the day they will diminish greatly and start to fall away. To thrive is to really be alive.

Various organised religions have contributed to this mindset that we deserve to suffer. Ancient sacrifice to win favour from gods is a practice going back thousands of years. Do we really think that our gods expect or want us to suffer in this way?

Prophets have advocated being kind to one another, yet for some reason we seem to think that does not extend to ourselves.

Some religions would have us believe that to be loved, we need to give up sex, to eat certain foods on certain days or at certain times, to sacrifice lengths of time in prayer or to worship, and so on. Our intentions and actions, in terms of how we treat ourselves and others, are surely more important than such things?

Unfortunately, many organised religions trade on our over-acceptance of suffering and pain. They sell on fear. 'Do as we say or go to hell' is a common belief structure promoted throughout history, mainly to demand your attendance and money. Organised religions insist on contributions from an often-struggling population, who pay money to avoid eternal damnation; yet the religious institution in question is likely to be one of the richest in the world, with a global property portfolio.

We are meant to attend church with our presence, not with presents in the form of money, for an already rich institution.

Sacrifice isn't for religion or employers alone.

Even in families, parents often sacrifice themselves for the good of their children. The prevailing belief structure that pervades is that 'I am less important than my children'. I pretty much gave up all my interests once I had children, under a sense of obligation.

Did anyone ask me to do this? No, I just felt I had to.

Later in life, when I saw how unnecessary this was, I started to live again. I realised that sacrifice was a self-imposed cage. It wasn't forced upon me by anyone else, but by my own limited way of thinking. Finally, I saw that I did matter as much as my kids; and to be honest, my kids loved seeing me happy.

Suffering validates us because our low self-esteem tells us we deserve it. If we simply survive, that's a major achievement, or so we tell ourselves subconsciously. Our sense of survival is a natural instinct, but so is our entitlement to pleasure and fun – we just block these out because we see ourselves as victims or martyrs. If we can sacrifice ourselves in the interests of others, then we feel validated. Ultimately, however, it has the opposite effect: too much self-sacrifice and it creates a great source of stress in life, contrary to self-love.

We can become slaves to what we believe are our obligations.

But if we change our thinking as a society, we will see that we are free to be whomever we want to be, and we don't need to suffer in order to matter. Freedom and choice are natural states of being, and we have the right to be what our hearts' desire.

Can you relate to this paradigm? Remember, happiness is a choice!

5.2.1: Life is serious, and it helps to worry

Commensurate with our core belief that we must suffer are the beliefs that life is serious, and that it helps to worry about it.

We have come to believe that seriousness is power and powerful. This is a long-held concept. We often associate serious things with a sense of fear or loss, and the work of powerful institutions or people. The need for protection enters our minds, and we move away from the energies of love and positivity. In these times, we lose our compassion and our need to win comes to the fore.

But I ask you this: why can't we tackle important things without making them serious? Surely, if we approach a problem with the energy of love, we can more readily focus on what is possible and align with our creativity, rather than being obsessed with what may be lost?

It might sound obvious, but when you are less serious you can't help but have more fun! It's a simple principle. Yet how often do we see our leaders having fun, and how would we react if they were? If seriousness equals importance in our minds, why would we admire fun leaders?

Life is constantly unfolding around us, and most of it we cannot control. It's a big world with billions of souls and forces interacting. When things happen to us that we don't like, we often take them very seriously. We worry, and we get stressed. This stress can then have significant and negative impacts on our wellbeing and environments. Our bodies can get sick as a result of worry and anxiety. To cope, many people turn to drugs, alcohol, or violence. This solves nothing and ultimately makes our lives worse in many ways.

The afflictions that diminish our health are called 'dis-eases' for a reason. When we are not 'at ease' with aspects of our life, we are dis-affected and can get sick. It is a major cause of many illnesses.

That said, many things in this world could of course be regarded as important and require our attention. However, our serious nature often comes from an inability to let go and accept what is. This does not mean that you will not experience emotions as a result of events in your life. Emotions are merely messages that you can contemplate to achieve greater self-awareness, or simply observe and enjoy. They are part of the privilege of being human, but they are a part we often try to suppress.

If only we could live a life of wonder, not worry, regardless of what takes place around us.

5.2.2: Wonder not worry

I try and live my life from the perspective of wonder, not worry. When anything happens that I witness or experience, it's liberating to view it with the perspective that, since it's already happened, it may as well teach me or another something valuable. My life has had many ups and downs, but once I was able to take this perspective every day, I was able to see what I could learn from each event.

Between the ages of 19-50, I suffered terribly from an intense muscular disorder. It was over 30 years of hell. Very few people ever knew I suffered from this painful experience, not even family members. My muscular disease showed me that I would suffer if I didn't live in alignment with my true self. It also taught me patience, compassion and resilience. These traits will now serve me well in the rest of my life. In effect, my muscular disorder was self-inflicted, although conventional thinking would not see it this way. Once I saw it as my teacher, not my torturer, it left me in peace.

So, we can face challenges in our life with a degree of importance, because they create learning experiences for us. However, to treat anything like its life-or-death adds little value to any situation, and just leads to further pain — unless of course it does put our physical bodies at risk of death.

It's normal for most people to overreact to situations and get stressed. But if we live from our hearts and the knowledge of what we really are, we will naturally take the perspective of wonder — not worry — in our lives.

Try it and see how much better life can FEEL!

5.2.3: We will eventually be abandoned

Our lack of self-worth reflects in our constant fear of abandonment, mainly by those we love.

We often feel that our lovers will eventually fall out of love with us and replace us. We may fear our parents will reject us, and even our community will reject us, if we don't meet the needs of others. Since we aren't perfect, we desperately try to fit in to avoid this suffering. This stems from a need to be loved and to feel complete within ourselves.

Abandonment, however, is a construct of the mind and is an emotive word. It typically aligns with a belief that you have been unfairly treated by someone and didn't deserve to be. But, lurking deep within the anger or pain that accompanies abandonment, is an inability to forgive yourself for not being able to keep that relationship or situation healthy and alive. You are, in effect, beating yourself up, while convincing yourself that someone else is to blame.

We direct our anger at the other person but, like most things, the way to peace lies within ourselves. The anger is a doorway to greater self-reflection.

Relationships are mirrors into our souls for both parties involved and, if they end, one or both parties need not perceive that as failure on their part; rather it is a chance for growth. Both parties can learn from a break up, after all it's the relationship that failed, not the individuals involved. Regardless of whether the other person faces their demons and self-reflects, the opportunity is always there for you. The end of a relationship doesn't mean anyone is a failure.

When I tried internet dating, I was amazed that many of the women I met just wanted 'a decent man'. It was like they had given up on finding true love or even someone who would fully respect them. Then it dawned on me. With around sixty-one per cent of women (in Australia, in 2021) claiming to have been sexually harassed or violated by men in their lives, and so many women being subjected to violence at the hands of men who said they loved them, is it any wonder they felt vulnerable, particularly in new relationships?

It's time men, in particular, grow to face their feelings when rejected, and not take their pain out on women or children when things go wrong. This is an urgent issue and needs addressing, given the extortionate violence, harm and even death it brings to families, particularly women. As a society, we really need to strengthen laws to prevent these types of events.

But real change won't occur until men learn to live from their hearts and conquer their limiting beliefs. Men need to do this, not women, lawyers or politicians. Facing pain and learning from it is the key, not blaming others. Men need to go inward, find love, and take that to the women and children in their lives.

If everyone were to simply love themselves enough, they would never feel they have failed in life. Failure is a totally irrelevant concept. If a breakup enables you to be stronger and more secure, you will eventually see it as a gift. It can make you happier and lighter, if you learn from it.

The greatest thing you can achieve in life is to transform yourself through greater self-awareness. The pain of so-called abandonment, especially when relationships end, can shower this gift upon us. Few other events can have this power.

The truth is you can only be abandoned if you abandon yourself. Love yourself and know you are worthy of love, and the world and your relationships will reflect this love.

It is often said that relationships end so that better ones can enter our lives. I certainly believe this. I wonder if you have ever experienced this in your life.

You don't deserve to suffer, but some relationships are stepping stones to that romantic love you have always dreamt about, where you will find true happiness.

5.3: There is a lack of resources

Collectively, people believe there are not enough resources in the world to go around and meet everyone's needs. This is a mindset of lack, and it leads to our never-ending drive to compete with each other.

However, this mindset of lack is nothing more than a self-fulfilling prophecy. What we fear we create! As we observe the haves and have-nots of the world, we reinforce the belief that: unless we compete and compete hard for the good things in life, we will miss out. It's an ever-deepening cycle that produces – what we see as – winners and losers, and it includes several associated limiting beliefs discussed below.

5.3.1: We must compete to survive

Throughout history, we have always obtained things we desire by taking or making. We can either create something ourselves or take it from others. Taking is obviously easier than making, and so power over others gives us access to what we desire, without needing to be creative ourselves.

However, there would be no lack on this planet if we worked together as a unified team. The planet is rich in resources, and we are gifted with great intelligence. The more we search for resources, the more we will surely find them. We, or more importantly our leaders, just lack the wisdom needed to create any unity of purpose. In most cases they lead us through manipulation, not a sense of purpose.

But wouldn't we create great abundance for all, and meet all our true needs, if we stopped being so competitive and became more cooperative?

This would require us to drop the whole idea of lack. When we see others with something we like, we tend to want it too, because not having it makes us feel we are less worthy or valuable than others. This is a construct of our egos.

Our hearts, if we can access them, know that we are already complete. There are things that we need to survive as human beings, such as food, water, medicines, shelter, and so on; but in truth our hearts and souls need very little to be happy.

Simplicity can be a great comfort for those who are truly happy, since it frees them up to live more liberally and focus on their true wants in life.

We have layered our desires over the top of our true needs and subconsciously labelled them as needs too. Yet most of us have never searched to find our true needs. Where I live, having multiple flat-screen television sets seems to have become a need!

The Covid-19 pandemic has shown us that we need much less than we thought to survive and be happy. Many businesses shut down during the various lockdowns, due to the lower levels of money and our inability to access their services or products following lockdown laws. But we survived.

Our sense of lack during the lockdowns was clearly demonstrated by our panic buying for goods that were in no real short supply, like toilet paper. People had to win over others, even if it meant having more rolls in their bathrooms.

For fifty-plus years, I was no different. I wanted more than I needed because material things made me feel better about myself. I eventually saw that I had more than I needed in life and was just as happy sitting in nature as I was travelling the world. I have now reset my sense of need, and hence my need to compete with others. I now embrace simplicity in my life far more than ever. Perhaps you have done the same, or would like to?

Our desire to compete can cause us to feel a sense of jealousy if others get what we wanted, but we could not afford it. This can lead to criminal behaviour or just plain resentment of those who have what we don't.

The bottom line is: if we think life is a big competition, and there are not enough resources for everyone, we will approach it from a place of fear, not love. This competition will manifest as a sense that some people win, and others lose, when the truth is we could all win if we work as a team. From this place, we could thrive as a community, not just survive.

We sometimes judge people who struggle in life as losers. But if we drop our warped sense of need, if we believe there are enough resources to meet the needs of all and work together, there could be a lot less so-called losers. This is our natural and happiest way to live, and it's a mere thought away.

5.3.2: We can exploit the weak

Our strong sense of competition has led our world into a place where there is a huge disparity of wealth. There are mega-rich billionaires at one end of the spectrum, and people in great poverty at the other end.

Covid-19 has served to widen this gap between rich and poor, with many billionaires in the right place, at the right time, getting richer by the hour, as mega-trends – like internet shopping – favour their business models. When poorer people received government handouts, they needed those funds to survive; whereas the rich were able to invest in assets and in turn get richer.

History is full of stories of wealthy people exploiting the less fortunate to build their wealth. Large corporations, including banks, have been shown to exploit unsophisticated customers who didn't understand what they were buying.

Today we see people in rich western nations outsourcing the manufacturing of certain goods, such as clothing, to developing countries where labour is cheap. In these places, such as Africa and parts of Asia, people are struggling to survive and get paid miniscule amounts of money to produce luxury products and consumables. The real profits are earned back in the richer nations at the expense of these vulnerable workers.

During the Covid-19 pandemic, when shops closed around the world, businesses in these wealthier nations showed no loyalty to these workers in these less developed countries. They just terminated their demand for goods and failed to pay for orders already placed. Such a decision reeks of selfishness and a lack of care for our fellow human beings. The exploitation of the weak is testament to our belief that it's acceptable to get away with what others allow, or what we can force them to do. Money is power unfortunately, or at least that's what we think.

There is a conscience springing up worldwide about the exploitation of the weak. Social media is bringing it forth more readily for all to see. Going forward, those people, businesses and countries that don't have a heart will find themselves under pressure to change.

If they don't, they may suffer a cardiac arrest of their own making and cease to exist.

5.3.3: Self-interest rules

Taxation systems across the world try to even out the financial playing field by taking more money from the rich to assist those less fortunate. But generally, there are no legal obligations on wealthy people to give to those less fortunate. This is fair, but the practice of sharing with others less fortunate than ourselves is generally not based on obligation, but on a person's values. Luckily, there are well-documented cases of mega-wealthy people sharing their assets with those who are less fortunate. But is this enough?

Money can bring a wonderful energy into our lives, allowing us to follow our dreams and meet our basic needs. But surely there comes a point at which we have enough money to be happy and can share some with our fellow human beings, or use it to benefit society and not just ourselves. Wouldn't we all benefit if collective wellbeing was more of a motivator in our society?

Our egos demand that we get richer and richer because this makes us feel safer and more worthy. Enough never seems to be enough when it comes to money. We don't need a law to force us to share, but we do need a new belief structure: that it's right and worthy to help our fellow humans in need, without the need for recognition.

Governments all over the world give welfare payments to the weak and disadvantaged to help them, and many developed countries give aid to developing countries to help them to progress. In 2005, after a massive earthquake in the Indian Ocean, Australia gave $1billion Australian dollars in aid to Sri Lanka alone to help them through the crisis. This was an amazing gesture, and its quantum shocked most Australians.

I applaud the government for doing it. We need more of it.

Despite all the charities doing their best to help the less advantaged, the world is still ravaged by poverty and full of under-privileged people, even in wealthier nations. We need to change our beliefs and became more open to sharing. It's the only way to a better world.

Even in elections, people tend to vote with their 'hip pocket' in mind. In other words, we vote for the candidates who will best give us what we want, typically money, rather than the health of the community in which we live. Could we all vote a different way?

Honestly ask yourself: how much does self-interest rule your life and the decisions you make each day?

5.4: We are alone, not all-one

One of the core sources of conflict and disharmony in this world is the belief that we are all separate, or alone – not unified as one race. This belief creates great pain and suffering, which is truly unnecessary.

This separation-based thinking needs to be replaced by a belief in unity at all levels in our world. It is a core belief structure that needs to be demolished if we are to achieve what we are capable of collectively and individually. The truth is: we are all one race, one big family, and not isolated individuals. We need each other to survive and thrive.

Our families, communities and countries demonstrate many harmful structures and interactions that flow from our lack of oneness or unity. The fact that the world is comprised of 195 separate countries, all with different laws and governance structures, is testament to this. Despite us all being the same, our communities are segregated. People tend to congregate only with those of similar backgrounds, as this makes them feel accepted and safe, even though this segregates them from others. In the same way, we tend to enter relationships with people who appear similar. We segregate children from different religions into different schools, claiming difference. We talk of black people, white people, and yellow people, just to name a few – highlighting difference, not unity. Our minds look for the differences in people, then we segregate ourselves from them. It is a figment of our egos. Our hearts would never make these kinds of judgements, for we are all from the same life force.

Inequality stems from our belief in superiority and inferiority, which is totally contrary to the concept of unity. Our tendency to judge and rank each other over our perceived relative worth is the great separator, and the cause of much unhappiness and violence in the world.

There is absolutely no basis for anyone to believe that they are superior to anyone else. Many people constantly seek personal inflation over true expansion.

That said, the sad reality is that some countries and communities have better access to resources, education, and technology, and this causes them to think they are better, and thus entitled to have power over other countries.

There are significant limitations that flow from our central belief that we are all separate.

5.4.1: We are not all equal

Inequality is a scourge on our human existence. It takes many forms. We all know in our hearts that it has no basis in truth, because we are all one big family. We are all human beings after all.

The belief that one group of people is fundamentally superior or inferior to another has led to great suffering and unfair outcomes for many people based on irrelevant differences such as:

- Skin colour
- Gender
- Religious beliefs
- Sexual preferences
- Physical ability
- Nationality
- Age
- Level of financial prosperity
- Perceived level of beauty
- Level of education

Persecution has been rampant since the dawn of time. But even with this knowing in their hearts, many people still consciously or subconsciously believe in different levels of worth among different groups of people.

How is this possible?

It's because of our preconditioned beliefs that have been handed down from generation to generation. Our subconscious minds have fundamentally accepted it, even if our hearts know that it is ridiculous. The only way out of this mess is to live from the wisdom of our hearts and change our thinking. Feel first, then think in alignment with your heart.

5.4.2: The king has no clothes

Let's consider fame. Originally, fame belonged to kings and queens, all of whom had a defined purpose. In exchange for taxes and loyalty, a monarch offered people protection and armaments, including a castle and armies.

However, we now elect governments to run our countries, and royal families have no actual power over so-called commoners, such that they are now little more than a wealthy famous family. So why do we still glorify them in the media and movies?

It's the same with celebrities. They may have at least acquired their status through talent and hard work, but they are merely doing a good job at what they do. So why put them on such a high pedestal? Are they really so admirable?

The story of 'The King with No Clothes' is a truism because many famous people are, in reality, no better than the people who worship them. It's time the masses saw this too and stopped swooning every time a celebrity or royal baby is born. Babies are born the world over, every minute, and they are equally beautiful!

Leaders – be they political or community leaders – need to be chosen based on integrity, strength and wisdom, not because they had particular parents, a big castle, a certain level of wealth, or are good at their job.

Let's consider dropping our preconditioned beliefs about admiring fame and royalty, and feel inside our hearts for a truer, happier belief system.

5.4.3: A virus for all

The Covid-19 pandemic showed us that we are all the same.

The virus did not care about country borders and infected people from all walks of life. It didn't just pick on a particular type of person. It even infected the leaders of the United States of America, the United Kingdom and Brazil, just to name a few. Even Ronaldo, arguably the world's best soccer player, contracted the virus, as did many other famous people.

Around the world, countries shut their borders to combat the virus. But we could also attack the virus as a collective, protecting the vulnerable in every nation by sharing medical technologies and vaccines. The World Health Organisation, or the United Nations, could have been a central point of coordination to fix the problem globally, rather than countries playing the blame game and allowing international self-interest to take centre stage.

5.4.4: Sexual discrimination is rife

A person's sexual preferences can also be held against them by our cruel society. It is irrelevant whether someone is heterosexual, homosexual, bisexual, transsexual or non-sexual; but throughout history people who are not heterosexual have been persecuted.

When I was growing up, homosexuality was frowned upon and often hidden. I recall homosexuality being a futile source of jokes and humour for comedians and television shows, who exploited the public belief structure that it was wrong or a lesser way of being. I also remember seeing the first gay and lesbian Mardi Gras parade through the streets of Sydney in 1979. Despite public condemnation, these brave groundbreakers had the strength to stand up for their rights and equality.

Thankfully things have progressed, and in 2019 gay marriage was finally made legal in Australia. Fairness is spreading as people liberate their minds and live more from their hearts. This needs to continue for us all to find happiness.

5.4.5: Religious truths can be divisive

Our history is riddled with religious wars and tensions. Every organised religion thinks it has the correct beliefs and the others must therefore be wrong. With more than 300 religions around the world, how can any one of them seriously think only they are right?

Many religions are based on the principle of a god-like presence or universal energy. However, at the end of the day, they are a construct of the human mind and are designed to serve the institution that governs them. If religious orders were actually connected to the divine, wouldn't there be only one religion, or a small number of similar ones? There is surely only one truth in the universe, not hundreds. Religion is often based on spiritual practices; yet most, if not all religions, are contorted and controlled by people. Every major religious text was written by someone – the Bible, the Sutras, the Vedas, the Quran, and Hadith, and the Tanach, Mishnah, Talmud and Midrash.

We have the right to belong to any religion we like and to support that organisation; but, the moment we believe that it is superior to other religions, is the moment that we have lost the plot.

Most people, like me, are brought up in a particular religion, because it's what their family or community believed to be true. We follow the religious teachings and practices to fit in.

This is a powerful form of conditioning. More people could consider exploring broader spiritual principles and consider what resonates with them, rather than what is expected of them by others in their community or family. Of course, this is their choice.

However, if people choose to follow a particular faith or religion, this would be done without the judgement of others, thus creating a more natural and happier way to exist.

5.4.6: Ageism

As I have grown older, I have become more conscious of the discrimination and subconscious mindsets that exist around age.

Once people get to a certain age, they are often rejected by employers, despite their high levels of experience and skills, and so they find it harder to get decent jobs. Accordingly, their standard of living can diminish.

The same goes for their love life. The accepted wisdom in life seems to be that we need to be romantically involved with someone similar to us. This includes race, age, colour, economic background, interests and so on. This can be practical in many circumstances, and age can have practical implications, but what if we looked more at feelings and at the truth of a person rather than how many candles are on their cake when deciding to date or employ someone?

5.4.7: Disabled people deserve empathy

The recent growth in the profile of the Paralympics, and other sports enjoyed by disabled people, is a sign that we are starting to give disabled people greater equality.

But why wouldn't we? Disabled people are the same as able-bodied people!

They have either been born with a disability or suffered an illness or accident to lead them to their current situation. But this could have happened to anyone.

When we meet disabled people we tend to discount or pity them. Why? The answer is that we have automatically rated them as below us, subconsciously.

We are all equal, no matter our physical condition. It's what is in our hearts that matters, not what we look like or how well we can walk or talk!

5.4.8: It's hard to be humble

I used to jokingly say to my kids that it's hard to be humble, until the day came that I realised I was wrong. It's the opposite in truth.

When we believe we need to achieve and be better than those around us to be valid and valuable, why wouldn't we find it hard to be humble in life? I have heard it said that, when you find yourself in the presence of a highly enlightened person, they are typically humble and non-competitive.

This is because they have let go of the beliefs that hold most of us trapped in our need to be important. For these evolved people, who have a clear understanding that all are equal in life, they find it easy to be humble.

5.5: My truth is the truth

As our egos strive to protect and promote us, we are regularly tempted to mould what we believe is the truth to meet our needs.

Truth is a concept. One person's truth is another person's mystery. When you are looking for collective truth, most look for hard facts. But what exactly can we line up and analyse? What can we prove with material evidence?

In some cases, this proof is possible to find, but often the truth is a matter of perspective, or a concept. Scientists, for example, tell us that everything on Earth is made up of atoms. So, if we look at an object, say a horse, it is an arrangement of atoms in a shape of what we call a horse. It's just a matter of perspective. A horse in a different language may not even be called a horse.

The deeper you look into the makeup of an object, the more you will see that it is only a concept of a truth we collectively accept. Truth can be tested by the understandings that we have and, if we have a collective understanding of something, it will feel like a truth.

Truth is therefore a concept that is agreed upon by a collective. What is true for me may not, therefore, be true to you. Different people have different views of the so-called truth.

Our minds can thus become confused by what exactly is truth, because our minds filter the information through their own belief structures.

However, if consulted, our hearts or gut do not lie. If we 'drop into' our hearts, we can become aware of a deeper understanding of truth. This requires us to feel more and think less. People often recommend that you access your gut feeling to make a decision. In that process, you are accessing your intuition, or the divine teacher within you.

It can also help to search for and acknowledge the truth of others, to challenge what we feel and find a more authentic collective truth. When we seek the truth of others, we seek to clarify understandings held by them, so that we can move forward and find a collective outcome that best suits all. When we do this, we will find a collective understanding of a situation, and consider and properly absorb the perspectives of other people – for what you perceive as true may be seen as untrue from a different perspective, and this is often valid.

Across our society, however, different versions of isolated 'truths' exist and are used to serve or justify people's egoic need to be right.

Our political leaders present their version of the 'truth' to avoid blame from the public, and to try and win votes. As a result, they can distort facts and present only selective good news. Governments often keep certain information secret, because they fear the public will not be able to handle it or will distort it to meet their own needs. This fails to give the public they serve due credit.

The media is another area where integrity in reporting is often questionable. Major media outlets often suffer from a lack of objectivity, revealed in the form of sensationalist news stories and a tendency to report the negative over the positive, because bad news sells better than good news.

The opposite may be the case in government-owned media outlets, because good news serves to benefit the perceived owner of that institution.

In recent years, the internet has seen a growth in non-mainstream media outlets, which often promote narrow interests.

No matter what the source, all media has a right to free speech. We as consumers just need realise that every media platform projects thoughts or views that are just that: perceptions of one organisation or person. None of it may be actually true!

Within corporate organisations, such as listed companies, the truth is often presented in a certain way to please decision-makers such as the board and senior executives. This good-news culture pervades the whole organisation, as staff adopt perspectives that protect and promote their position or role.

From my years in business, I frequently witnessed leaders presenting only good news stories to preserve their reputation and financial rewards. This made it difficult for senior stakeholders, including board members and even regulators, to make the best decisions, because they were receiving stories from a self-interested perspective.

In many organisations, there is a tendency to 'shoot the messenger' or person who brings forth a different perspective that contradicts the truth of another. This is a cultural norm that needs to be addressed, because an organisation that doesn't consider different perspectives and views will atrophy in the hubris and good-news culture that it otherwise accepts and rewards.

In fact, at all levels in society, we need to search inside our hearts to find a truer empathy for the contradictory views of others. We need to listen to the perspectives of those others, for once we know why another party sees things the way they do, only then can we find a way forward that best suits all parties involved.

This is where wisdom meets logic, and a so-called truth can yield to the best interests of our collective family.

Our obsession with having 'the' truth – a singular and only truth – only harms our ability to trust one another and create harmonious relationships.

Trust is closely linked to our ability to be vulnerable about our fears, doubts and opinions with another person or group of people. When two parties are vulnerable and open up about the perspectives that are true to them, trust springs forth. This opens the door to magic to be created in any relationship.

Our attachment to the need to be right therefore needs to be replaced by an exploration of understanding. This will help us determine the best interests of all involved. We will be richer and happier as a society when we can soften our obsession with being right and making others wrong.

5.6: We have the right to judge others

Judgement is the great separator in our society. Our collective lack of self-esteem, and our conditioning to compete, lead us to a place of non-acceptance of others. We constantly sit in judgement of others because criticising them, using our own benchmarks of what is acceptable, allows us to feel better about ourselves. It inflates our egos but denies us great inner peace.

We do not 'live and let live', although we think we do.

Our judgement of others is so ingrained we do it on auto pilot, often all day long. We judge others because we think everyone else should be like us.

Our media does it as reporters search for headlines and ratings.

Our government representatives do it to score votes.

Many of our parents did it while we were growing up.

Instead of judgement, we could choose a more conscious way of living, by simply observing, or witnessing, the ways and lives of others. We can participate in this world and the communities we live in by observing without assessment, without judgement, what others are doing or saying. This is awareness. Judgement is not!

When we live as a whole person with our hearts and minds in sync, and not just in our minds, we are full within ourselves and therefore able to accept others for who they are. We are all equal. We are fundamentally all the same. We are all on a journey of discovery that will see us making mistakes. All of us!

We all have subconscious beliefs that cause us to react to a given situation in a certain way, and deep wounds from our lives that distort our realities. They trigger inside us under pressure and can lead us to do or say things that we regret or may even be illegal.

We can observe these actions or choices, but judgement serves to put oneself above another through condemnation, and ultimately it betrays the fact that we are all equal. It flies in the face of unity. In fact, it slaps it.

When we condemn another, it artificially inflates our sense of importance.

At its core, our judgement lacks compassion and empathy, and using it means we have not properly considered another person's perspective or right to hold an opinion. All people have the right to choose their life and level of happiness. There is no love in judging or controlling others because they own their own life, not you!

Not judging does not mean that mistakes go unpunished. We are all responsible and often accountable for what we do. It is clearly not possible to let everyone do whatever they like at any time. The law is in place for a reason, and sometimes punishment or correction is needed to rehabilitate a person who acts in a damaging way to others.

When someone makes a mistake, they will sometimes see the errors of their ways and self-regulate. However, major mistakes may require significant correction to change that person's thinking.

Unless judgement is fair, it can seriously harm the person it is directed at and impair their sense of self-worth. Each time this occurs, our collective lack of self-worth as a society is diminished.

Judging others badly is energetically expensive for us all and introduces a negative into our lives that would be best to avoid if we want harmony. We have a choice: to 'live and let live' with forgiveness and empathy; or the James Bond way of 'live and let die' with a licence to judge and destroy.

Judgement, particularly in the form of condemnation, is a normal part of life. We hear it and we see it every day. It may even be directed at us, and most likely is. However, this kind of judgement is not loving and comes from our own fears and insecurities that we are not enough. This is a complete falsehood, no matter what story our lives have to tell.

When we live more in our hearts, we can move from judgement to compassion, because within ourselves there is nothing missing, no holes to fill. We are whole when we offer compassion – not judgement – and therefore we bring ourselves closer to others.

When we more comprehensively apply the code of happiness to our lives and become more authentic, there can be more uniqueness and less collective sameness in our society. This can only work if it is not strangled by judgement.

We tend to think those who judge others harshly are strong and powerful. We think they are high in self-esteem. But those who judge the loudest and hardest are hiding their own internal battles with insecurity. They do so to present themselves as strong and important, but essentially, they are hiding their own vulnerability. These people, and many among us, do not understand their own potency as a loving person. As a result, they promote themselves through judgement. It's easier than changing themselves or accepting others.

So, the next time you feel yourself judging, be swift to check in and feel why this is the case. Ask yourself: what am I missing that I feel the need to judge another like this?

The shift from judgement to compassion starts with yourself. If we are one big family, which we are, let's truly care about each other.

The reality is that, although we constantly judge others harshly, we are also our own worst critics. We constantly berate ourselves and put ourselves down if we don't meet the perfectionistic standards that many of us set for ourselves.

We all want to feel secure and in our comfort zones. We all want to win and not lose, and when we perceive any kind of loss, we unleash harsh criticism on ourselves. This negative self-talk constantly brings us down to a place of the lowest common denominator.

Let's stop berating ourselves and rate ourselves as wonderful for simply being. Just being alive is worth celebrating each day! You don't need to wait until your birthday comes around to celebrate the wonder of you. If you doubt that, listen to the buzz in your body and the beating of your heart. You are a miracle of nature regardless of who you think you are or what you do!

I urge you to listen to the thoughts and words of others every day. As you do, you will begin to see how entangled our world is in judgement, and how we can all end this: by living without judgement, of course.

5.7: We live in the past or future

Life is lived in a series of moments. We live moment by moment, and this string of moments unfolds to create our lives.

Unfortunately, most of us don't know how to live in the now. We live in the future or the past, and our consciousness constantly bounces from one to the other: future/past, future/past, future/past. It is how our minds are programmed. Rarely do we concentrate on the moment we are actually in.

Our focus on the past is often full of a mix of emotions with bitter and positive memories. We feel shame, guilt and anger about the 'story of our lives' (see below). We cling to our story, and its imperfections haunt us.

We can also be so busy planning our futures that we forget to live in the present. We so want a positive future that we feel compelled to control and plan it, even though that plan may relate to events that ultimately never come to pass. If we think we can tell the future, let me tell you: we can't. It's only our egos that want to believe we can.

When we live in the now – the present – our energy shifts to one of allowing our life to unfold rather than controlling it. This allows our sense of adventure to take over and we can respond to the opportunities and challenges that life presents to us in each and every moment. When we already have it all planned, we potentially block the full potential that our life possesses.

In effect, we cap our potential in search of certainty, and this so-called certainty is impossible to achieve!

When you transcend the idea that you need certainty in your life, you invite the power of possibility to plug into your life with great potency.

I wake up every morning now and throw open the curtains and wonder what life will throw at me that day. It's far more liberating than having everything pre-set or planned within an inch of its life. Who wants to watch a movie where you already know the plot and how the movie ends? It takes away the mystery from the movie!

The future and past are simply stories. The only time that matters is now.

So why do we live in the past or future each day?

I used to be a master of this type of control. I had glimpses of how my obsession with planning my life came from my mind and was driven by fear. It took away the mystery in my life and restricted its full potential, and in turn my happiness. My expectations, once not met, only caused me personal anguish and regret.

Life coaches and mentors often teach us to plan, plan, and plan. They say we need to set targets and know where we are going if we want to reach our goals and succeed. This approach can have some merit if we want to live a limited, controlled, and safe life.

I prefer to live with a fresh, ever evolving dream! Dreams can become an intention. I may work towards the dream, but I am not validated by its achievement, such that if my expectations are not met, I will not be upset. My dreams are intentionally broad, opening up more potential outcomes. I encourage you to avoid any controlling, limiting plan, and start to dream instead.

Expectations are without doubt the enemy of fun in our lives. Misery comes when we can't meet the expectations we set for ourselves.

How many times have you set expectations that have failed to materialise, and how did it feel?

Let's look more deeply at our unhealthy relationships with the past and the future.

5.7.1: Letting go of the past

If you are like me, you have had things go wrong in your life that you have regretted. This forms part of your story and it's a story we all struggle to let go of, despite the event now being over. In effect, our stories are like illusions we can let go of at any time, if we choose to (although this is difficult in situations of abuse). It is no more than a choice.

Most of us carry different emotions attached to our story. Of course, we also have positive memories, but these can often be overwhelmed by our painful ones. Regret is an emotion that offers no benefit to our lives. It's best to learn from our mishaps and mistakes and move on.

I have carried many painful memories throughout my life, and the most powerful and damaging emotions have centred on my experience of perceived betrayal. With some painful experiences, including a series of difficult experiences with my parents, I carried deep pain associated with being let down. In the past few years, I have come to see that I hadn't forgiven people for the events of my past. But deep down I also realised that the one person that I actually needed to forgive was myself. Ultimately, I was in charge of my life, not others. My self-esteem had been dented by what I saw as failures, and my ego wanted to find someone to blame for a story I felt was less than ideal in many ways.

My inability to let go of my supposed failures held me back. In effect, I was repeatedly stabbing myself every day with daggers of shame and regret. My ego was in a loop, constantly searching for a better outcome, even though this was impossible.

I could not change the past.

In my 50s, I woke up to the wisdom that within these supposed failures dwelled the key to freedom. In every event that went wrong, there were lessons for me to see. These events, once I looked closely at them, showed me where my self-worth was lacking, and my subconscious fears were playing out. They were a beautiful mirror into me. I took full responsibility for my life at this point. This awareness was the 'gold' I needed to see, and it opened the gateway to the release of my pain and the restoration of my self-esteem.

Today my mindset is very different when it comes to difficult issues I must face. I now see every event in my life as either an experience of great joy or an opportunity for great learning, and great learning *is* a source of joy. The secret to life is to bring the energy of joy into every moment. En-joy-ment is the true secret of success, and the energy of joy within us can open a door to a better life.

In this place of deep self-reflection, everything can become joyful, and you can free yourself from the cage of regret. There is great freedom when you put down the knives you once used to stab yourself with, and instead use them to cut the chains that held you tied to the past and defocussed from the now.

We've all heard that history constantly repeats itself. Some say it rhymes. But when we learn from the past, we can stop history from repeating itself in our lives. This requires a new mindset in which you embrace adversity and ask it to show you how you can change to prevent it from reoccurring. Awareness in its purest form dissolves our patterns of self-sabotage. Nothing in life is truly wrong. It all serves with deep purpose.

The mind is like a steel trap, and sometimes it doesn't want to let go of past events. Remember, it sees its job as protecting and promoting your value. In this way the mind likes to blame others, or make you the prisoner of regret, encouraging you to play safer next time.

A key secret in finding happiness in your life is to take full responsibility for that happiness. Your life is your choice, and others choose theirs.

How many of the perceived failures from your past do you cling to and constantly blame others for? Letting them go isn't easy, but it is so rewarding once you do.

5.7.2: Allowing the future to be better

The conventional thinking of our time is that we need to plan to succeed. As a child we are asked what we plan to do when we grow up. As we age, we think we need to be able to articulate a life plan. Will we get married? How many kids will we have? Where will we retire? Our planning has no limits it seems!

The business world is awash with plans, budgets, and targets. There are strategic plans, operational plans, sales targets, and financial plans, just to name a few. Most staff plan what they need to achieve in the year ahead. In this sea of plans, creativity is replaced by pressure. Much time is spent planning to plan, rather than doing. It's a plan-fest. Plan-mania, you might say!

As we age, we also feel we need a retirement plan and even a funeral plan. We take away the mystery of life and replace it with plans, multitudes of plans. Some people even plan aspects of their death or funeral. My mother did!

Most people work their whole lives in jobs they don't really enjoy, so they can one day stop, retire, and escape obligation. The journey to that retirement is often loaded with a sense of obligation and limited fun. However, our preconditioning tells us that this is the way life should be. Our weeks at work are full of dreary days in the office, so we can come alive on weekends and public holidays, and for a few precious weeks every year when we can holiday. We are not being in the now. We are giving up our current happiness in the hope that the future will be better.

But this future may never come; or, by the time we get there, life may have painted us a very different picture. Mine certainly did many times.

When you holiday what do you holiday from? You can't take a vacation from yourself, just the circumstances you are creating in your life. Wouldn't it be better to be happy in the now with who you are, rather than trying to escape or forget your life temporarily? This can mean facing issues and circumstances in your life now, not hoping they will miraculously go away in the future.

Our hearts know the path in life that we want to follow. Our minds, on the other hand, act out of fear and want to keep us safe. If we plan with our minds rather than dream with our hearts, we will most likely end up playing safe and following the collective norms expected of us through social conditioning. Our hearts can see the adventures we desire. Our minds want us to stay in the comfort zones we have known, even if they have been bad. It's 'the devil we know', as they say.

Whereas, if we allow our hearts to dream a big bold vision of what is possible, we can unfold in the now, with that bold vision acting like a lighthouse on our sea of possibilities.

If we restrict our visions to a hard plan with every detail itemised, we take away the mystery and the possibilities that may be far greater than our mind's fearful objectives. Did we really come to Earth to live out that predictable movie, or would we prefer to be in an adventure or action thriller with a mysterious ending? I know now that I came here to be bold, not just fit in, and I am now fully committed to this mantra till the day I leave this life!

'Now' is the only time that matters. We cannot live in the past for it is done. We cannot live in the future because it can only ever arrive in the now. When we get there, it will be the now, not the future!

Why do we readily give up on our current happiness by hanging onto the pain of events that are over and done with? Why plan to be happy in the future, when that future we imagine may never come?

We need to allow our 'now' to bring us the joy we desire. Why wait?

Do yourself a favour and notice each time you think about the future or the past. When you laugh with joy, and when you notice it, bring yourself back to the now you are in, say these words to yourself, 'I'm here now and that's all that matters'.

You, and those you are with, will benefit from your enhanced presence, particularly those you love.

5.8: Money matters more than love

It is often said that money makes the world go around. While there is great truth in this statement, the obsession of many people with making money and acquiring things creates complexity and emptiness in our lives. It certainly did in mine for many years.

The world suffers from greed, as many in the population strive to enhance their lack of self-worth with money. To have money gives us a perception of power, control, and importance in our lives, because it can often buy us what we believe makes us more valuable. It even gives us access to and power over others, should those of us with money choose to use it that way.

We all take money so seriously because it values us in a sense. We don't have much fun with funding, you might say.

Many human beings spend much of their adult lives focussing on earning as much money as they can. They believe that the more money they have, the more worthy or valuable they are as a person. This in turn will bring them happiness and love, so they think.

I carried this mistaken subconscious belief for many years, having heard my mother criticise my father, for much of my formative years, about his income earning capabilities. This made me mistakenly believe that to be loveable you had to be a good provider for your family and be seen as successful by your friends.

Today, men and women all over the world place this same burden on themselves.

Money in itself is a great concept and is very important. It gives us a mechanism with which to transact with each other. Money is not therefore an evil thing in itself, and having an abundance of money can be a wonderful thing, used for purpose and positive loving pursuits, or experiences. After all, if life is to be enjoyed money allows us to have fun.

But there are whole industries, products and offerings that support the premise that the more money you have the more valuable you are. Prestige cars, clothes, houses, jewellery, resorts and even classes of airline seats are a testament to reinforcing the belief that we are only as good as our wealth.

How many times have you strived to buy an item thinking that, once you get it, you will be happy? Then, when you get it, you realise it didn't make you happy for long. So, you go in search of the next purchase, hoping that it will bring you the joy you seek.

The acquisition of physical items and money cannot bring you self-worth, because self-worth can only come from inside your own heart. When we find the connection to our true selves, we realise that self-love and fun is what we primarily seek and not material wealth. Money is wonderful but it's not core to our essence, like love.

The fundamental distinction here is between need and want. When we need money to prove we are valuable and make us happy, we can never have enough. The more we have the more we feel we need to get. Our appetite for money is insatiable because money can never fulfil the need that drives us to seek it. It's a mismatch on a monumental scale, the whole world over.

When we want money but don't need it for validation, we are in a much healthier place. Once there, we can stop making money when we have enough, we can share it with others in need or use it for deep purpose and enjoyment. There, money can be magical because its energy is being applied by the wholeness of ourselves and our fulfilment, not for the enhancement of our egos.

Without integrity and fairness, money and its pursuit can cause great pain in this world. Much crime and unfair business practices take place in the pursuit of money. Gambling causes great family pain as people strive to strike it rich quickly. Invariably gambling ends in tears, because gambling is mathematically designed for a collective loss so that the administrator, such as the casino, can profit.

Money unfortunately often comes at a great cost to our lives and our sense of being. It shouldn't, but it often does. We often sacrifice things that truly matter more, in order to get it.

The world is in love with money, but money isn't love and never will be. It can never replace love as our primary desire in life.

Modern businesses are full of people sacrificing themselves and things dear to them for money. This is not a criticism, I did it too because of my conditioned upbringing.

Employees often work overtime and suffer from a great fear of losing their jobs, because subconsciously much of their validation comes from having their job title and the income that goes with it. They fear failing to fulfil their roles as providers for their families.

This belief structure means they can be manipulated by employers determined to maximise financial results, rather than caring about the welfare of their staff.

Our obsession with money has created financial structures and institutions that are overly fragile and complex because they are unsustainable and frankly not real. Even the money we say we 'make' has become a commodity with little basis in reality.

Imagine if we could learn to approach funding with more fun and less seriousness in our lives, we could finally be rich in our hearts and better balance would be possible for us all. When we can relax and have fun our true worth can a-gain be the windfall we actually seek.

You need money to survive, but if you reflect deeply, do you devote too much time to making money at the expense of love in your life?

Money and our obsession with it have led to several associated damaging belief structures that leave us as slaves to our bank accounts and, more accurately, the debts that keep us in chains.

Let's consider the key ones:

5.8.1: We can consume whatever we want

We have developed an entitlement mentality to money as a society.

Our current levels of consumerism are not sustainable in the long run. It is destroying our planet and the fabric of what we could be as a society. The rate at which we are consuming is excessive, and global warming is giving us a major warning at present. The pollution we are creating and the destruction of jungles and forests for timber are clearly taking a toll on the planet.

Earth can meet our true needs, if we control our population growth and plundering resources at all costs; but it cannot meet all our wants.

Our wants are endless. We just keep consuming and wanting more and more. This is a very normal human instinct, but I wonder what we are actually seeking in the search for more?

'He with the most toys wins' is a common expression. It's a competition best avoided and easily avoided once you reach a place of integrity within yourself.

Our true needs, on the other hand, are straightforward and don't overly tax our resources.

If you think about our actual material needs, the list is relatively short. Shelter, food, clothing, water, medicine and health services, power, sanitation, communication tools, education, and some forms of transport are our key needs.

Covid-19 has made many of us reassess what we actually need to survive. The designation of essential services included the very things mentioned before as basic needs. For some, this experience has been liberating and has given them an opportunity to see the virtues of a simpler, less expensive lifestyle. For others, the withdrawal of their luxuries, indulgences and social outlets has created significant stress.

Coronavirus shutdowns across the world have shown us how disproportionate salaries are for many essential workers. Key workers such as nurses, teachers, supermarket workers, aged care workers, food producers (like farmers), bank tellers, and so on, were vital to our communities, yet most are low paid, earning less than many non-essential workers who weren't really missed during the shutdowns.

Let's take a close look at our priorities as a society and reward these people better for the important work that they do. Their happiness is our happiness, for seeing them treated with greater respect increases the respect we can then have for ourselves.

5.8.2: We must protect ourselves from greedy people

Our obsession with money and its associated greed have left many of us with a lack of trust when we transact with others in our communities. We often feel a need to protect ourselves from this greed and the hidden belief that our levels of wealth define us.

We are often wary of being ripped off as people try and part us from our money. It is a circular process. We want the most money we can get for our services when we sell them, but we want to pay as little as possible when we buy something. It's a dance led by our individual levels of greed.

There are businesses that will charge us more than they need to make reasonable returns, simply because they can. Conventional thinking tells us if we have a monopoly in a market we can charge more. The simple principle is that: the more competition in a market, the lower prices will go, as sellers need to compete for sales.

The belief that we can charge whatever we can get away with is endemic in our society and has led to the need for governments to step in to protect consumers. Certain organisations with products we think we need – like banks, petrol distributors and energy companies – are often accused of price gouging to make unfair or super-profits. The recent Royal Commission in Australia exposed aspects of this in the financial services sector. Government legislation has been required in most countries to protect consumers from greedy sellers.

We spend our lives behind locked doors, protecting things we own. Our cars, houses, businesses, and even our computers must be protected from potential thieves who know it's far faster to take money than to make money. I have been physically robbed seven times in my life, and scammed, so I know this one all too well!

Imagine a world where this was not necessary.

Security is necessary at present and comes at a stifling cost to us all. It's sad but easy to understand its origin. If people believe they are more valuable the more money they have, and the less there is to go around, this will continue to occur.

Mindsets are both the problem and the solution.

5.8.3: The twisted relationship of money, power and sex

The relationship between money, power and sex is one that is also unhealthy in our society.

Many people want money, power and sex for validation. They make us feel more worthy. If one does not have sex, for example, we may feel we have lost our ability to procreate. This is a very fundamental human drive that we feel powerfully in our bodies. It is instinctive and can drive us to unhealthy wants. Similarly, if we do not have enough resources because we lack money, we may feel that we are in a powerless position on multiple fronts, and this will drive us into unhealthy behaviours.

Power, money and sex can be all wonderful energies if they are used in the right way. There can be harmony in the relationship between empowerment, abundance and intimacy, if they are subject to the right set of values.

However, when power and money give us power *over* another person, the two become linked in a bad way. The concept that a person with money has power over another, simply because they have money, is a perverse concept of the mind.

Those most vulnerable are those with a mindset of lack. They never believe they have enough money, sex or power to feel validated or whole, and this can place them in a space where others can easily manipulate them.

Many of our social structures program individuals or small collectives of people to feel like they're not enough. Many doctors, hospitals, schools, social events, and so on, are only available to those with certain levels of wealth. This can again leave people with a vulnerability to be manipulated.

It is important therefore that we understand our relationship with sex, money and our own empowerment as a society, so that power, sex and money are no longer used to control others.

The sex scandal involving Harvey Weinstein is a well-documented example of a man with money and power in the entertainment industry, abusing his position to gain unfair and immoral sexual favours from women. History is littered with these types of abuses, and the list of allegations is extensive, even involving the Catholic Church.

When we know who we are because we have gone inward to find it out, our tendency to either control or be controlled by money, sex or power is diminished, for we need none of these to feel whole. If we are complete and need nothing, we open ourselves up to receive what we want, not what others force upon us or tell us we need to sacrifice to get.

There is nothing wrong with having money and a state of abundance, as these are completely natural and available to all, as long as we drop the idea that only a minority can be the 'haves' and the majority be the exploitable 'have-nots'.

5.9: We don't own our own lives

Many of us believe we cannot allow ourselves to be our true selves in life. Instead, we allow ourselves to be directed or owned by the views of others, such as our parents. We fundamentally lack sovereignty, and in this place, we allow ourselves to be told what to do. We want to fit in and be accepted.

This mindset is absorbed at a young age. We are told we are good if we do what we are told and rewarded; and if we don't do what we're told, primarily by our parents or teachers, we are called 'bad' and punished. This pattern makes us compliant and teaches us that our lives are not ours to direct and own.

But if we don't feel we own our own destiny, we won't take responsibility for it, and so we subrogate key decisions in our lives to others, normally to those who we feel have power over us, greater experience, or perhaps whom we want to please. This lack of responsibility pervades many parts of our lives and blocks us from discovering who we are and how we want to exist.

The belief that we don't own our own lives has a flip-side. In the same way that we allow others to control and direct our lives, we often believe we have the right to own or direct others. Of course, this is not the case. There is no love in control, and it reflects deep insecurities in those who feel the need to control others.

My life followed this pattern until a few years ago. For most of my life, I gave my energy and time to become successful at things I didn't really like doing to please others. I chose a career in accounting and finance rather than following my career passions, because my parents thought I should. Really, I wanted to be a doctor, journalist, or work in consumer protection. I abandoned my true passions. It was my fault and I own that now.

I am sure I am not the only person in society who has followed a career they didn't really want. Ask yourself if you have done this or still are. Don't judge yourself if you have. It's normal. An estimated 95% of people are in careers or jobs they would prefer not to be in. I was certainly one of the 95% for most of my life!

However, by societal measures, I was a success in my career. Of course, my heart knew otherwise, and I spent much energy suppressing my true desires. My body paid the price and was a battleground for stress.

The impacts of not living a life in alignment with who you truly are can be profoundly damaging on your life and the people around you. It caused me many years of great physical pain.

At the age of 19, I developed a serious muscle disorder that impacted my life for over thirty years. I thought it was just bad luck and, despite years and years of expensive medical treatment on the symptoms, I didn't get relief until my early 50s when I awoke to the fact that the key driver of my health issue was stress. I was living out of alignment with who I truly was.

When we don't think we own our lives, we subrogate responsibility for it. Our attempts to fit in to the world around us make us vulnerable to unhappiness and poor health, including poor mental health. When I had my muscle disorder for all those years, I also disowned the pain in my body, such was the extent of my self-sacrifice. If I had owned that pain, I probably would have become emotionally broken and vulnerable. I didn't think the world would appreciate that, and I feared rejection.

Unity is a great attribute in any society, but we can be unique and united at the same time in our quest for happiness. This takes acceptance and love.

When we don't think we can be ourselves, we don't really bother to find out who we want to be. We become who we think we *need* to be. We allow ourselves to be owned in different ways. We become who we think our romantic partner wants us to be, so we will continue to be loved. We work the way our boss wants us to work, so we don't get fired. We allow our governments to take away our freedoms, because we think they have ultimate power over us. Many people expect their government to provide them with a living, choosing to ignore the fact that this is ultimately their responsibility and their opportunity to claim self-determination or sovereignty over themselves. We drink alcohol and take drugs to be like our friends, and to give us the freedom to smile and have fun. We follow the current fashion to make sure we look like others look. We are robots programmed to fit in. Zombies might be a better description.

It's endemic in our way of being. Then we judge those around us who are different and don't match the norms! If people dress or otherwise present themselves differently, we judge them unfairly. We all have the right to choose the life we want. Satisfying others is largely irrelevant in our personal choices, as long as we obey the law.

We don't often see how much we fall in line with the way things are, just to fit in. We sacrifice ourselves to not stand out, but the cost of this compliance is great. We suffer. Our health suffers, our energy drops, our happiness declines, and ultimately, we don't enjoy life as much as we could. It's a very expensive opportunity cost.

Ongoing debates over vaccinations is an important one relating to sovereignty. I have always taken vaccines, but it's everyone's fundamental choice to decide whether they inject a substance into their body. Science is one thing, the right to choose our own lives is another. This is a basic human right that needs to be respected.

Contrary to popular opinion, I believe freedom is a fundamental right, not a privilege in life, unless of course you break a sensible law.

We need to own our own lives. True freedom awaits those people brave enough to listen to their souls.

Are there any aspects of your life that you have subrogated to others to make them happy, not you?

5.10: Our bodies don't matter

Our bodies are amazing creations, and what they enable us to do is nothing short of a miracle. We only get one body in this life, and it's the 'vehicle' we spend our whole lives inside.

Despite this, and despite all the medical advice we receive – in the media and other forms of communication – about health, diets, exercise, sleep and drinking habits, most people fail to take adequate care of their bodies. They simply ignore the advice and put their bodies at risk. Of course, I have done this too, at times. We ignore our mental health and suppress our pain with alcohol, drugs and mindless recreation, rather than address that pain. We basically cross our fingers and hope that bad health will only apply to others.

'It won't happen to me,' we say to ourselves.

We take little responsibility for our health, preferring to focus energies on other priorities, like money and work, because these things make us feel more important and get noticed.

If you ask most people if their health is important to them, they will, of course, say 'yes'. However, when it comes to it, they often will not take the advice they are given, and they will accept less than ideal health. In effect, they don't take full responsibility for their own health because their subconscious belief is that other things define them more!

The trade-off between health and wealth has been particularly stark during the Covid-19 pandemic. At a macro-level, we were forced as a society to choose between our economies and our health.

We need to get better at making a balanced choice on an individual level each day of our lives. This also applies to societies and countries. Why can't we choose both – supporting our economics and our health – with sensible risk management practices and wisdom, and strive to achieve that balance with our hearts and minds?

To some extent we seem able to disown our bodies and take little responsibility for them. Our bodies provide the link to our hearts or souls. They house our feelings and allow us therefore to feel love and to know our truths. They are our pathway to the expression of intimacy with another. Without our functioning bodies, nothing is possible, because we are dead!

Despite our logical understanding of this need for good health, we live in a world where we devote great energies to our minds and not our bodies. We will invest hours each day into cerebral work or study, and we will only squeeze in exercise or sleep if we get time. If we have a health problem, we look for a quick fix in the form of a drug or operation to change our situation.

Even then we often look for others to motivate us or pay people to give us the discipline to care for our bodies. We pay to be trained by personal trainers, when we probably already know what to do to get fit. We simply don't take enough self-responsibility and therefore apply the requisite discipline to make it happen.

We get so busy and focussed on other things that we cut corners, eating takeaway or unhealthy food, all the while listening to the voices of other people who tell us it's alright.

There is a herd mentality at play here. Peer pressure encourages you to do what others around you are doing. If we are all unhealthy together it makes everyone feel better about themselves. It's another layer of conditioning.

I did an executive health check in my early 50s and was told I was in the top five per cent of my age group for fitness. The doctor then went on to tell me not to get excited about that result because it was a low bar to clear. Many people are not very fit at that age, after years of neglect and ambivalence.

Social conditioning encourages us not to prioritise our health, particularly as we get older. It only makes people feel insecure about themselves. What if we collectively adopted better habits and took responsibility for our health?

Here are a few associated beliefs that spin off from our beliefs about our bodies.

5.10.1: Alcohol and drugs help us cope

In our society, alcohol and drugs have become our crutch. It helps many to cope. It allows us to relax and is socially encouraged, particularly in younger age groups who see it as a passage to adulthood.

But alcohol is a masking agent that allows us to escape our true feelings. Yes, it can help to release our minds for short periods of time and have fun, and this can be great; but it also prevents us from growing in life when it is overused.

Perhaps governments want this because when people mask their pain with substances, they may not demand change and can be more easily controlled?

When we feel unhappy, however, it is best to face this pain, as it is often a signpost to our limiting and often subconscious beliefs, many of which are just adopted from others. But what many people do is use alcohol and drugs to escape the pain in their bodies and minds. It gives them temporary relief and a way to avoid facing the pain.

The trouble is that the pain comes back, often more intensely, so we need to keep drinking alcohol or using substances to project the image of ourselves we want others to see.

What goes up must eventually go down!

5.10.2: Age must weary me

As a culture we expect our bodies to fall apart as we age. In many ways, we behave in a way that makes this belief come true.

However, our body's cells completely regenerate every eighteen months. Therefore, if we are living in a healthy way, the ageing process can be much slower than we believe.

We put real limitations on our bodies as we age because of our mistaken beliefs. We reduce our exercise levels because we are conditioned to do so. When I am around people who are over fifty, I hear their constant references to their ailments, aches, and pains. It's a common topic of discussion. With this mindset, is it any wonder that our bodies atrophy badly, given that we become what we believe we are or should be?

Age is a function of the man-made concept of time, and therefore ageing is a function of the passing of thought. I wonder what might be possible if we changed the way we think about it?

Science tells us that there is no reason why the human body can't survive to about 120 years of age. But why would it, if we talk ourselves into believing a much lower number is our likely lifespan, like 85. We become what we think!

If we live with passion our whole lives, there is no reason we can't survive well past 100.

I would love a dollar for every time I have been told that I exercise too hard for my age. It's all in the mind. That's the problem.

We need to live more from our hearts where our energy levels are unlimited, regardless of our human age.

Why should the number of candles on my birthday cake determine my level of health and fitness? It can be the other way around!

5.10.3: Illness is purely physical

We generally see the world as a physical place, and this shows up in our considerations of health and wellness.

But what about the link between emotional wellbeing and physical health? There is a stronger cause and effect here than most people recognise.

In recent years, as I have grown in self-awareness, I have observed the link between my mental and physical health. I have seen how my beliefs and insecurities impact on my health through my cellular structure. Once I found out who my true self really is, I hardly had a day of genuine sickness.

With this awareness, I have turned more and more to nonconventional or holistic health providers for cures rather than traditional western medicine. This includes Reiki, acupuncture, herbalists, and Chinese medical practitioners. These providers work with the energy flows within and around our bodies, rather than just physical tissues and bones.

Some conditions have been solved by a holistic doctor, even after traditional medicine could not find the solution.

The extremely debilitating muscle disorder I mentioned enduring for most of my life is called Deficiency of Functional Occlusion Syndrome. This disorder is hell on Earth, and I would not wish it upon my worst enemy. Some textbooks don't even reference it, but for me the disorder started when I was 19 years old and did not cease until my early 50s. It resulted in muscle cramps throughout my body, regular migraine headaches, and itchy skin associated with never-ending pressures on my nervous system.

I do not regret having this disease, despite its unimaginable impact on my life, because it has taught me much about myself, including the power of patience and resilience. It has also taught me great empathy for people with chronic pain and terminal illness. Thirty-plus years, in my case, was a long time to be sick.

But the biggest thing this disease taught me was that I created it. I was its architect and the air that it breathed. I gave it life and, no matter what treatment I got for it, I was in truth the only cure. It only went away when I saw its lessons and I gave it permission to leave. Then, I finally saw that I did not have to endure this pain, and my beliefs shifted accordingly. I went inward, and it went to the exit lounge.

The greatest lesson this disease taught me was to be holistically healthy. I needed to be in integrity, not just fit. I spent much of my life living out of alignment with my true self, and this brought on the disorder. I didn't follow my heart's desires, and my suppression of pain associated with this sense of self-betrayal was eating up my body from the inside out. The anger I felt put pressure on my body, and it manifested as a muscle disorder.

It started at 19 years old, because this was when I commenced my career and studies in accounting. I never wanted to follow this path. Deep down I wanted to be a doctor, among other things.

The pain peaked in periods of my life when I was out of alignment with my heart, either through relationships or work issues.

When I eventually knew myself, I was able to release my sense of self-betrayal and all the pain I had been dangerously holding in my body. Now I am free of the disorder because I am living the life I choose, not the life I thought I needed to live to satisfy others.

I encourage others to consider if they are causing their own physical issues. Bad backs can be associated with burden in our lives, for example. I had chronic bad backs for years and spent many hours and dollars visiting medical specialists. None of it worked because they were only treating my symptoms, not the cause of my pain. Once I became truly happy, the pain instantly ceased, and I now never have back pain whatsoever. I'm like a teenager again, just with grey hair!

Many (but not all) diseases in our bodies have a link to our belief structures, unless of course we get hit by a bus. I encourage you to rethink your role in your health while you still have it to fix. Don't delegate it to others!

5.10.4: My house is my home

Most people live in a house, and these vary significantly in shape and size around the world. We clean, decorate and care for our houses because we consider them to be our homes. 'Home is where the heart is' is a common phrase used by society.

I have moved house many times in my life, close to twenty times. If it's taught me one thing, it's that a house is a house. My body is my only true home, even if it's only for the course of my life. It's where my real heart is.

Why wouldn't I care for my true home with the best nourishment and exercise? When I focus inward, not outwards, that's the home that matters; not the one made from bricks or wood.

When a victim who has lost their house in a natural disaster is interviewed, they will invariably say that they may have lost the house they lived in, but thankfully they are still alive. We need to put the health of our bodies over the quality and cleanliness of our houses each day. Do we need a flood or bushfire to strike before we understand this?

Of course, houses can be full of love, but they are less likely to be if the people inside them are not healthy or happy.

5.11: Change is bad and must be avoided

Most people fear change and prefer to stay safe and sound in their comfort zone, even if it's less than ideal. Again, it's 'the devil we know' as is commonly said. Too few people seek to grow and expand by challenging themselves. We place a greater emphasis on being safe in our lives, than we do on following our dreams into an adventure. On a subconscious level, we believe that change may threaten our lives by making them worse. The mind screams, 'Get it wrong and we may die!' So, we listen, subconsciously.

There is a common expression that 'it will be what it will be'. The concept of 'allowing' change is in our vernacular, yet we seldom allow change to take place. We resist it, and through our obsession with control we try to allow only the change our minds *think* are in our interests.

The truth is we often don't know what's in our interests until after change has occurred. Due to our layers of conditioning, we don't know who we are, let alone what life path is best for us.

Resisting change is also inconsistent with our very beings, because over the course of our lives surely we *should* grow and develop and fundamentally change. As we grow, we can eventually outgrow a situation, such as a job or relationship, and therefore may want to go to another level. At times we may need to express ourselves in a new situation or relationship to challenge ourselves and embrace the unknown.

We need to see past our fear of change, past our unhappy situations, and past the thought that we might go backwards and lose what we have. We need to expand to a place where happiness is our benchmark of success, not our normal conditioned benchmarks. Because isn't the unknown more exciting than the known? After all, where do you think adventures are more likely to exist?

I have of course lived through this human tendency to fear change myself. With no faith in who I really was and a world of possibility before me, I tried to control every aspect of life to ensure I did not lose the things I had. But this defensive way of living left me stressed and unhappy. In the end, by focussing on the negative, I brought it forth into reality. I stayed in relationships and jobs too long, even though deep down I knew they didn't fulfil me. I feared the unknown rather than embracing it as an exciting adventure. This was a ridiculous way to live because, on the rare occasions that I followed my heart and made changes in my life – that deep down I wanted – I was much happier and at peace, even if it meant that I experienced some pain related to the change, as well as the reactions of others.

When I lost key relationships, including two marriages, and was forced out of senior jobs, I felt betrayed and emotionally shattered. Yet even then, in time, I came to see that I was ultimately better off and happier because I was able to re-choose my life after each event and make changes more aligned with who I am and what I wanted to do.

These days I embrace change much more and I never fear it. I believe my heart, if I dare to listen to it, has a dream for me and I need to allow this dream to unfold. I must not resist it because it is in my interests.

Facing change takes bravery and normally leads us to a better place in our lives. As I mentioned before, if you ask most people when they have grown most in their lives, they will cite a difficult time that they endured and describe what they learned about themselves. Unfortunately, we humans do tend to grow mainly through times of adversity. It's here where we find our greatest strengths. But it doesn't need to be this way. We can grow in positive loving times, once we learn how.

I have experienced both, growth in good times and bad. My growth in good times has, to be honest, been a recent phenomenon, as I have opened up to the real me. There is no need to suffer to become happier and lighter in life.

But to grow in the good times we need to approach change in our lives with an open mind and an open heart. We need to wonder what we can learn from it, not worry that we will suffer as a result. This is easier said than done initially and requires a different way of thinking. It certainly requires a need for self-compassion and self-acceptance when we change our path in life. It needs us to trust in our own hearts.

There are also many associated belief structures that play out because of our fear of change.

5.11.1: To trust too much, is to lose

Betrayal is an emotive word, but it describes an emotion that we've likely all experienced. We have all lost something we didn't want to during our lives, and the outcome is that many of us have become wary and watchful for signs of betrayal. As a result, we subconsciously don't trust, either ourselves or others.

Fear does not live in our hearts, it lives in our minds. Therefore, if we love from our hearts trust will always be present.

Business circles in the past ten years have become full of the catch-cry that change is the new constant. This may well be the case, but from my experience nearly everyone I worked with resisted change deeply. Regulators and progressive CEOs had to force it on many employees.

Imagine how much positive change could be made with the right mindset! We rarely lose when we trust the power of change, for change is the universal law of refreshment.

We need to trust that what is happening right now is as it should be. When we take this mindset, we can embrace what is possible in our lives.

The universe does not make mistakes, even if we think it does.

5.11.2: We must plan our lives to avoid pain

This brings me back to planning. Human beings love to plan. Rather than live in the present moment, we frequently set expectations about what we want out of life in the future.

But this is fraught with misery.

When you set expectations, you open yourself up to a high probability of perceived failure and disappointment. I say perceived failure because it is not actual failure. Our minds, despite their best efforts, cannot predict the future with any real accuracy, unless we live in a bubble of repetition. Things will happen around us each day, and life will unfold whether we like it or not.

Expectation is not only the enemy of fun, but also the enemy of potential. When you transcend your ideas of what is certain, you invite potential and possibility into your life.

With eight billion people in the world, why would we ever think we can achieve total control over our destiny?

As time goes by, you will change and the world around you will change, so why lock yourself in and set yourself up for perceived failure?

My advice is to wake up every day, wonder how the day will unfold, and be ready to react and flow as it does. Any other way of being is to assume that you know what the future holds. Frankly you don't and can't!

5.12: We are humans doing not being

We have become humans doing, not human beings.

In the western world we have buried ourselves in deadlines, urgency, fear of not getting things done, priorities, and the idea of time. Time has become a commodity that rules our lives. We are its slaves.

Most people you meet will say that they are bereft of time. How often do you hear people say that they are time poor, have spent too much time on something, they are short of time or need to make up for lost time? These are common expressions, and they show just how often we think of time as a commodity we need to get more of. Our language around time reflects our obsession with it.

The truth is, we have all the time in the world – if we choose to take this perspective. When I worked in the corporate world I would often get into lifts with colleagues and ask them how they were going. Their response was typically the same. They would tell me that they were so busy it was ridiculous. Most likely, they said this because it validated them and made them feel needed and safe. Their greatest fear was probably not to be needed, so they revelled in being under pressure and being martyred by the sword of commitment.

Our perception of time dictates our experience of it. If you believe that the time you must accomplish a task is limited, you will feel rushed and time poor.

However, if you re-evaluate the 'truth' of time, you will see that it's your choice as to whether it owns you or you have sovereignty over it.

In the recent Covid-19 lockdowns, many people forced to work from home enjoyed the extra time that they felt they had due to no longer commuting to work. No extra time was created. We still had 24 hours in every day, it's just that these workers used their time in a different way. Many broke the chains of slavery put in place by time as they perceived it.

To change our relationship with time, we need to change our perception of the things we want to do in life. We need to consider what things are urgent and what things are our actual priorities. Our minds create an idea of what we need to achieve by when, within the confines of the ticking clock.

Clocks rule our lives. I used to be obsessed with clocks and had one in every room of my house. I could not go out without wearing a watch. I had different watches for different occasions. I was obsessed with time.

These days I no longer wear a watch. I do what I want to do when I want to do it, rather than being a slave to time. It's my life to own and manage and I, as a rule, don't let the time on a clock drive it.

If you are unhappy with your relationship with time, forget the concept of time management and multitasking. Both concepts can keep you trapped in the world of time. They might allow you to be busier and get more done, but ask yourself if this is what you want. Why are we trying to manage a concept created by our egos? You will find it far more beneficial to manage your behaviours around time. Take a step back and work out what you want to do and when. Ask yourself if the things you are currently doing are necessary. Do they add value to your life, and are you genuinely interested in doing them? Your life is precious. Don't waste it!

Most of us are running around enslaved in obligations we don't want to do. Our life experience as a human being is intended to be rich with enjoyment, not buried in commitments. Great pleasure can come from being our true selves and doing what we love, not doing what others want us to do. Our happiness should not be the by-product of a schedule, or dependent upon doing what we think others want.

To experience the richness of your life, change your behaviours, do what interests you and what is of value to your life. You could also determine when and how you participate in those activities and discuss this openly with your loved ones.

We can all get to a point of inefficiency where we feel out of control with time – efficiency and time are very different. To be efficient, what you are doing needs to have true purpose; and to make it happen, tasks often need to be done in the right sequence, by the right people, in the right moments.

Your life is a collection of moments, and how you choose to experience these moments becomes your life story. The tale that you will tell on your deathbed will be determined by the joy and the experiences that you had along the way, not by a list of things you begrudgingly got done. Try not to become dictated to by others or social norms.

Our experiences are meant to expand us, not deplete us and make us feel as if we wasted our lives. Most of us use our time to generate greater self-worth. If we already have self-worth and know who we are, we don't need to spend as much time trying to prove we are valid. The end result is more time to enjoy and be what we truly are: happy human beings in love with life, not stressed-out humans doing what they think they must.

We all need to be fully present in our lives, no matter what we choose to do with our time. But we can't do this when we are doing multiple things at once or doing something we don't enjoy, and we just want to get things finished. This creates stress in our bodies and leaves us feeling emotionally depleted.

When we are doing what we love, time is no longer an issue because we feel whole within ourselves. In this beautiful place, our hearts and minds are both engaged as one, and this unity can bring forth our divine gifts. By following your passions, you can create great outcomes for yourself and the world!

We all feel a sense of stress if we don't get everything done that we wanted to do in a day. I used to suffer from this before I changed my perception of time and my purpose in life. My principal purpose now is to be happy. Time used to be a barrier to this, so I no longer allow it to 'tick me off'.

Ask yourself if this applies to you. Does it make you a lesser person because you don't get everything done on a given day? How many of the things you thought you should do, did you want to do anyway?

Think about nature. We are all a part of nature, so next time you look at a sunset, a beach or perhaps some trees gently swaying in a breeze, ask yourself: what role does time play in the way nature operates? The answer is it doesn't. Nature has no clocks. It works off energy, the changing of the seasons, and the movement of the Earth around the sun and moon. The leaves on a tree don't look at a calendar to determine what day they need to fall off a branch. They fall when the energy is right for the tree to shed them. The tree doesn't try to put them back on because it thinks they fell on the wrong day. It just is.

So why don't we live aligned with our own energetic feelings? We are slaves to commitment and time, not our energy levels and desires. We push ourselves when we are sick and may still go on to work or exercise. We push through situations with no sleep for days or weeks on end. This only reduces our intrinsic creativity. In deciding our actions, we need to be more conscious of our feelings, rather than the clock on the wall. Are we here to be happy or just get things done? Your heart already knows the answer to that question!

When we are tired, we need to rest. When we are energised, we can express. There is no shame in resting or enjoying life.

Stop looking at clocks all the time and forget about feeling guilty when you are merely honouring your body. It matters.

Money and getting things done are not the only things in life. Our obsession with accumulating assets and being a success can cause us to constantly push ourselves, often beyond our limits. Time is not money, despite our views to the contrary.

Loving ourselves means accepting that we are natural beings; and that we, like the tree, can adapt to the energy in our hearts. This is our natural state.

With so many things on our plates in our so-called modern world, we often think that the only way to get everything done is to have a plan or list to control our workloads. The plan becomes another thing we must do or manage! We plan to plan! Misery becomes our master.

Any plan we have needs to ideally be a simple plan, so we can focus on the things we have decided we would love to do, rather than the multitude of obligations we feel we need to meet.

Do you meet your own desires every day? It's time to be, not do! Allow the energy of joy to dictate your every moment. Enjoyment is the key to life.

When did you last let the energy in your heart guide your day, rather than your diary and the needs of others? Why not give it a go?

5.13: We must reject and fear the feminine

Our world is currently dominated by male leadership. Females are generally under-represented in leadership roles. Although this is changing gradually in some countries, it still has a long way to go to reach a point of balance.

Over the course of history, men have traditionally believed they are superior to women, and have feared feminine power. Many men simply can't relate to the feminine, and so they reject it.

On a metaphysical level, everyone has what are termed 'masculine' and 'feminine' traits or energies in different proportions. It has nothing to do with the 'male' and 'female' physical genders of how a person is born.

That said, cisgender women typically display more of the feminine energies and cisgender men typically display more of the masculine energies.

Below are some common masculine and feminine energies. I did not invent these – the internet contains many articles where experts have documented them. We all carry these energies to different degrees. Can you spot the ones that best define you or your loved ones?

Common Masculine Energies	Common Feminine Energies
o Righteous	o Compassionate/caring
o Competitive	o Collaborative
o Protective	o Nurturing
o Goal-orientated	o Empathetic
o Factual	o Intuitive
o Monotasking	o Multitasking
o Impatient	o Patient
o Assertive	o Forgiving
o Bias for action	o Express emotions
o Independent	o Understand interconnectivity
o Individual success	o Collective success

Our conditioning has led to a world where many cisgender men are considered more capable and valued in certain jobs than cisgender women, resulting in an imbalance in favour of cisgender men in our societies. Call it inequality.

We have lost our belief in the power or value of feminine energies, such that we do not readily accept or reward them as we do masculine energies. This is causing mayhem on our planet and at the same time is grossly unfair. Women have been denied equality and leadership roles because energies or characteristics such as compassion, care, nurturing, and collaboration are seen as too soft to get the outcomes that people believe they need to be successful. How can I get rich if I am collaborative and caring, when everyone around me is so competitive and selfish? Their subconscious minds whisper to them, 'Surely I will lose'.

If life is a big competition, with not enough spoils to go around, is it any wonder we suppress feminine energies that we convince ourselves are too weak to compete?

Yet intuition, for example, is such a powerful and underestimated gift that will often allow for better decision-making than facts and a focus on action. We tend to think with our minds, and search for control in all we do; but this leaves little space for a heart connection to guide us through life, through the feminine energies.

However, intuition can more easily search for the collective wellbeing in any decision and provide a solution that has a win-win outcome for all involved. A masculine-oriented action-based decision is more likely to be assertive and look for victory for the party making the decision, rather than search for the common good. Which is better for our communities?

Society has tended to manoeuvre women into roles of child and family nurturing. Although this is something those with feminine energies often excel at, conditioning has unfairly demanded these roles be done by all women, when in fact women have the right to choose what path they follow, the same as men.

We also do not reward nurturing skills, even though they are incredibly important to our societies. Families are the backbones of our communities, and children are our futures. Why do we deny the importance of this and focus so much on the accumulation of wealth? It's in our 'win at all costs' mindsets.

In 2019, I visited Egypt for a holiday. I was taken aback by the country's suppression of women. Few women were to be seen in jobs, and they appeared to be engaged only in household duties rather than applying their gifts to the commercial world. This is far from natural.

For centuries now, the business world and political leadership has been largely robbed of the power of feminine energies. How ridiculous! Surely the most powerful force of all is a combination of fact and intuition, competition and collaboration – masculine and feminine energies working together in balance?

A great family, a great society, a great country and a great world can come from leadership better balanced in this way.

Greater success will be achieved through embracing feminine energies in all that we do and in equal measure to the masculine.

In recent years we have seen legislation bringing women's rights more into balance. Companies, at the behest of regulators, have set targets on the number of women in leadership roles and on boards to force change and bring more feminine energies into play. This has had positive results, and I commend it as an initial starting point.

However, these kinds of targets would not be necessary if we understood the need for a natural balance of energies in our leaders. Who cares what body they are in?

The world is in truth a balance of masculine and feminine life forces. In the most simplistic example, the sexual interactions of a male and female can create a new person. When energies come into balance across our social fabric, true magic can and will return to our families, societies, and the world order.

Like everything in life, true harmony and progress will only be made when we live from the wholeness that comes from our hearts and minds being in sync.

We need to change our beliefs around men and women's relative functionality and abilities. It is time men consciously and subconsciously stopped thinking they are superior to women.

Our bodies are different, but it's the masculine and feminine energies that need to be understood and employed with wisdom in our world. Companies that apply this principle will have a huge advantage over those that don't. True happiness will be achieved when the masculine and feminine stand together as allies, not competitors!

5.13.1: A new type of gentle-man

In the past, we have often referred to men as being gentlemen. But how many of our men are actually gentle?

Growing up as a male I was taught that, to be successful, I had to be a winner at all costs. How good would our society be if we expected men to be gentle and kind, as well as smart and wise? How good would our society be if our men had the following traits?

- o Fearless but non-violent
- o Respectful of women and children as equals
- o Working for the collective good
- o Able to have constructive debate
- o Not judging or condemning of others
- o Respectful of different opinions
- o Always kind and caring
- o Able to admit failure
- o Potent but not needing to be important

5.14: Men and women are totally different

We often hear of the 'battle of the sexes'. This statement reflects the general belief that men and women are fundamentally different and in competition.

As I mentioned above, beyond our physical differences men and women are completely equal – we are all humans, all the same. The differences we perceive are based on preconditioned belief structures that we have inherited from history, but they do not serve us. In fact, preconditioned beliefs put limitations on the lives of both men and women.

I grew up in a world of gender segregation. Where I lived, girls and boys went to different high schools and undertook different social and sporting activities. There were also social norms around what men and women should both do.

Historically, men have been seen to be more suited to roles requiring physical strength, such as farming, hunting, and fighting; and women have been seen to be suited to nurturing activities, such as childrearing and domestic chores. However, with today's technology, these traditional gender roles can now be abandoned and change fully.

We need to look past the belief that men and women are fundamentally different.

5.14.1: Women make better parents than men

To my great shame, I was preconditioned to believe that women were more able parents than men, and were therefore more important to their children than their fathers. This was based on the historical fact that women in our society, and in many other societies around the world, were seen as the primary caregivers within a family, while men were the financial providers.

I lived this paradigm for much of my life. In my second marriage, my wife was mostly a stay-at-home mother, while I worked full time in corporate roles. My wife was well-prepared for the experience of raising children, as she had anticipated this role for years. I wasn't. She excelled at it. When I had my first child, my reaction was to feel a greater sense of obligation as a provider, rather than as a father. This was subconscious and reflected the fact that my wife gave up well-paid work to care for our children. This made me the sole breadwinner in the family and sent me into overdrive subconsciously on money. At a time when I should have been enjoying the role of a father, I was away, working harder than ever to pay the bills.

I believe my wife may have felt abandoned and alone on the parenting front, and I equally felt abandoned and alone in the role of making money. Both are of course critical roles and can be shared.

Having now snapped out of my preconditioned spell, I can see that children need exposure to male and female energies to grow up in balance. Both are equally important. Fathers and mothers offer their children different perspectives and skills, although these will vary from family to family due to the different proportions of feminine and masculine energies experienced by both parents. The same principles would apply to same-sex relationships where children are being raised.

When my second marriage ended, I chose to have equal custody of my four children, all under the age of 18. This made life extremely challenging for a while, but it was one of the best decisions of my life. I worked flexibly, and on alternating weeks I was their sole parent, as was my ex-wife on her week. My employer was incredibly supportive and progressive because they recognised the importance of flexible working. I cannot thank them enough.

The need for me to engage more with my children also enabled me to forge a much stronger relationship with my children than I ever would have achieved under the old family paradigm. I have received accolades in the press for embracing flexible working and caring for children as a senior business executive. To be honest, though, I see lots of single parents, particularly women, doing the exact same thing as I did, and on much lower incomes than I had, and they got zero praise or help. This is tough and unfair.

Even within secure relationships, mothers often carry the burden of the home duties because they are seen as the most-able providers of care. This is just a preconditioned belief structure and has no basis in reality. As a collective, fathers really need to understand this better and take on an equal share of household duties. They say that a 'woman's work is never done', and in many families, this is unfortunately true because of the preconditioned attitude men traditionally have about embracing parenthood fully.

What I learned was that, once my children were beyond breastfeeding, there was nothing that my wife could do that I could not. It just took me far too long to work this out!

As a single man, I continue to parent with great energy, and it is now a wonderful part of my life. I only wish I had seen this earlier.

I encourage everyone to change their thinking about parenthood. I was forced to do it by circumstances, but if you are a parent reading this book, perhaps you can do it voluntarily?

5.14.2: Men like sex more than women

When heterosexual men get together, they often criticise their female partners for not wanting as much sex as them. I have heard this so many times. The old joke is that once you marry a woman, she won't want to have sex with you again after the initial honeymoon period.

The myth that women don't like sex as much as men is rubbish.

Women I have spoken to have confirmed my view, although I recognise that this is virtually impossible to prove one way or another.

It's true that men carry testosterone in their bodies, which can make them extremely sexual. However, women are also driven by their hormones, which can drive them to connect with their partners through sex.

To think that women desire sex less than a man is inauthentic and unnatural.

5.14.3: Emotion is a weakness

I am not a psychologist, but many Australian men growing up in my era were taught to suppress their emotions – unless those emotions were anger or pride! If you cried or expressed how you felt in any other way, you were seen as weak. The men I knew were embarrassed to be caught crying and instinctively tried to cover it up. We feared being written-off by people if we were overly emotional. Emotion has become increasingly rejected as weak by our society.

Thus, I grew up in fear of emotional potency. This does not mean I had no feelings. I just learned to disregard or suppress them because of societal norms. I saw the damage emotions could do to others when they were not controlled.

Australian women of my era, on the other hand, seemed less influenced by this preconditioned view, and generally accepted that they could embrace and express feelings of sadness, fear, and vulnerability more readily than men.

However, every human being has emotions. We all experience joy, fear, anger, sadness, and disgust. The Australian men I grew up with only became masters at suppressing their feelings, because accessing and expressing them might have harmed their status, or so they thought.

Of course, different cultures have different preconditioned views of emotion, such that many Australians struggle with other nationalities, such as Italians and South Africans, who generally seem much more expressive and direct. Perhaps you could say more authentic?

Australians may claim to be laid-back, but this merely reflects how our culture tends to suppress our feelings, because we want to be seen as calm and in control.

We need to drop our fear of emotions and really value our feelings, for they are rich in wisdom. Human emotion is a gift, a great privilege of being human, not a burden. It distinguishes us from other beings. It creates great colour in our life, and feelings are a great source of information from which we can grow. They are a signpost to our beliefs and subconscious fears and desires, if we allow them to surface.

I am trying to do this more and more in my life.

When we suppress our feelings and emotions we create stress, and we can do great damage to our lives and our bodies.

We can also damage relationships because issues and opportunities go unnoticed and are perhaps not openly discussed.

It's natural to feel.

Men and woman alike need to allow each other to feel and express, for here lies the possibility of an authentic loving relationship, better sexual parity, and ultimately – happiness!

5.14.4: Caring for children is easy work

One of the lowest paid roles in our society is parenthood. Not only do many parents, particularly women, give up their careers to raise children; but they are often left in a poor financial position as a result, with financial reliance on others, lower annual incomes, and low retirement savings.

In my corporate roles, I often spoke with women who were both corporate workers and mothers, and invariably they would tell me how much harder it was to parent than to work for an employer, despite the stringent demands of organisations. As corporate workers their efforts were recognised with salaries, bonuses, awards, and so on. But what did they receive when they are at home raising children? Certainly, no money – unless they were receiving government subsidies or child support. No bonuses. No awards. Hardly even recognition for the importance of their work.

The work of a parent is critical – a life or death role in many ways. The worst that could happen for me when I was a corporate worker was that someone lost money. But if a child carer has a bad day, someone could get sick, lost or die.

So why don't we give parenthood and associated roles relating to the care of children the credibility they deserve?

The simple answer is that we think raising children is easy, particularly for women because we think it's natural for them. We don't really value it enough!

Yet our children are the future generation of adults and leaders. Raising them well is critical.

Currently, both men and women need to have the right to be a primary caregiver, and the importance of this role needs to be recognised for everyone. It can't be seen as an easy way out of working. It's hard work and needs to be more highly valued by society.

5.15: We love with a checklist

Our conditioned minds love in a conditioned way. After all, that's all they are capable of doing, unless they are connected to the wisdom of our hearts.

Unfortunately, most of us carry a checklist into our romantic and even family relationships. The number of ticks on our checklist often determine whether we think we love someone – 'think' being the operative word.

However, true love is a feeling or an energy, and can only come from one place: our hearts. It cannot be found when we look for it; it finds you. It is heaven-sent and cannot be created by our brains. It comes from within.

Yet our entire dating world is becoming based on, and obsessed with, finding love on our laptops and through electronic checklists. This can only lead to unhappiness.

5.15.1: What is unconditional love?

I have done a lot of reading on the topic of unconditional love and, from what I understand, it's a very rare phenomenon and few people actually understand it. We certainly don't apply it to ourselves very often, given our tendency to believe we are unlovable.

The key factors needed for unconditional love seem to be:

- The energy, or vibration, of love
- A total commitment to the other person's wellbeing and our own
- Freedom (not control over another)

- Trust (always)
- Full acceptance of another
- The equal exchange of giving and receiving between parties
- Honest and open communication
- Quality conflict resolution

Can many of us honestly say we have experienced a romantic relationship like this?

To date I haven't, but I hope to one day! In my past romantic relations, I've had real issues with expressing how I feel through open and honest communication. I have been on both sides of this silence, and I am now committed to changing this as best I can in future relationships.

As I mentioned earlier, our minds unfortunately constantly rank and rate the people we meet to determine whether they are better or worse than ourselves. We also rank potential suitors when we meet them, according to our checklists, to assess whether we are worthy of them, or they are worthy of us.

This evaluation process is a great separator and can block true love. Fail the initial mind-based test and potential love is scuttled!

We need to ditch the checklists.

Wouldn't it be better to feel with our hearts and bodies to see if love and chemistry are potentially present in a meeting? If so, we could then move on to create romance from a base of love, not the other way around.

5.15.2: Our search for fairy tales

The dating world is full of people seeking to meet the person who will be with them forever. As mentioned earlier, it's the fairy tale we all seek, and our romantic checklists contain our version of the roadmap to happily-ever-after. The current high divorce rates in the western world (around forty per cent in Australia) indicate that our ego-based way of loving is not working.

From a young age, and throughout our lives, we are subjected to love stories that show us what love is supposed to look like. It all starts with childhood Disney movies depicting 'forever love', with men and women meeting a princess or prince and falling in love in a castle of dreams. We are indoctrinated at a young age!

Thus, heterosexual women search for the dashing, handsome, wealthy prince who can save them from their mediocre lives; and heterosexual men dream of the beautiful loyal damsel they can save and hold in their arms happily ever after.

That said, in 'Beauty and the Beast' and 'Aladdin', the key characters fall in true love and win the palace, but only after they have released their egoic and selfish forms of love and learnt to love from their hearts in an unconditional way. Next time you watch these two movies, watch them with fresh eyes. Their deeper meaning is wonderful once it is witnessed with awareness. They tell a much more positive story of love.

Our movies and television shows, including fairy tales, promote the story of a never-ending cycle of separation then unity between lovers. We love this constant story plot and play it out in our day-to-day lives. Lack of communication, misunderstanding, and the egoic mind create the separation; then love defies all to create unity and reunification.

But our minds constantly sabotage the prospect of harmony because most of us lack the ability to see our neediness at play and our inability to love unconditionally. We are the architects of our own demise.

We could be teaching kids at school how to love unconditionally, not just how to do algebra. I wish I had been taught about it. It may have saved me from two divorces.

That said, what if relationships are not necessarily forever, and instead we believe that people come together for purpose then move on? We could get our minds out of the fairy-tale story of happily ever after.

A relationship might be forever, or it may not be, and surely either situation can be socially acceptable. We learn from every relationship regardless of how long it is. If trust and freedom are critical parts of any relationship – and if they are based on want, not need – then surely a relationship stays together out of desire, not because we once made a promise and signed a document in a white dress or fancy suit.

Life changes, we change, and to be locked into a relationship forever, once it has served its purpose, needs to be seriously reassessed by our community. How can we stay committed to a relationship that deep in our hearts we are not committed to? Marriage could be seen as a construct of the mind to ensure certainty and security, though I respect that there will be varying views on this subject.

As our children experience more fulfilling family life and witness unconditional love, so this can snowball through future generations.

Either way, we need to ditch the fairy-tale checklist.

5.15.3: The rise of online dating

In the modern dating world, online dating and dating agency practices have allowed us to take 'checklist love' to new heights.

We don't just meet people and feel into their energy and our shared chemistry anymore. We now fill out an online form and send forth an advertisement of our best features into the online ether. We post the best photos we can of ourselves into the advertisement, then we hide behind a stream of emails and texts until both parties have enough ticks on their checklists to feel sufficiently compelled to meet in person.

If we don't get enough ticks, we discard that person, push the delete button and try again.

Some people email and even date multiple people at a time, knowing that they have a high level of anonymity behind their computers. With one swipe or a delete button, the relationship can be finished. Love without compassion – that is not really love!

The online dating world is full of fear. It's competitive and lacks much authenticity because it is mind-driven.

Of course, during the Covid-19 lockdowns in Australia, people had little choice but to use online dating, which accordingly spiked by five times its previous usage. That's a lot of checklists and touched-up photos.

But we can improve the content and focus of dating sites. At present they focus on the 'story' of a persona, and whether one person has the interests, hobbies, and qualities to be similar enough to another to possibly complete them.

What if the dating questionnaire showed a deeper insight into a person, rather than what they think is their ideal partner or first date? Could they describe the depth of the relationship they desire, their hopes and dreams in life, and their core beliefs and values? A little more substance in the information would be so beneficial to the users of some sites.

We need to change the online dating checklist.

5.15.4: Our conscious and subconscious checklists

Most of us have dreamed up, either consciously or subconsciously, the kind of person we hope to fall in love with and be with forever. We may even have written it down. I know I did once, until I snapped out of my conditioned mind and replaced it with an outline of the type of relationship I wanted to create with a woman, not a checklist of the qualities or physical features they had to have in order for me to love them.

We generally have a checklist designed to find someone like us. We normally seek someone who is a similar age, nationality, religion, location, and has the same interests and hobbies. Some people's checklists focus mainly on physical looks; others place a lot more emphasis on a partner's levels of achievement.

We also often want to couple with someone who will meet the expectations of those around us, such as family and friends. We fear that if we date someone too different to us we will lose face in the eyes of those who most frequently influence our thinking. In effect, we subrogate to others our right to choose who we want to be with, then we wonder why so many relationships fail.

By the same token, too many parents, family members and friends think they know what would make us happy in relationships.

But no one can actually know how another person feels about a lover (or any other subject, for that matter), so what right do we have to tell others how they should feel? Can't we see that this is impossible?

In effect we use conscious checklists to find love, then we subconsciously use the checklists of others to vet the potential partners we meet. It's conditioning at its worst, and it's keeping divorce lawyers rich.

We need to ditch our conscious and subconscious checklists.

We need to love with our hearts, not our minds. When two people in a relationship love with their minds, mind-based rubbish can diminish their love, as the mind cannot help but analyse others and look for fault. Fault can be easy to find because, at a human level, we are all imperfect. From this dangerous place of finding fault, resentments are established and can grow over time, unless we have a healthy way to clear conflict.

Alternatively, when we love from our hearts, we accept others without judgement. In this place our differences are diminished because we see others without condition. They glow in our perception, and we can't help but glow back in their presence. Two glowing lovers are unmistakeable together. Do you know what that looks like?

If our hearts allow it, we will each find the right person to love – someone who has the same level of self-esteem to help us on our journey through life, someone who we are meant to be with for our own growth. Our hearts and souls will use great power to bring us together, along with the mutual hook of physical attraction. If we use our mind-based checklists to manufacture love, then subconsciously vet suitors with the approval of others, the relationships we create will likely end in tears, because they were never meant to be in the first place. These types of relationships are based on need, not want.

It is important that we allow relationships to unfold, and to listen intently to our hearts, not just our minds, as this will allow us to make the right decisions. The views of others are fundamentally irrelevant.

Our tendency to look for logic, before we feel for love, can impair our chance for happiness and true love. It needs to be reversed: love over logic.

5.15.5: Compatibility counts

A point to note here: to be in a loving relationship that lasts, we do need to be compatible with the other person. It may not be practical to develop a relationship with someone in a distant location or a different walk of life. Sometimes relationships just don't have the right timing or make practical sense, even if we wish they did.

Here the logical mind may play a useful role, once love is felt between two people.

5.15.6: Checklists in perpetuity

Once formed, we rarely tear up checklists and consign them to history. Instead, we carry them through our relationships, our insecurities and our assumption that love will complete us, leading us to constantly refer to the checklist as our relationships progress. If our partner slips and does not continue to meet the score we once gave them on the original checklist, even if circumstances have changed greatly beyond control, we may end the relationship. Our partner 'changed' too much.

However, surely all people should grow and thus change over the course of their lives? Ditch the original checklist and feel!

5.15.7: Our versatile checklists

We don't just apply checklists to romantic partners, we also apply them to other people.

We may rate our friends based on who they are or become and discard them if they change.

We may even love our children to different degrees, depending on their respective levels of success. Do you have a favourite child or feel that a sibling received greater love than you did?

What if we put our checklists away and loved with our hearts, not our judgemental minds? Judgement separates, acceptance unites.

5.15.8: The sabotage of checklists

When I became single in my 50s, I attended two online dating courses and one dating course in person, because I had not dated for over twenty years. What I experienced was somewhat useful, but it worried me that people were being taught to present themselves as something they weren't in order to attract each other. Frankly, the key point of the coaching seemed to be to teach you how to appear super-confident, even if you weren't, because that's what most people had on their checklists.

What has gone wrong with our world that we must teach people how to say 'hello' to each other? The answer is: a lot!

But the truth is that people are scared to approach each other for fear of rejection, as the fear of rejection is intense. Why? In this modern age, surely everyone knows the only way to meet people is to say 'hello' and take it from there.

We all want the same thing: an authentic and loving relationship. The only way to bring lasting happiness to a relationship, and therefore to your role in that relationship, is to be your true self with the other person. Confident or not! All we need to be is our true selves.

As I mentioned earlier, often when a human being meets a prospective romantic partner, they are tempted to pretend to be what they believe the other person wants them to be, in order to gain favour and create the illusion of compatibility. This can typically last for a couple of years, until the couple can no longer sustain the pretence – we cannot pretend to be something we are not forever. It is inauthentic, exhausting and our integrity simply won't let us. How many relationships have you had that ended after this two-year deadline?

I have been both the perpetrator and the victim of inauthenticity and non-expression of feelings in relationships, and in both dynamics it caused devastation at the end of the relationship. In effect, the desire not to hurt each other with honesty causes much greater pain in the long run. I'm therefore now committed to authentic sharing of feelings in all future relationships!

Checklists can sabotage honesty, the sharing of authenticity, and thus the blooming of a lasting love.

5.15.9: Artificial ways to impress the judges

Two industries that thrive on our egoic way of dating are: the fashion and beauty industries. We say 'clothes maketh the man'. I believed this, and at one point engaged the services of a style consultant to improve my dress sense and attractiveness. I was a lousy dresser, so it helped me to a point.

I'm not criticising these industries because looking good is often reflective of strong self-esteem. It is a problem, however, when it is built on vanity and fear.

Did it change the substance of who I was?

No. However, we do see getting dressed up as a way of attracting a partner and being highly rated by others. I was definitely in fear when I first worked with the style consultant. I would not be now.

People can spend a fortune on haircuts, beauty products and outfits to maximise their appeal. Manipulated by industries and unfair social expectations, many of us can spend hours, and much money, trying to improve our looks – but does it leave us feeling fulfilled?

This is a major form of subconscious conditioning. There is a degree of madness in trying so hard not to look natural.

We need to always respect our bodies and dress in a way that aligns with our true sense of self.

We just need to witness when our egoic minds waste money to make us more attractive, when just being the healthiest, most natural version of our true selves is what most people find attractive.

The energy between people generates real love, not the clothes or haircuts.

Ditch the beauty and fashion checklists.

5.16: Leadership is only about getting results

As a rule, our leaders are incentivised, programmed, and chosen to get results, rather than to care about how we get those results. This reflects our obsession with competition and winning.

However, this current model of leadership is hindering our progress as a race, because we simultaneously live in hope that our leaders will truly care about us and lead with authentic wisdom and intelligence. We are thus constantly let down and disappointed by those selected to lead us.

What we require is to be led by those with sound hearts and minds, working in unison; by those who can see what others can't see; by those with foresight and insight, not just the ability to do what is logical or what was learnt in academia or books.

Wisdom like this is a form of knowing, based on intuition, and comes from intelligence beyond the mind. Those with wisdom are typically balanced and in touch with their minds, bodies, and spirits. They care and make decisions for the benefit of the collective, not just themselves. They are service-minded, not selfish. They are often one step ahead of the herd, and prioritise achieving important outcomes, not promoting their own importance. Here true potency lies.

Insight and intuition come from within, and only leaders who know their true self can have the surety of what they represent.

Are leaders born or taught? The answer can surely be either, but regardless of the answer a great leader needs to have one key ingredient: self-awareness.

Unfortunately, most leaders are the product of the normal societal conditioning and are therefore built to fit into the system that created them. It needs to be the other way around, with leaders shaping society.

To be great, leaders need to see beyond what is obvious and normal, and know with insight a better way to go forward. They will love those around them but act in the long-term interests of the majority. This may make them unpopular with some, but they will have the strength to make hard decisions for the collective good. They need conviction and the ability to sense or feel into decisions, not just think.

Our current model of leadership is based on outdated stereotypes that comply with our egoic need for material success. The leaders who can generally get these material results are wrongly put on a pedestal, rather than being regarded as part of the team that they lead.

Unfortunately, we have leaders who use fear to get results, rather than those who use love and care to create the conditions for a team to succeed.

There are several associated outdated beliefs about leadership that need to be crushed because of the deep importance of leadership in our lives. Unless they are, we risk continuing in a place of profound unhappiness and mediocrity.

5.16.1: Old straight white men make the best leaders

Our subconscious bias, including our lack of respect for feminine energies and gifts, have directed us to think that older, well-educated, rich, straight white men make the best leaders. If we look at the collective of leaders of western countries during my lifetime, it has largely been white men in their 50s, 60s and 70s. Of course, there have been exceptions like Barack Obama, who became president of America at just 48 years old.

Still, we have this commonly held view that age must bring experience and skill to a leader, and therefore without age a leader is not equipped to handle difficult situations.

Of course, it should not matter how old a leader is, if they have the wisdom and a strong open mind to do the job properly. Likewise, it should not matter about their sexuality, colour of their skin, or gender.

We need to drop the inherent bias towards straight white men and simply look for leaders with the right mix of compassion and assertiveness in their leadership abilities.

We also have a bias towards leaders who are rich. Why? Because we think if they became rich, they make us rich too. Unfortunately, this is rarely the case.

But what if we looked for leaders who balanced heart and mind, no matter what type of body they inhabit?

5.16.2: Leaders are superior to those they lead

Society seems to hold a collective belief that the leaders who get results are more important than the people they lead. This simply isn't true, and hints at a lack of understanding about the role or characteristics of a great leader.

In every business I've worked in, the senior leaders got paid much more than everyone else. At one stage I was one of them. When things went well, those leaders got recognition and money. They were well rewarded and therefore felt validated. When things didn't go so well, their first option was to get rid of people who worked for them, rather than take personal responsibility for any problems.

For this reason, among others, many people aspire to be leaders because they see these personal benefits. This doesn't mean they are suited to the role, or that the role matches their passions or skill sets.

For example, people who excel at creative roles often step into leadership roles because their technical or mental abilities are so highly valued, and no one wants to lose them. But they end up leading poorly and failing to the detriment of all, because they lack true leadership qualities.

Leadership is not something everyone is cut out for. It can be learned, but true leaders need to exhibit the right balance of skills and qualities for someone to be effective at it. Thus, we need to even out the financial rewards for workers and leaders, and to attract leaders for the right reason: because they're good at leading.

Our organisations need a better balance overall in the way they value workers and leaders, as they are equally important. A business cannot be effective without the workers who make the business run *and* the leaders who set strategy, vision and motivate people.

Is it fair that senior leaders earn ten, twenty, thirty times that of the people working for them? No. Many workers, because of perceptions of seniority, earn a low salary that makes it hard for them to do anything other than survive and live from pay-to-pay. The leaders typically have much more advantage in life, because their bigger salaries give them material wealth. But is it the CEO who keeps a bank running, or the tellers and IT specialists who keep the lights on and the customers happy? We all know the answer!

I have been in both senior and junior roles, so I have seen the world from both sides. The recent Covid-19 issues showed us how unfairly we treat many essential workers, paying them extremely modest amounts of money. This includes supermarket workers, teachers, nurses, bank tellers, and so on. I was once married to a schoolteacher. I know firsthand how hard they work and how little they get paid. If these people truly keep the lights on in our economy, why do we make them struggle so much to survive? Ask yourself: why do so many of us have so little conscience about thriving, when we know, if we bothered to look, how many others around us are struggling to survive?

Self-interest is the short answer. We are programmed to want to win.

Another issue with the relationship between workers and leaders is that, when a company goes through tough times, it's the workers not the leaders who are the first to pay with the loss of their jobs. If loyalty is at a premium from the top down, it's not surprising that the staff do not project loyalty upward after being let down.

We have pyramid structures in our modern world, which has some logic; but the pyramid is inverted when you look at individual salaries. When will we start looking more closely at the true contribution workers bring to an organisation and our lives, rather than the immediate monetary benefit that can be measured from their hard work? When will we reassess our model of leadership?

A leader is accountable for a team of people, but is no more important than the people they lead. They may earn more because of the demands or legal responsibilities of the role they are in, or hopefully because they have the right mix of wisdom and experience; but we still need to change our thinking on remuneration because it is currently inequitable.

Substance and balance are needed, and leaders need to understand that they will get better results if they inspire and bond with their people in a common direction, not enslave them with fear, so that if they make a mistake or don't get results every time they will be replaced.

Loyalty earns loyalty, and the best results come from leaders with the right skills, including self-awareness and wisdom.

5.16.3: Leaders have the right to control us

Our mindset around leaders also says that they have the right to control us, and therefore we must do whatever they say, even if we have lost faith in their judgement or abilities. We often endure questionable leaders for far too long, even after they have shown gross incompetence. Why? Because we underestimate the true power of the people in forcing change.

In most cases, leaders are there to serve the masses, not themselves; and when they don't act in the collective best interests, they need to be removed by us, the people they lead. Our political systems often don't have sufficient mechanisms to make this possible.

The world has, thus, been plagued by dishonest and incompetent leaders throughout history, who have retained power through manipulation and force. These types of leaders do not lead with heart, and there is no place for them in leadership roles going forward.

Resentment of governments by the people who vote them has always been common. A great symbol of this resentment is the tall fences and security needed to protect such leaders from their own people!

This would not be necessary in a world based on benevolent, honest leadership, where true respect exists.

It is not uncommon for political leaders to be given leadership opportunities based on a series of promises. Normally politicians are voted into power under a fanfare of promises but disappoint voters because they spend more time managing their own reputation and trying not to make mistakes or voting on party lines, rather than being fearless and supporting the common good with wise decisions.

Many of us are apathetic about our leaders and just do what they say. We deceive ourselves into thinking that our leaders have complex jobs and must be smarter than us, but this is often not the case. This belief structure needs to shift. We typically prefer to wait for years till the next election to change inappropriate leaders, rather than make a stand and demand a change early on. Apathy is alive and well!

Social media is making it more possible to take a stand on issues and generate differing views on issues for our leaders to act upon. We need to harness these new tools to have our say in the world.

The power of social media has never been more evident than during the Covid-19 pandemic. People had no choice but to connect on social media and have collectively realised the true power of this medium. Of course, it can also have a dark power if misused.

It's the natural order for us to have rights to our own sovereignty as people. There is a limit to what we should accept from egoic leaders without wisdom, before we stand up and be counted.

Leaders need to know, the world over, how to lead with wisdom for the masses, not for their own benefit or reputations. We need stronger mechanisms to make this possible, so we don't have to wait years to see change take place.

Incompetent, ego-driven leaders can't lead us to success, and therefore are in competition with our best interests as a society.

Great leadership can help us to thrive and escape the clutches of our obsession with the need to just survive.

How many wise political leaders can you name, who you think genuinely cared about the people they led?

5.17: Everything that matters is matter

The common belief is that we live in a three-dimensional world in which most things appear to be solid, including our own bodies. We believe in things we can touch, but for most people this is where we draw the line.

Despite lots of human experiences to the contrary, and despite the apparent faith people have in life after death, many do not accept the existence of things they cannot physically see or touch. The possible metaphysical realms of our existence are collectively denied or questioned by millions of people, because the evidence is not often physical.

Why do we fear what we cannot see or touch, and reject what could give us great hope in our lives?

I believe that I am an eternal being and in truth never die. So, for me, death is simply a rebirth and is not to be feared. To believe in this concept, however, I accept that I also have to believe in a universal field of energy, or perhaps 'god'; or that perhaps everything in the universe is just energy or light, and we are only light waves vibrating at a specific level of intensity? Maybe parts of us – and the world – are only solid because those particles of light are vibrating at a slow enough rate to make them three-dimensional? The possibilities are endless. Just as endless as our visions of the stars, the beauty of our planet, the stunning serenity of sunset or sunrise, and so on.

Our logical minds seek physical evidence before they believe in something. This is what we have been taught or conditioned to believe. But our hearts know differently.

Our minds think that we are physical beings who can choose whether or not to be spiritual. What if we *are* spirits who have chosen to be physical for a certain period of time? In this paradigm there would be no such thing as spiritual or non-spiritual, because we would all be spiritual with just different levels of self-awareness.

If there is an infinite intelligence, perhaps some of us can connect to that and get help? Perhaps we can communicate metaphysically, make love metaphysically, and communicate with people who have passed over?

In this changed way of thinking, the need for the physical diminishes and possibilities open. You can't take anything physical with you when you die. You will only own it temporarily in this life, so why stress out about what size house you own, what car you drive, or what clothes you wear? You might want material possessions, but the joy they bring is temporary, so there's no point buying them for validation or to raise your sense of importance.

Because we live so firmly in our minds, most people too readily accept the conditioning they have learned from others with a purely physical mindset.

But what of all the people around the world who meditate and understand the benefits meditation brings. By quieting our minds, we can connect to our hearts or souls. The power of meditation is immense if you open yourself up to it. It allows you to go within and find out who you really are. It has really changed my life for the better.

5.18: Death is the end

For most people, death is their greatest fear. It's a fear that lurks powerfully in the subconscious mind. It's the ultimate unknown.

We are also constantly exposed to death in our lives. We witness it not only as a natural event, but also through our media outlets. Some of us may have even witnessed it through our involvement in conflicts, wars and accidents.

Of course, death is not something we invite into our lives. But it can also be something that – consciously or subconsciously – holds us back. We are so scared of all the deaths we see around us that we play it safe in our lives. Too safe. We limit the adventures we might have, and in its subtlest form our fear causes us to not trust those around us. Many of us, me included, have probably led conservative lives, and held ourselves back from interacting with certain elements of society or opportunities because we fear losing our lives.

For example, I always wanted to jump out of a plane, but my fear always stopped me until 2021, when I literally took the plunge. It was exhilarating.

Our fear of death can cause us to hide our energy for life, or light, under our 'rock'.

The fear of death not only holds us back, but it is such a mystery to us that we choose to consciously ignore it in our lives. We know it's unavoidable in the long run, but it's a topic we suppress in our thinking and conversations. We all want to die in our sleep at a ripe old age. But what then?

Collectively we want to believe in life after death but, again, to do so we must surely also explore the concept of a universal intelligence.

There are more than 300 religions in the world, and many of them preach different beliefs about eternal life. The Catholic religion, in which I was brought up, taught me that there is a God, but we only live once before we return to the afterlife, to heaven or hell. Many religions believe in reincarnation, or the belief that we return to Earth multiple times to reach enlightenment. The point is that beliefs are variable, and none of them can be proven definitively.

Of course, there are also atheists who have no belief in any universal energy. These people believe that, at the end of this life, it's all over and there is no such thing as eternal life. We simply cease to be.

Many people are also not sure how the afterlife will operate for them once they die.

All this adds up to a collective doubt or fear that has many people not wanting to die, even if they are living an awful life, because they don't know where death will take them and what its consequences will be. This will likely make people cling to life and be cautious about how they live, and not allow themselves, or loved ones, to pass on – even after their desire to live is gone. I experienced this in conversations with my mother before her death at age 88.

Also, if a person believes there is no life after death, they may think there is no accountability to a higher power, so whatever they can get away with in life is not going to result in them carrying any enduring debt. This could result in a more selfish attitude being adopted in life and a singular focus on the physical things in life. After all, if your heart and soul are not connected to any higher intelligence, why would you bother trying to live your life from a place of love? The answer is: you may not, and you are more likely to live from your ego, focussing on money, surviving and winning, not loving. Many people live this way, even many who call themselves religious.

If you only believe in things you can see or touch, life can become a purely physical random event that you need to control, or risk becoming irrelevant forever. Whereas, what's the worst that could happen if you open yourself up to possibilities? It can free you up from believing you need to control everything in life. You can explore the idea of fate or synchronicity.

I call this the energy of allowing (as opposed to controlling). When we allow events to unfold, we can more readily learn from them and enjoy the experiences that take place. We don't need to wrestle with everything that occurs, because we can trust that experiences will guide us forward. We just need to trust that change is ultimately in our best interests.

Our fear of death also leads us to seek to be remembered by the world once we pass on. This leads us into the creation of personal legacies linked to our name for all to witness. Two ways we do this is by having children to carry our names, and by having a tombstone with our name forever engraved on it.

The world's population is now about eight billion people. In 1800, it was only one billion. This is a phenomenal and arguably unsustainable rate of growth. It is estimated that by 2050, the world's population will grow to more than fifteen billion people. I have contributed to this with five children.

Why do we reproduce so rapidly, despite the obvious looming consequences for our world and our planet? One reason might lie in the fact that our minds fear that we will be forgotten after we die. So, we seek to create new people who will survive us, carry forward a memory of who we were, and preserve our assets into the future. We spend so much energy in our lives creating wealth that we don't want to leave it to someone we don't know or who won't honour our lives.

We also create cemeteries or burial grounds to remember our dead. Isn't this a waste of valuable land and resources? When I die, I am happy to just be remembered and have my ashes scattered in a natural place, not put in a wooden box or a brick wall to take up space. My loved ones can remember me without killing flowers and placing them on a tomb.

We need to drop the need to leave physical reminders of our life and accept that our memories are much more important. Isn't it enough that on our deathbeds we are able to remember what we contributed to in this world, and cherish our own contributions, rather than what others think?

It's bad enough that life, for most of us, is a competition before we die; does it also have to be after we depart?

It's normal for us to fear that our stories will end the day we die, and most of us don't have a sense of comfort about what happens after that. We stay in our comfort zones, afraid to take risks, and cling to safety. We believe there is no assistance from a divine power, so we seek to control our lives fully. We fail to live from love, because we see no accountability to a universal energy. We don't want to consider what happens after we die, so we keep our heads in the sand.

But belief in possibilities can be liberating and can free us to treat life as an adventure. In this place, we can be free to follow our true passions and desires rather than play it safe. This is where the magic begins.

We have an opportunity to open our hearts and minds to consider more possibilities? Simply ask your heart if there is eternal life. If you listen closely, you may be surprised by what you feel. If you listen closely to your body, you may feel a life force literally buzzing inside you! Be that buzz!

5.19: Life is a random event

Many people believe that life is a series of random events and that we are at the whim of luck or misfortune.

Others believe that everything in life happens for a reason or purpose. Consistent with this, our lives therefore have reason or purpose. We are not here on the Earth just to make up the numbers. Life is not just a spectator sport. So, we need to get on the field and make the most of our gifts and opportunities! Play and have fun!

Which approach will have us living a happier life?

Many of us take the negative perspective that the world is out to get us, and therefore we should hide and play safe or we'll perish. But life is what you make of it, particularly once you know who and what you are, and all your life force can take you on a wonderful journey of discovery.

It's important that each one of us looks for the purpose in our lives. We all have unique gifts and great talents we can bring to this Earth, but few of us are seeking to find how we can uniquely contribute to this world. Only our hearts know the answer to this question. No one else knows our special or divine purpose in life. No one else knows what our heart is here to express. No one else knows what sets us on fire. No one else can tell you how to live. No one! So why do we let them?

Instead, we become what everyone around us becomes or wants us to become. Life churns out people like a cookie cutter churns out biscuits. We put up our shields and rattle our sabres to anyone who threatens us. We don't trust others until we see sufficient evidence that this is possible. People we meet are untrustworthy until they prove otherwise.

Alternatively, how would life feel if we followed our true desires and worked towards our ultimate purpose, rather than ignoring that purpose and leaving it to sit in the shadows of possibility? I have experienced this and, let me tell you, following your dreams is a path full of joy and happiness.

Why not go inward to find out for yourself? You are the only one who can. I suspect you will be delighted by what you find.

When we don't follow our heart's desire, we are constantly redirected back to it by life. When we carry unfortunate self-images and subconscious falsehoods about ourselves, we will constantly stray off our true path because life delivers to our level of self-worth. Water, as they say, finds its own level. The self-love in our hearts will periodically redirect us back to the path we were intended to follow, and it may do this in ways that feel uncomfortable and challenging.

Human beings typically only change when things – in their minds – go wrong. In this place we summon the strength to say 'no' to more unhappiness, we bring our hearts to the fore, and it allows us to use this different heart-based operating system to reboot our lives.

Pain thus unfortunately becomes our coach in life, rather than pleasure. It is possible to learn from both, but wouldn't it be better to learn with the love in our hearts rather than the fear in our troubled minds?

If things have not worked out perfectly in your life so far, just know that you have been traversing stepping stones of love that can bring you great self-awareness – if you dare to turn them over and look for the messages of love underneath.

Life can have deep purpose for us all, even if it's only to experience and learn. When we search inside our hearts for truth, we can start to learn through joy rather than disaster. This is where magic can begin.

When you surrender to the truth in your heart, it is extremely liberating. In this place your life lives you; you don't have to struggle or force yourself to live it. Have you ever noticed that often the best things happen to you when you're not even trying, or you're completely relaxed and are having fun?

What could go wrong if you relax, have fun, and see what unfolds?

5.20: We are separate from nature

Science tells us that human beings (or homo sapiens) are highly intelligent primates that have become the dominant species on Earth because of our superior intelligence. It further states we have evolved from the homininae subtribe of animals, comprised of monkeys and gorillas.

In other words, we are animals and a part of nature, like any other being on this planet. We share common biological traits with many other animals, including having a brain, nervous system, and so on. Everything within our bodies is comprised of the elements of nature, and we rely upon the goodness provided by Mother Nature for our survival. Our bodies are entirely comprised of earthly elements. We need air, water and sunshine to survive, and without soil we would have no food. We need the planet and its interaction with the sun for our very survival.

Despite all this, many people clearly behave as if we are above nature or not a part of it. They believe this as a result of human conditioning. I often hear people say, 'I love to be in nature'. But you *are* nature, and you can never leave it.

Many people think we can do whatever we like with the planet that sustains us, with the other animals that co-exist alongside us, because we are separate and above them. When it comes to nature, we have a superiority complex. This has led us to an unsustainable level of consumption of natural resources and left our planet sick and depleted.

This surely must end, yet it won't until we stop believing we are separate from nature.

We often refer to ourselves as landholders when we buy land. This reflects our belief that, with money, we can own parts of this planet. Some cultures, like indigenous Australians, believe that the land holds us — we don't hold it. This is definitely food for thought. I, like many people in the world, 'own' land; but I believe I am 'renting' it off Mother Nature and she is my landlord. As such, I must align myself with her requirements to sustain my rental agreement with her.

Our arrogant attitude to nature leads us to some key associated beliefs.

5.20.1: Nature has unlimited resources we can exploit

There is much evidence that our planet is in a bad way. Human beings have largely treated the planet like it has unlimited resources, and our belief seems to be that we can take more and more from the Earth to suit our desires.

Our obsession with money and modern lifestyles has led us to an unsustainable situation on both a macro and micro level.

The constant consumerism we create means factories continually access natural resources to make the products that we want. Those resources include timber, which necessitates the felling of thousands of trees each day — trees that would otherwise cleanse our atmosphere, creating the oxygen we all breathe every minute of our lives.

Life has become more complex and consumer based. It lacks simplicity. Our planet is the victim of this obsession; but eventually we will be the victims, once Mother Earth has had enough. She is in charge here, not us; and whenever she rebalances, we pay the price for our neglect!

Our planet has the resources to easily meet our needs in life but, as I mentioned before, not our escalated wants. Our wants are endless. The more we seem to get, the more we want; and our wants will likely never feel met, because they can never fill the void in our hearts. Our wants vary by person and therefore are countless.

Our needs, on the other hand, are relatively straightforward and will not overly tax the planet.

I am not pointing the finger at others here. Up until my 50s, I worked hard to make money to spend on material things. Buying things gave me a sense of satisfaction, though only for short periods of time. I even cut down trees to make my house more valuable and my family richer.

But during the Covid-19 shutdowns, multiple television segments on the news showed a healthier planet emerging. Pollution in many places diminished, and animals started to return to locations normally filled by human beings. This shows how quickly our planet might recover if we reduce our unsustainable lifestyles.

All too regularly, we witness natural disaster after natural disaster, as the planet continues to consistently rebalance itself in the face of our selfish way of living.

5.20.2: We can mistreat other animals

There is no doubt that human beings are the dominant species on the planet. We have higher intelligence than other species and have developed technology that can be used to control other animals.

The animal kingdom is largely driven by instinct. Animals eat and prey on other species that they are preprogrammed by nature to pursue. They only eat what they need to survive, and don't kill for fun or entertainment as do we humans.

They are programmed by nature. We are programmed by the unnatural beliefs of the egoic mind.

When you consider how we treat other animals, it's often terrible. We hunt for fun. We make animals race so we can gamble on the result, even though it often kills them. We sell animals for profit. We put them in zoos so we can enjoy a day out with the family. We keep them as pets until they no longer suit our lifestyles.

We constantly destroy the habitats of other species, so little do we really care about them. It is believed that the Australian koala may be extinct by 2050, because of the rate at which we are destroying their habitats. This is a sad situation.

We treat animals as if they have no intelligence, no feelings, and no rights. When will we wake up and realise that they matter as much as we do? We share this world with them as fellow travellers. We are all just having a different experience, with different levels of consciousness and different physical bodies. We need to have more respect.

It is sickening to see animals shipped all over the world for food and stored in terrible conditions prior to their death. We can be very heartless when it comes to other animals. But they have a right to a natural life. Once we recognise that, think of the joy it will bring us to see animals happy. Their happiness is our happiness.

5.20.3: It's best to live in cities

Humans tend to congregate, more and more congesting in cities. During my lifetime in Australia, more people have moved out of rural areas, resulting in declining populations in these areas, which often then suffer economically. On the one hand, lower populations make country-living quieter and more natural. But on the other hand it compromises lifestyles due to the limited economic and social opportunities that eventuate.

Living in cities has historically been seen as providing more opportunities for entertainment and employment, meeting the need to earn money, consume and enjoy the escapism that recreation in cities readily creates – shops, theatres, restaurants, and infrastructure such as stadiums.

In late 2020, I had the opportunity to live in the Sydney inner city suburb of Ultimo. Residents were so friendly and connected. I was also pleasantly surprised with the number of small parks and gardens giving people access to nature. Living in Ultimo proved to be an enlightening experience, helping me to see that city living has merits.

However, there are also many downsides to such a life. In cities we live close to other people and are influenced by their noise and activities. We more readily endure traffic congestion, pollution, queues, transport disruptions, violence, crime, and so on. We are surrounded more by concrete and less by trees. Cities are moneymaking epicentres, with big populations easier to sell to, thus creating mass consumerism. As we congregate in cities, the prices of properties escalate, particularly in sought-after areas. This puts pressure on housing costs, and families are forced to work harder and for longer hours to afford rents and mortgage repayments.

The pressure to earn more also puts pressure on relationships, and families suffer from breakups and divorces. As these breakups occur, so more housing is needed because the broken family now needs two homes, not one. And so the merry-go-round of consumerism goes on, and life gets more competitive and intense.

Access to fresh air and sunlight can also be limited in big cities. Workers get jammed into buses and trains to reach their places of employment, and our proximity to others makes us more likely to catch viruses and bacterial infections.

Indeed, Covid-19 has shown us the extreme health dangers of living in big cities. Is it any wonder that some of the biggest cities in the world were the hardest hit by the virus, including New York, Los Angeles, Paris, London, just to name a few?

In Australia the virus hit Sydney and Melbourne hard because they had the biggest populations and received most of the overseas visitors. This enabled the virus to spread more readily. States like Western Australia, South Australia and the Northern Territory were more able to control the spread of the virus due to lower population concentrations and, to some extent, their isolation.

Another aspect of the pandemic was the demonstration that working from home can be just as effective as going into crowded city offices every day. Employers have learned to trust their workers to get things done, without direct supervision. Traditionally, businesses have congregated in cities dominated by skyscrapers and industrial areas.

This might now change.

It's already changing. Sea and tree changes have become increasingly popular since Covid-19. The pandemic stopped many of the events that people are able to experience more readily in the big cities, such as concerts and major sporting events. With these derailed, people came to see more clearly the virtues of living in rural or non-urban areas.

If our wonderful technology can be applied properly to our working lives, there is no reason we can't now continue to live in less populated areas, where we can be more at one with nature, given that we are natural beings and part of the bigger ecosystem.

Our hearts sing louder in nature, not in concrete jungles; although where we live is of course a personal choice and one that we are all entitled to make. It is natural for us to be out in nature, connected to the elements, such as the Earth, ocean, sunlight, and fresh air. As natural beings, we thrive and feel alive in nature and can more easily access our hearts. Yet we tend to regard this as a low priority and only have this experience when time allows, typically on holidays or weekends. Have you noticed how many major cities have a central park, or many parks, where people gravitate to relax and recharge, somehow knowing they need nature to feel refreshed?

But pause for a moment and consider how you feel when you experience a beautiful sunrise or sunset, a day on the beach, or the opportunity to experience the view from a mountain range. I'll bet there is a part of you that feels free and at home. Time stands still. This is because you are nature and, in moments like this, you sense your return to this state. You melt into the environment. You find happiness.

When we as a society lose our obsession with having to validate our sense of self with big houses and protecting ourselves from our fear that others will take from or abandon us, we can change the way we live. A more collaborative society would more likely choose to live in smaller communities, more closely aligned with nature, and sharing the skills and resources they have at their disposal, without having to compete with each other.

Sharing common land to grow food, and trusting each other more to respect what's produced, would be examples of what might be possible. These types of shared vegetable gardens exist in some communities, but they are rare because we would prefer to buy rather than grow what we need. We are too busy to get our hands in the soil.

I'm sure great town planners could quickly create physical communities to match a mindset resolving around a greater sharing of resources.

When you are in your heart's centre, it doesn't matter where your physical home is. In this place you are already home. We can therefore of course choose to be happy regardless of where we live.

However, to find your way back to your heart, nature is a wonderful guiding light, and being near to nature is where we as a species are meant to live as often as we can.

Do you feel yourself relax in nature, and wonder how you would feel to live in nature each and every day with your family?

5.21: Technology is critical for our happiness

Technology is a double-edged sword. It can be a game-changer and improve our lives immensely, but it can also enslave us if we are not careful. Both outcomes already occur in our lives.

The human mind has a great capacity to invent new and exciting things, given its incredible intellect. Since the dawn of time, and particularly since the industrial revolution in the 1700s, we have created new and wonderful devices to make our lives better.

Who could go past the invention of the wheel in shaping the world, or electricity for that matter? Imagine the chaos in this world without traffic lights! The list is endless.

The introduction of computer technology in the 20th century, along with the launch of the internet, changed our lives in a vast way. Businesses and individuals alike have benefitted from the incredible capabilities that computerisation has brought forth.

Smartphones and tablets have changed the way we interact with each other and have allowed us to carry a whole bundle of different technologies in the palm of our hands. How often do you see cameras around people's necks these days? Not often, because everyone has a phone with a camera, which they generally carry wherever they go. We even do our banking from our phones.

Technology is a time saver (once you get it right) and can take away the need for human effort. We can change the channel on our television sets without getting out of our chairs, unlike when I was a child. We can even turn on our lights and air conditioners before we arrive home. Today's world is a lot more advanced than the one I entered in the 1960s!

But have we become too reliant on, and vulnerable to, computers in our lives? Technology seems to be shaping our society rather than the other way around.

We are now facing the early stages of artificial intelligence, and this may create even greater opportunities, as well as greater risks to our lifestyles. Imagine a world where computers take control, as has been portrayed in movies. This may seem far-fetched, but you never know!

Everything in our life has benefits and trade-offs, positives, and negatives. So how we use technology will ultimately come down to our belief structures about it.

Young people have never known life without many of the mod-cons we now take for granted. What are their belief structures about technology?

Many people are becoming dependent on their smartphones, in often unhealthy ways. For example, our ability to communicate human to human may be at risk through our reliance on texts and email. Surely this way of communicating can lead to great misinterpretations between people. I have certainly experienced this. With the millions of texts and emails being sent around the world every day, it's hard not to imagine how many are being misinterpreted!

Whereas, when you speak with someone face-to-face, or over the phone, you can feel the energy and intent of the other person. It is far more personal and intimate, and you can sense the energy of the conversation. Body language and energy is easily transferred between people when we communicate person-to-person. This is critical, yet these connections are being lost to computer connections and modems.

People are also often braver behind texts and emails, because it's easier to be blunt when you're not directly exposed to another's energy. But we run the risk of going too far with texts. I know I have done this in my life, so now I try to only use electronic communication when it's a transactional conversation.

Our children are growing up with active social media that acts like a permanent paparazzi in their lives. Anything they do, including things that are less than ideal, can be broadcast to the world in seconds. This can cause them great worry and stress.

Technology also costs us money to run each day. Imagine how many devices need to be charged across the world every day with electricity. This puts pressure on the planet, but also has to increase our energy costs. People constantly lament their energy bills, but it's no surprise those bills rise with so many devices now in our homes and offices.

When I was in school, there was a view being espoused that computers would change the world and allow us to all work less. The reality is the opposite! It has sped up our lives and put greater time pressures on us all. It's now virtually impossible to escape work, even on weekends, because of all the messages and emails that follow us wherever we go, and they don't stop. They even follow us on holidays. In some ways, holidays have just given us a different location from which to answer our emails and texts!

The greatest double-edged sword of technology relates to weapons. Modern defence forces around the world spend trillions of dollars each year on weapons. They are primarily for defence, but the nuclear arsenal of the world is so powerful, it could destroy the world many times over if misused.

Technology in the form of weapons is a terrible thing. The gun culture in some countries has made those countries incredibly unsafe.

Our belief that we must create the latest and greatest technology to protect ourselves is a huge waste of money and resources and has just left the world in a very dangerous place in which our very existence is at risk, along with the existence of other creatures on Earth.

Our obsession with technology is potentially detrimental to the fabric of our lives. It fits very closely with our obsession with money, consumerism and avoiding true intimate contact with other people.

In all the technological bombardment of our lives, are we losing touch with the things that matter? Getting out in the fresh air, sitting under a tree, swimming in the ocean or seeing a real sunset – they have been replaced by virtual versions!

In 2020, a study in Australia showed that kids were gradually losing their ability to jump compared to kids 30 years ago. Is there any wonder when all they have to do these days is jump virtually?

If we rely on technology too much, it can make us lazy and harm our health.

Gamers may be being physically impaired and desensitised through their overuse of computer games. How many people can you shoot on a screen, and how many cars can you crash, before your mind sees these kinds of activities at a subconscious level as non-threatening and normal?

The Covid-19 lockdowns showed us the potential of the internet and its ability to connect people. But if we let technology overcomplicate our lives, make them busy and detached, we will lose key things that we already lack in life: contact with our sense of self and the unity of being connected to other souls.

Technology deters us from going inward and searching for true happiness because it provides so many opportunities to go outward. True happiness can only be found inside ourselves – not on a screen or on a keyboard.

We need to realise this, and log into ourselves and our heart-based operating systems. We are the only ones who know the password and can access our own search engine.

5.21.1: The more information we have the better

The boom in technology in recent decades has led us firmly into the information age. We have so much information at our fingertips; it surely has reached the point of overload. There is so much data and information in our world, and it grows exponentially every day.

We know so much about so many things, but so little about ourselves. We know more about our planet each day, but has this stopped us wrecking it?

Perhaps it is time we replaced the information age with the transformation age.

Sure, enjoyment can come from watching a movie on a flat-screen television or playing a game on your computer; but real happiness comes from the joy of transforming yourself. When you take the time to access your own heart, and to direct and star in a new movie that is your ideal and intended adventurous life, you can feel immense self-empowerment.

5.22: Money is always real and unlimited

Money is an important part of our lives, but many of us sacrifice too much of our happiness to make it, especially since many monetary assets are not real.

Indeed, our obsession with money has led us to create complex economic structures – services and products that are beyond the comprehension of the average person. Our financial structures are, to some extent, based on illusion, as our egoic minds strive to create assets with limited basis in reality. Even money has become unlimited and thus, to some extent, fake. Money cannot be unlimited.

The rise of Modern Monetary Theory (MMT), as it has been coined, basically justifies an endless creation of money, and is mired in illusion. MMT is based on a belief that you can create as much money as you like and not decay the true value of currencies.

Due to complexities involved, I cover the subject of money in much more detail in the next chapter, under 'Economic behaviours and structural concerns'.

CHAPTER

6

The Impacts of Our Limiting Beliefs on our Financial and Social Interactions and Structures

The twenty-two limiting beliefs that flow from our social conditioning, and from our mind-based operating systems, have a major impact on our world, societies and families.

At an individual level, they leave many people unhappy and unfulfilled with their lives.

But the ripple effect on our societies is also huge. Those beliefs drive social and financial interactions with many unloving and unintended consequences.

Our fears have created a complex and volatile world, where competition and stress abound. We are used to this mayhem, and so we accept it as normal each and every day. But this is not the life most of us crave. We don't understand what is possible, because we don't know who we truly are, as individuals or as a race. Until we find a collective path to knowing ourselves, we will continue to suffer from a diversity of social and economic problems.

The opportunity for transformation lies in changing ourselves. When we transform ourselves, we can't help but influence others, and set off a chain reaction of transformations. Our habits create our habitats, remember!

Set out below is a summary of some of the main social, economic, and environmental problems that flow from our current twenty-two core belief structures. Some of them I have touched upon earlier in this book. Others I will now explore, focusing on the more critical ones.

We are at a crossroads in society, and need to address the source of our problems: our limiting belief structures. Unless we change them, we will have far less wonderful places left to enjoy.

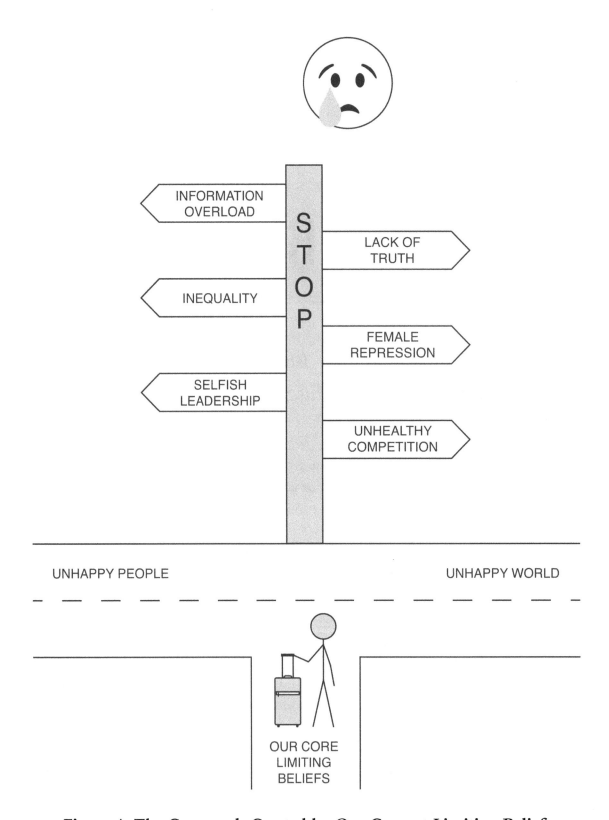

Figure 4: The Crossroads Created by Our Current Limiting Beliefs

6.1: Common threads of discontent

There are several outcomes common across social and economic areas that we all experience as a result of our limiting beliefs. These are:

1. *Inequality*

Our world is rife with judgement and inequality. This plays out in social settings, but also in an unlevel playing field economically. Our business world has traditionally given economic advantage to straight white males. I am one of them, and I'm sure this has unfairly helped me in life at the expense of others.

It is hard to break out of any cycle of disadvantage. Once a family achieves a certain level of wealth, their children then get the benefit of that wealth, including better health, education, and nutrition. For those in the cycle of poverty, it's difficult to escape; and generations become trapped in the same circumstances, believing that they can do no better.

The rich, on the other hand, get richer and enjoy the social and economic benefits this brings.

We need to change our beliefs around equality. The Black Lives Matter movement in 2020 was a great effort in waking up the world to its insidious discrimination; but inequality is not just about colour. It takes many forms, fuelled by our need to judge each other constantly.

We can talk all we like, but until our belief structures shift, inequality will remain in our world. Laws and money can only change so much.

2. *Lack of truth*

Truth is always relative, and therefore there is no one truth, just different perspectives. However, our inclination to disrespect the views of others, and twist, deny or avoid speaking objectively, infiltrates all levels of our society.

Politicians, heads of state, business leaders, the media, and individuals all like to 'spin' their views and distort the facts to enhance their own reputations and financial situations.

It's hard to fix something if you can't see the reality of an event or issue first. Whether this relates to your own personal development or issues in a nation, an obvious assessment is needed to start the ball rolling. Who knows how much your views may be contorted by your own conditioning!

People don't practice enough personal responsibility and accountability. It's always easier to deflect blame onto others or circumstances rather than admit your own failings. This is a by-product of our egoic minds. Our hearts never lie and will be compassionate to the views of others, but our minds will do whatever they can to protect us and make us think we are important. This blocks our opportunity as a race to be potent and thrive.

As a society, forgiveness is not seen as a strength. Our tendency not to love ourselves leads us to want to see others fail and to judge them harshly. This makes us feel better about who we are. If life is a big competition, why wouldn't we behave this way?

Self-awareness relies on honesty. Our media outlets tend to lead us down a path of worry and concern by focussing on bad things. Why? Because bad things sell newspapers and get ratings. The bottom line is that it's all about money, not love.

When we start being more honest about the facts and stop trying to hang everyone who makes a mistake, we will start to see the benefits as a society of facing realities. In this place we can listen to each other's perspectives and come together for the common good.

If we listen to each other with compassion, unity is possible.

Isn't it better to be happy than right?

3. *Female repression*

Our society's obsession with valuing money, getting things done and competing with each other, rather than nurturing and caring, has led women to be repressed and pigeonholed into certain jobs. It is still a major issue in most cultures. Progress is too slow.

In Australia, gender inequality is recognised and has been apparently outlawed. This hasn't affected life in practice, and recent stories about alleged sexual indiscretions in the Australian Parliament show the depth of this issue in our society.

Socially and economically women suffer at the hands of a male-dominated world. Violence, sexual abuse, and the repression of women are major issues around the world and will not change until everyone fully recognises that women are equal to men as human beings.

There are certain cultures in the world where the repression of women is worse than others.

The scourge of sexual abuse against women is exposed more and more every day. This repression must stop. But this will only be possible if our beliefs shift.

Men and women are equal. Without men and women creating together, we have no world.

4. *Unhealthy competition*

Our world is one big competition. We are all out to win, and this shapes our economies and societies and creates ongoing tensions between nations that all want to have the greatest influence in the world.

Competition is dominating our lives at the expense of collaboration. Instead of being supportive of the collective community, we compete to win. Self-interest is the order of the day.

Off the back of our need to win arises crime, an obsession with profits in businesses, the abuse of workers, and exploitation of our planet in an overworked, stressed world. We spend our lives locking everything up, including ourselves, because we don't trust our fellow human beings. We need to protect ourselves from others, and regulators and law enforcement agencies the world over must protect the public from unscrupulous people, as well as businesses out to make as much money as they can.

We all need to survive, and in some parts of the world this is a great challenge. But when we finally see that the world has given us a great abundance of resources to support our survival, and if we share more than we have, there *is* enough for all to have a dignified life. This, however, will require new wise leaders to surface and take centre stage.

The competitive nature of life leads us to hoard what we have and not share with others. This occurs at all levels of society, including nationally. When more of us become self-centred, not selfish, we can begin to thrive collectively.

What if we backed off somewhat on our obsession with competing? There is nothing wrong with success and wealth, if it is derived with integrity and used for honourable purposes. But our intrinsic lack of self-worth has tipped the scales too far towards winning at all costs.

How many of us are thriving only because we take advantage of those struggling to survive? Why do we not feel the limiting nature of this and its inauthenticity?

5. *Information overload*

Our investment in technology has helped us in many ways, but also hindered the quality of our interactions. We also go outward and jam our brains constantly with information to the point that we can't possibly remember or use it all.

We need to seek more transformation, not information, in our lives.

If overused, technology can prevent us from being present with our true selves and nature. We are losing our ability to relate person to person, and to communicate with real intimacy and feeling.

Our obsession with doing, and not being, sits nicely with our obsession with technology and information. Technological devices, while keeping us connected, can overstimulate our minds and desensitise our awareness. We do what we have been programmed to do, just like computers. Our operating systems become much like theirs.

Computers have opened up a relatively new form of crime in cyber-crime. Criminals can now steal from people and organisations from anywhere in the world. Nations can spy on nations and attack their financial systems by bringing down their key computer systems.

It's not natural to be this way. How can it be?

6. Selfish leadership

There is no such thing as a bad team, but there are bad leaders. Most people, although being conditioned, want to be led in the right direction. They will often follow the leader because they don't trust their own judgement.

But most leaders are under a spell of self-service. It's a form of self-interested competing. Leaders get recognition, get paid more, and feel validated with the power that leadership brings. In most walks of life, leadership is a form of manipulation for personal gain.

Bad leadership frustrates us all. So does leadership in isolation, where leaders don't work together for the common good.

Leadership urgently needs an overhaul. Great leadership comes from the power within us, not the belief that we need power over others.

During the Covid-19 pandemic, Australia witnessed its senior leaders working well with each other, under a relatively consistent framework. They also communicated regularly with the public. This has seen their popularity spike to previously unseen levels. However, at times and increasingly, politics arose, and backstabbing took place once mistakes were made. This disappointed the public.

Why did it take a crisis to get our national leaders to work so closely together? Finally, they had a common enemy, a common cause to focus on.

On the contrary, we saw American leaders failing to follow a common direction during the pandemic, and the results were disharmony and fracturing of communities.

On a world level, most countries went their own way on the pandemic, with little international co-operation. Even the work to develop a vaccine took the shape of another competition. Every country and pharmaceutical company wanted to be the first to find the successful vaccine and to make their people safe, irrespective of what happened to people in other countries. Why? Because it was worth a fortune. Again, self-interest and the obsession with money (over health) came to the fore. Money makes the world go around, unfortunately, but it has also tilted it off its intended axis.

Only collective leadership focussed on the health of all people will defeat the virus and others. If we separate to survive, the chance for unity and collective wellbeing will elude us. Again, our obsession with survival will bring us to our knees.

We need leaders with wisdom, as well as cerebral intelligence, who can lead with their hearts and minds in unison. They are rare but, as Nelson Mandela showed, they do exist.

6.2: Social interactions

Our family units, which are the fabric of our society, are suffering from our deteriorating society, and the amount of time we focus on doing and making money at all costs.

Mental health issues are also on the rise, as is substance abuse. Stress is being caused by the huge priority we all place on work, and our health is suffering.

We may have more money, but the pressures of rising property prices, debt, and the costs of living lead our children to be without their parents for longer and longer periods. This leads to less effective mentoring in life skills. Guilty parents give money to their children, not love, and this has unintended consequences.

With both parents out of the home working, families can lack leadership. In times gone by, families lived more as extended families with retired grandparents living with the family. In Australia at least, this has been replaced by a network of retirement villages and nursing homes, and parents paying strangers for childcare.

Extended families are a free resource that has been largely abandoned. This is equally unfortunate for grandparents, who are put into institutions rather than invited into the family home, because many people no longer have time to care for the older generation. Retirement homes and nursing homes can be extremely confronting for older people, but do we really care enough? Out of sight, out of mind!

Many people are unhappy and in pain, but rather than face this pain and say no more to it, they try and bury it with drugs and alcohol. This just defers any chance of their truly knowing themselves and finding out what really makes them happy, then expressing that. Dutch courage has replaced real courage in many cultures.

Society has many virtues, and many people are kind-hearted. However, the problems faced by us all in this ever increasingly complex and competitive world are significant, and won't change unless love takes over from fear, and we recognise the greater need for unity, not separation. We are one big family, not distant, insecure cousins in a race to own the most toys, and content to tread on each other to get them.

Our conditioned minds are not going to lead us to a better society unless we step back and search inside ourselves. This will allow our true priorities to be expressed and open the door to happiness.

6.3: Economic behaviours and structural concerns

We are focussed so heavily on money and profits that our lifestyles have become unsustainable. World debt constituted by governments, as well as personal and corporate debt, is at staggering levels that continue to grow every day.

In 2020, government world debt alone was estimated to be US$254 trillion, an astounding sum that most likely can never be paid back. Only inflation can erode it.

In the next five years, the Australian government debt is forecast to reach AUD$1.7 trillion, and that's just Federal debt.

In 2020, the total debt of the American economy was estimated to be $84 trillion US dollars and is the equivalent of three and a half times the income levels of the entire nation. The debt of the American government stands at close to $30 trillion US dollars in 2021.

Our children will inherit all this debt because someone eventually has to pay it back. But how many children or young adults understand the financial markets in the western world? Financial literacy is low because the economy is too complex for the average person to understand, yet we all need financial services. Tax systems, in particular, are ridiculously complex, such that we all need experts to help us navigate them.

We live in a world of consumerism, and many of us seek the next sugar hit to feel good about our lives. Our unsustainable lifestyles rely on the ever-increasing growth of debt to fuel them. We are borrowing money (or being given it by governments, in some cases) that may not exist, to buy overpriced assets and spend on often frivolous wants.

Around the world, Covid-19 has exposed our lack of investment in health systems. Could we not redirect the billions of dollars spent every year on the military or space exploration, into health to improve the lives of the collective populations here on Earth? Doesn't it make sense to fix this planet first, before we go looking for the next one to live on?

The world has been split between the haves and have-nots, with the rich getting richer and the poor getting poorer. During the pandemic many people used government handouts to keep themselves afloat, whereas the rich invested it into stocks, property, and cryptocurrencies. This situation is unfair, and it's time we created a more level playing field in our economy.

Our economic structures are sick and on life support, and unfortunately, due to our largesse, this is self-inflicted. We need to move to a simpler and sustainable way of life. We are paying the price for our sense of entitlement, as is our planet.

There are many economic structural outcomes aligned with this.

6.3.1: Profit is king

The concept of profit is one that needs deeper consideration. Businesses are obsessed with profit, and it drives them to make damaging short-term decisions that harm long-term customer loyalty and distracts from what is possible. The organisational and market obsession with profit is out of balance in society.

Like individuals, most organisations are first and foremost judged and validated on their ability to make money, particularly publicly listed companies, which are valued on stock exchanges.

In recent decades, there has been a push to use 'balanced scorecards' to incentivise management to achieve more than maximum profits. Measures such as customer satisfaction, staff satisfaction and risk factors have been applied to provide greater balance in business operations. These are getting greater scrutiny from boards, shareholders, and business analysts.

However, it's hard to break the mesmerising power of profits. When large organisations release their results every six months, headlines in the media and market announcements are generally focussed on whether profits have gone up or down. This stems from our core belief that money is what matters in business, and therefore what validates an organisation.

How many media reports about big listed companies focus on those companies' achievement of purpose? Purpose is always overshadowed by profit.

However, we forget that without a real purpose a business will eventually atrophy as it becomes irrelevant. If a company focuses on profits too much and loses the trust of its customers, it can risk either losing or diminishing its market position. Companies, like people, cannot survive forever without a heart. Today, people – particularly younger people – thankfully look for integrity in business more than they did in my generation.

Throughout my career, I consistently noted how focussed most executives and staff were on their salary and bonuses. This led to the current year profit being a massive priority. Staff mistakes, or decisions that put that profit at risk, were not tolerated. The employees involved were harshly dealt with, even if they had taken actions with the best of intentions.

Profit is king and it sits on a thorny throne. Markets expect ongoing profit growth from companies, even in times of great economic stress. This is tantamount to greed, and unfortunately leads to inappropriate behaviour by companies, the victims of which are normally customers, suppliers, or staff.

Profit created through the manipulation or repression of staff or customers is not sustainable going forward, because our world increasingly demands integrity at all levels.

An individual can have multiple relationships with a business. They can be an investor, staff member and product owner. This web of interrelationships is profound and makes it imperative that we moderate both the corporate and community obsession with profits. Companies need to understand that 'what goes around, comes around'.

Have you ever felt that an organisation has taken advantage of you without just cause? I'm sure you will agree that this needs to change and be replaced with fairness.

6.3.2: Middle-man mania

As previously mentioned, economic theory tells us that rational buyers always want to buy at the lowest price possible and grab a bargain. A rational seller always wants to sell at the highest possible price to 'make a killing'. Often neither party cares about the other, and the fairness of a transaction is often not a consideration.

Agents and brokers sit in the middle of many transactions, let's call them middlemen. Banks also act as middlemen between the government and central banks, and we the people. Their job is to bring two parties together and create a sale. They exist largely because buyers and sellers cannot communicate openly or effectively, and often don't care about the welfare of each other. The middlemen encourage this situation for they know that it validates their reason for getting paid.

Many things are sold this way, with middlemen making money by earning a commission by representing the buyer or the seller (or themselves). Insurance, real estate and mortgages are common products that are sold using middlemen.

The commission earned is basically a leakage of value from the asset, and in an ideal world this could be avoided.

Let's consider real estate agents. They have a valid role to play, but it's often exaggerated. If the market is strong, property sells itself. The agents largely care about their own income and therefore just want a sale to take place. They often have limited knowledge of the property they are selling, and rarely seek to attain knowledge before selling the property. Agents try to encourage competition to drive up the price, taking advantage of the human tendency to compete. Auctions, if used, create a time-pressured event in which competition peaks and buyers have little time to make important decisions. I wonder how many properties have been overpriced through this artificial environment.

In some Australian states, sellers also have the legal right to bid for their own properties in auctions. Frankly this is madness.

In the ideal world, buyers and sellers would simply talk to each other about the sale. They could negotiate a price and terms based on fairness and each other's perceived value. By wanting to reach a fair price, both parties would be allowed to move on without the need for expensive estate agent commissions. Both would benefit!

To get to this point, however, both buyer and seller need to care about the other and be capable of listening. Where I live in Australia, this does not exist in property transactions. Buyers and sellers likely never meet. They may know each other's names, but that would be about it. All correspondence occurs through agents and lawyers, who feed off the disconnect.

This structure is devoid of empathy and care. How could it be otherwise when you never meet the party on the other side of the transaction? Even if we did, if all we care about is winning, collaboration to achieve a fair outcome is unlikely.

Perhaps it could work better if agents had the purpose of securing sales at a fair price to buyers and sellers or had a role of offering a valuation based on expert opinions, for buyers and sellers to discuss. Unfortunately, this is not their purpose under existing practices. They rely on competition and the impersonal nature of sales to create their roles and wealth.

It is the same with other middlemen.

6.3.3: The 'small-print' mentality

The world relies on legal contracts for many transactions. Typically, contracts are drafted by the seller and signed by both buyer and seller.

I doubt many buyers read contracts in full, except in the case of large expensive purchases, because such contracts are often long wordy documents, with small print written in legal speak. And, even if you don't like the terms and conditions as a consumer, you generally have no power to change them, even if you were to spend money on your own lawyer to get an opinion. Your only alternative course of action is generally not to buy the product or service.

When buyers sign contracts, they want to trust that the seller will be fair when an issue arises. However, this is often highly optimistic, because the seller's behaviour is probably ruled by the contract and the contract was written by their lawyers to suit them in the first place.

Recently in Australia, Royal Commissions have investigated banking, insurance, and aged care industries, and have identified many examples of consumer manipulation and unfair product terms and delivery.

Imagine a world where businesses truly cared about their customers, and honoured the trust they were awarded in the first place, rather than needing to be forced to do so by corporate watchdogs. The marketplace for products could be fair, and we would not need the legal minefields and regulations we currently all have to endure.

Our business world is drenched in complex legal processes and entangled in consumer protection legislation, which an authentic caring society with a bigger heart and a smaller wallet could live without. It is fuelled by fear and greed. It all comes down to our belief structures, and these can be changed in an instant.

6.3.4: Our complex markets

Human beings have created complex financial markets and structures to regulate, create and value money throughout the world.

As mentioned above, the average person does not understand the complexity of financial activities and how money flows. They therefore do not understand the risks associated with money, and the fact that money is influenced by so many factors. This is not a criticism, because there are complex webs of financial factors at play. But people do believe that the money they own is real and, once they earn it, it will be there when they want or need to use it. They trust that banks, financial institutions, and governments are safe.

Unfortunately, financial markets are subject to volatility, like we have been witnessing throughout the Covid-19 pandemic. Throughout history we have gone through cycles of boom and bust in financial markets. People who thought their money was safe have lost it all in an instant.

Do we really want to continue to live this way?

6.3.5: Confidence is everything

There is one big factor that determines whether there is a perception of wealth in world economies or not. This is the level of confidence. When confidence is high, lots of money seemingly changes hands and asset values rise. In normal circumstances, as the demand for money rises, inflation occurs as sellers put up prices.

When confidence is low, people stop spending money, and the flow of money slows. People, through their own fear, will not buy assets or goods and services, and prices fall. In this situation, inflation is likely to be low or even negative (known as deflation), as lower demand dampens prices.

So, wealth levels are heavily influenced by confidence. The value of your money and what it can buy, or sell, is fragile to say the least.

History is littered with economic collapses known as recessions, as well as deep long-term recessions known as depressions. Often what causes these terrible financial situations is people themselves. Their excess greed can create the reality they do not want. It's self-induced. Boom and bust are unhappy bedfellows.

Of course, bad economic conditions can be caused by other factors such as the availability of natural resources, wars, climatic changes and natural disasters like floods and droughts.

Confidence is, however, a potent factor.

Do we really want to have economic structures and asset values that one day appear to be sound and booming, but the next day are collapsing, when nothing changed other than our perceptions? I don't think so!

6.3.6: Are our assets real or illusory?

Asset values (including currencies) don't just rise because they should. They rise on the back of supply and demand and, as mentioned above, confidence. The stock market is a great example of this. It is fundamentally a massive gambling site. People buy and sell stocks either hoping or expecting that stock prices will rise or fall. It is largely based on people's expectations of the future – a future they really can't predict, although they think they can.

Unless stock prices continue to rise, there will typically be winners or losers depending on when you buy or sell. Stockbrokers and analysts prey on this volatility and make a living out of the market volatility that plays out. The volatility in the market is more important to them than the absolute stock prices, because the volatility and uncertainty drive the demand for their services.

Then you have assets like derivatives, which are not real in themselves since they are based on the values of other assets, and which can exaggerate gains and exaggerate losses. These assets are based on two parties who are happy to trade because they have opposing expectations of price movements. Simplistically, one will lose and one will win. Again, this is a form of gambling.

Cryptocurrencies can be virtual assets depending on the substance behind them, and their value is often based on human perception, not reality. For as long as everyone holding cryptocurrencies wants their value to rise, they probably will; but only until significant doubt sets in, and confidence is lost. Turn off the electricity and these assets can cease to exist, unlike assets you can touch, such as gold bullion and property.

Large western capitalist economies are heavily based on its population's confidence levels. For wealth to be created, these economies are not supposed to slow rapidly or stop. Once this occurs, asset values are likely to fall appreciably as fear grips the population. In this situation there are likely to be more losers than winners as people stop spending money out of fear.

In effect, the human fear of financial collapse is self-generating. We create that fear, causing wealth levels to fall, perhaps significantly.

With human emotions in charge, asset values can swing violently over relatively short periods of time. Herd mentality comes into play and people copy each other, fearing they will be left behind. Human beings believe there is safety in numbers, so if we follow the herd, we will be at less risk of getting hurt. The herd, of course, creates its own destiny and may run itself off a cliff, because the herd is operating on collective fear or euphoria.

Traditionally, asset types that have more validity in a time of financial crises are the assets that you can physically touch. This includes precious metals like gold and silver, and property since human beings need to have a roof over our heads, and 'God is not making any more land'. Whether we rent or buy a property, we all need shelter and a place to sleep. Demand for houses can thus be impaired but never totally extinguished. Gold, silver, and other precious metals are rare and solid, and have long been sought-after in all civilisations because of their beauty and their ability to be moulded and used for other purposes, such as jewellery or ornaments. They also have use in technology, medicines, and manufacturing.

Property and precious metals also make sense. If the world as we know it ceased to exist instantly, and all human life became extinct, what would have any use or value to any extraterrestrials who come to Earth? They would arrive to find property and natural resources. Would 'created' assets like derivatives, and even money in the banking system, have any value? Of course not. It was just a form of exchange and had no true value, once the belief in its value had gone. It only has a value based on human fabrication and belief structures.

No one really knows how cryptocurrencies will behave in a major financial crisis. I can't know either. Some see them as a safe haven if government-issued money loses value. I believe it will be determined by what they are backed by and what their utility is.

This all adds up to a financial system that is fundamentally overly complex, volatile, and fragile. When we are overly optimistic, we create asset values that are overpriced; and when we are negative, we create asset values that are most likely underpriced. It's like a giant wave going up and down as herd members follow each other. It is most obvious in the stock markets of the world, because unlike other assets, like property, stocks can normally be bought and sold quickly. This makes the stock market incredibly fragile and susceptible to the whims of human emotion. Cryptocurrencies seem to be the same, if not worse.

One danger the world faces at a time of financial collapse is that if we create too much new money with printing presses, or just by releasing digits onto computer systems, when we come out of the depths of despair and people start spending again, high inflation could set in, and the value of money might crash. This is already evident in 2022. This could make goods and services ridiculously expensive and diminish the true value of debts. In this situation, banks may collapse as the assets they hold become less valuable. A truism is that the value of property is largely determined by what the banks will lend against it. This puts banks in a position of great influence over our current financial world.

Governments, which really represent entire populations, can go broke just like big companies and individuals if they live beyond their means, or try and create assets that do not actually exist. It's not serving us as an ideology to trade so much on emotion and to trade assets that have so little validity. This is not natural. Surely, we would prefer an economy, and for that matter currencies, with much more stability that grows gradually and does not go through boom and bust.

Money also seemingly creates itself. Central banks lend money to banks, which then lend it to customers. These customers either invest or spend this money, which finds its way back into the banking system to be re-lent. So, the same money gets lent and re-lent and reinvested multiple times. If this merry-go-round of money stops, where do the true assets reside? It's only if the system stops that we will get the answer to this question.

There is so much money in computer systems in this world. Do we really know what value it has? Do we really know what underlying assets support that money? Human beings continually create, value, and circulate money, which is fundamentally steeped in emotion and expectation.

Up until 1971, world governments applied what was called the Gold Standard in the creation of currency. Any money created was backed up, by a level of about 40%, by stores of gold. United States President Richard Nixon removed this system, meaning that most countries could create as much money as they liked.

As I write this book, the American government is printing and releasing about $4 billion US dollars a day. Other countries are doing something similar. This is a magic trick, based on pure illusion, like pulling white rabbits from hats. Money only has value if it is created from productive work and value-adding activities or assets.

If we continue with our current unsustainable lifestyles, we will eventually break this system. At some point we will need to accept a falling of asset values and a move to simplicity, to remove illusions that exist. Alternatively, we will need to reintroduce the benchmarking of money to real assets like gold, to give money a basis in reality.

To work properly, our economy needs everyone to spend money, so we all have a role to play and can earn an income. We all need each other in life and economically to survive.

A properly working economy also needs to have a simpler economic environment, where economic structures are less likely to behave irrationally.

If we all knew our wholeness, the role of money would also change in our lives. A simple change in our thinking would change our economies. When you know yourself, you desire more of yourself and less of everything else, including money and recognition. In this place, materialism falls away as an unhealthy need in our lives.

With greater care for each other, greater simplicity and more equality, there could be enough resources on this planet for us all to have enough and be happy.

In short, our economic structures and interactions reflect our competitive ways of being. The thought that life is a giant competition for money, and that money defines us, has left us in a complex, harsh economic environment where we have lost sight of the illusions at play.

Our hearts want simplicity and economic collaboration, not our unsustainable broken economies where a minority have and the majority have not. We need a change before the whole system collapses under the weight of fake wealth and unfair systems. The consequences of this kind of collapse would be catastrophic to say the least.

6.4: World order is out of order

The world is a sovereign collection of more than 300 countries. It is largely un-united and cooperation by nations is largely optional.

Organisations such as the World Health Organisation, the United Nations, and the World Bank exist to bring united benefits to the world. However, they rely on the cooperation and goodwill of nations to both fund them and allow them to meet their intended purposes.

There are some people who advocate for a central world government, instead of the loose collective of countries that exist today. No matter what structure is in place, it won't matter if our belief structures are not right. Imagine a world government that has the wrong intentions, values, and leaders. At least now we have a selection of well-run countries in the mix.

World tensions are high and always have been. The world's superpowers including America, China and Russia are constantly asserting themselves and using their scale and strength to manipulate others. Trade wars and embargoes have been waged at different points to try to control the activities of other countries. The Middle East has long been a hot bed of tensions and conflicts. Different religions and ideologies, such as the clash of communism and capitalism, make for a world where unity is unlikely, because the different ideologies clash through judgement. Competition abounds between countries, just as it does between individuals.

Throughout history, countries have chosen to go to war to resolve differences. But war should never ever, ever, ever be an option. Both victor and vanquished ultimately lose as human lives are lost and human souls are forever stained.

Will countries (or people) ever stop looking to win and have power over others? The answer is 'yes, of course', but only once the belief structures of leaders and countries shift from competition to collaboration.

If you look at the world, you will see the haves and have-nots that are so noticeable in all walks of life. Countries with great resources like Saudi Arabia (oil) and Australia (minerals) have high standards of living despite their small populations. But how many countries share resources with others? They only sell resources if the price is right. Is this enough?

In a world where many people have no food or shelter, while other countries have multi-billionaires and companies bigger than countries, when will we learn to share better as a race?

The answer is: only once we see that we are all one big family and not competitors. Each country is entitled to its own sovereignty, but we need to exercise this individuality while also caring for other nations.

6.5: Environmental mess

I have already touched on how much we abuse and exploit our planet. Our world is becoming more and more polluted and subject to the painful impacts of climate change. We are taking advantage of other animals on this planet, and not giving them the respect they deserve.

Why do we treat other animals with such contempt and believe they have no feelings? It's a preconditioned belief structure that we are more important than other animals. We need to grow beyond this belief. We would not live this way if we accessed our hearts as much as we access our minds.

There are environmental activists and institutions around the world working to protect animals and the planet. But they are largely driven by the passion of select individuals and charities that care deeply about the environment.

The coordination of environmental programs seems to suffer from the same lack of unity that we see in other walks of life. It's the younger generation, led by individuals like Greta Thunberg, who seem to be the leaders here. Their high sensitivity to environmental issues is remarkable and reflects their ability to understand the importance of a clean planet. They just need better support – without needing 20 years of scientific evidence and the promise of more votes or profits – before anyone acts.

We need better-coordinated programs to improve the planet, across the world. It's our home, and at the moment we are defecating on our own doorstep. The Paris Agreement to address climate change is a positive step, but again it is optional.

How many animals do we need to send into extinction before we change our way of thinking? If we don't care for Mother Nature, how long will it be before she gets rid of us? We are temporary renters on the Earth, and the planet would survive and probably flourish without our presence. If we don't get our act together, we may well be evicted soon!

We are supposedly creating a more sustainable way of living, but when I look at the amount of packaging I end up with in my bin at the end of the week, it's clear that we need to do more to save the planet. Most things sold in our supermarkets and shops come in plastic packets. It's ridiculous! We need to spend more energy on replacing litter rather than sorting it!

We make things to only last a certain period of time before they need to be replaced. Once they fail to meet our needs, we dig a hole and bury them in the womb of Mother Nature, leaving it to her to break them down. What if we put more effort into making things that last, rather than things that are disposable? Mother Nature should not be used as a rubbish tip because we are lazy and greedy.

When we see that we are a part of nature and not above it, Mother Nature will start to improve her own health without getting rid of us.

Time is, however, running out.

CHAPTER

$$\overline{\overline{}}$$

7

$$\underline{\underline{}}$$

How to Find Your Greatest Happiness

In the first half of this book, I have shown what is causing our lives to be so difficult and often undesirable. Some readers will relate to the life of obligation and despair described. I lived it for years.

Now I will focus on how we can transform our lives and make them far more fun and enjoyable.

7.1: Own your own transformation

How do you go about removing your conditioning, then applying the code of happiness to your life, as I have done?

Firstly, you need to change the way you think and in turn the beliefs you hold. This is a choice. We create our own life, not the life of another, and here lies the key to transformation. We start by changing ourselves first, by owning our own experience, and not letting others think they can or should tell us how to live. We are sovereign beings, and we all deserve to be happy. It's all about taking responsibility for ourselves.

We don't need to change others and try to make them happier. This is a form of judgement. Their happiness is their choice. It's better to be happy and role-model possibilities for others to see and feel.

This is a journey you will find most rewarding and will never regret. When you find the happiness within you, your heart will recognise it, and want it more and more.

Did you see any of the limiting beliefs and recognise them as applying to you or your circumstances? If so, why not consider how you can adopt a new way of thinking.

We are beings of love, wanting to experience joy in each and every moment of our lives. So why are we wasting our lives in such a conditioned place of despair and fear? Most of us have been under a spell we didn't understand. We were determined to survive. Let yourself step into the sunlight, for that is where your life is meant to be lived.

Do you remember when you were a child, and you were told to go out and play? In some ways, playing was your job.

How would you like to release your inner child again? How would you like to find your inner graciousness to discover new fun in your life?

This is possible at any age. It's a gift you can give yourself. All you need to do is drop the belief structure that, once you become an adult, you need to be serious and worry about life.

Children are spontaneous, curious, open, free and creative. You can be too, if you want to be. Your inner child is still within you waiting to play again. He or she has been waiting for you to organise some games they can play!

Anticipate spontaneity in your life and it will be so every day. It's just a belief away, like everything else.

7.2: Wholeness is the key

To be whole and authentic, we need to live with our hearts, bodies, and minds as one. The truth of 'watt' we are (see below for the spelling of this word!) and how we want to live resides in our hearts. Our hearts can feel and transmit these feelings to our bodies and minds. Our minds are experts at organising and implementing what we ultimately believe and think. Our bodies are our antennas, and they are the vessel that allows everything to take place. Our bodies allow us to live a human existence and hopefully to live it well.

With our hearts, bodies, and minds in unity, we can know ourselves and become what deep down we know we really are.

I have used the word 'watt' not 'what' above, although it may seem grammatically wrong, because you are like a light globe. What I describe as your heart is the energy of life that animates you as a human being. You are the energy of life, and can allow it to be expressed, lighting up all your experiences. If you allow yourself to be turned on, you can be a radiant light in an often-dark world.

Who we are is less important than what we are. When you stop caring about who you are and drop your need for importance, your true potency can come forth, and from here joy can be with you every moment of your life.

Our natural state is love, not fear. We can live with no fear, believe it or not. Most of us have just not experienced it, yet! Our journey to a lighter, brighter planet is through love and acceptance, not fear and judgement.

Our hearts know the way to happiness, if we allow them to lead us in our lives. But the journey to this magical place means letting our egoic minds play their natural role as the implementer, not the leader.

Happiness comes from being in integrity with your true self and being understood by others. Trust me, this is a journey of discovery you don't want to miss!

To make the change that is needed, we must first search inside ourselves. We cannot demonstrate in the streets for a change we have not made within ourselves first. As we change one-by-one, the ripple effect on our families and societies will gather pace.

If enough people discover who they really are, our world can make momentous change.

When we all know what and who we want to be, we will no longer need to be told who we need to be. Imagine a world full of law-abiding people all being authentic and living from a place of happiness. No judgement, no racism, no wars, just acceptance and sharing!

Happy loving people don't start fights or steal from each other. They care about their fellow human beings and know who they are. They don't need a big house or a fast car to feel worthy of love. They know they can only find true happiness and love inside themselves, and don't need the outside world to give it to them to feel whole. They know they already have it within them.

But how do we get to such a place?

How do we override our egos and change our operating systems?

Here I can share my own journey of the last six years in the hope of helping others who want to find their happiness.

7.3: My experience with knowing myself

I went to a high school in a suburb called Normanhurst in Sydney. Sketched into my school blazer was the school motto of 'Know Thyself'. These words sat on top of an embroidered phoenix. Little did I know how profound this message and image would be in my life.

7.3.1: Rebirth and resurrection

The phoenix is an ancient Greek symbol of rebirth. In mythology, it is a bird associated with the sun that rises from the ashes of its predecessor to attain new life. Herein lies the opportunity for every one of us individually, and collectively, to be reborn or resurrected and rise from our own ashes.

Many great stories in history contain the essence of resurrection as their core message – that as human beings we always possess the ability to move to a higher level of consciousness or way of being.

Two great stories come to mind in the lives of Jesus Christ and Osiris, an ancient Egyptian pharaoh who ruled with love and is much admired in Egyptian folklore.

Both Jesus Christ and Osiris lived from a place of love and light but befell terrible deaths at the hands of people with egoic fears, and a desire to take away their influence in society. In their stories, both could not be denied and rose again to prove we are all capable of rebirth when we live from a place of knowing ourselves.

We are all loving beings at our core, and this gives us our greatest hope, for it is possible to bring our self-love and self-awareness – which we all possess within our hearts – into our own lives, then express it into the societies in which we live.

At the end of the day, we are all equal, but we are at different stages of knowing who and what we truly are.

7.3.2: My journey to a lighter place

The past six years have been a combination of the most difficult and wonderful times I have ever experienced in my life. Pain has been both my tormentor and my best friend. By facing my pain and considering how my beliefs have been conditioned by my upbringing, I have been able to shine a light on my own shadows and transition my life to a lighter and happier life, rich in possibilities.

I feel much freer as a result, and I am fast becoming a more natural and authentic version of 'Mark'. I am only Mark because I was given this name at birth. I am truly a different person now, who has found my real essence.

My journey along the path to greater self-awareness has taken two different forks. A hard one that partially worked, but which was long and tedious; and an easier, faster route that I wish for all of you.

Until recently, I documented every single day of my six-year journey in bound journals, so that each step I took was shared with both my heart and mind. It also allowed me to readily record my journey along the stepping stones of love, which I now see I took with other people. I no longer need to journal my experiences to the same extent, for my mind now knows its place as my implementer, and my ego is deeply transformed.

I am but a microcosm of our society. I am flawed and have a roller-coaster of experiences. I have laughed and cried, loved and hated, won and lost. I am no Jesus Christ or Osiris – born pure of heart and mind, and free of conditioning. I have had to fight my own demons and hacked my way through a jungle of despair to get to the clearing I am now starting to explore.

I was fully conditioned by a deeply wounded family and society, emerging from the shadows of World War II.

My mother was saddened by her abandonment by her father after his six-year stint in the war.

My father carried the scars of responsibility following the early death of his father, which required him to leave school early to support his mother and younger brother, when he was the smartest child in his year at school. He became broken at a young age and was a nervous wreck for most of his life, suffering from an overload of responsibility from which he never really recovered. He could never accept his own imperfections, and this depressed him.

All readers will have their own stories, and perhaps you too can relate to having a sometimes difficult life.

7.3.3: The simplicity of it all

The journey to lightness and happiness is simple. Unfortunately, it took me five years of deep self-reflection and tears to work it out. There are many books that will tell you all about your psychological schematics and the subconscious damage you sustained as a child, which has set you on a course of self-destruction.

I read some of these, and I even saw a psychologist for several months. I pulled myself apart in the hope that I could put myself back together. I worked on my personal belief structures and sparked the pain of perceived failures. I cried myself to sleep in the hope of waking up happier. My life was never meant to turn out the way it did, or at least that is what I told myself. I beat myself up all in the name of becoming a better man. It did help, to some extent, but it was not a pleasant experience, and I don't believe this is how healing needs to go.

Many people are obsessed with doing what they call healing. Some so-called spiritual people nourish their egos on the back of this often-painful introspection to gain greater self-awareness.

In a sense these imperfect people go constantly in search of their faults to find and eradicate their misery. I too once thought I had to suffer to reach a point of great happiness, releasing the grief I once buried and was afraid to face.

But when you try and find fault in yourself, you perpetuate the myth that you are deeply flawed. The truth is that the real you is *not* flawed. Knowing yourself helps you to dis-cover this. You are pure love if you allow it to fill you up and take you to a lighter place and broader perspective. This is just a choice.

It's all a matter of perspective. Life is a wonderful learning experience, a univers-ity of expansion. But we can graduate from this university and go on to experience a deep love for ourselves. When we start to see our mishaps in life as nothing more than stepping stones to greater self-awareness, and celebrate their wisdom, we enter a new place of freedom within ourselves.

We still need to face our past experiences and issues, but we can do it in a positive way. Once we allow awareness to step in, it will dissolve our conditioned beliefs through the intelligence of our hearts.

The limiting belief structures outlined in this book are important to consider. I urge you to consider them and, upon deep reflection, consider which ones you can change out of enhanced awareness. Discuss them with your loved ones, if that helps. This starts the process of clearing away the veil that you have unknowingly placed between your mind and your heart.

It's important that you don't beat yourself up for holding onto conditioned beliefs. We all have them. We can't help but have them really. In some ways, we only carry them because we have strong minds that learned quickly how to adapt to our environment. Honour this strength.

A key secret to removing your conditioned beliefs is to allow your consciousness to bring them forward for clearing or awareness. You don't need to chase them, especially if it is painful. Just give your heart the freedom to show you the ones you can let go of and allow the magic to take place. It will bring each conditioned belief forward in divine timing.

Meditating or going inward helps. Sometimes awareness around a conditioned belief and the impact it has on your life can be emotional and challenging, for it will show you what you wrongly needed, feared, or were attached to in your life, according to conditioned views you adopted. But know that they are only emotions, and they will pass, most likely with your whole self feeling lighter and brighter every time they recede.

So, when you spot the conditioned beliefs that have caused you pain, question them; laugh at them, if possible; consider their origin; and, as you see through them, commit to letting them go. Cry if you need to – you need to let out any residual energy attached to that belief. The mere act of awareness will ultimately dissolve them from your consciousness and your experiences. Celebrate every step you take to knowing yourself better and more intimately.

I followed the slow painful path of trying to change and beat myself up for being conditioned, because I didn't understand how simple and joyous self-transformation could really be, particularly when you apply compassion to your story and forgive yourself for whatever went wrong. It is possible to get there in a much more joyful way. To become enlightened, it's best to be light, be happy and enjoy the journey. Relive an experience, feel the release of energy, then let it go and celebrate your new awareness.

Once the penny dropped for me, my life changed quite quickly. I achieved more in a short period of a few months than I did in my previous five years of 'healing', just by allowing my heart, not my resistant mind, to take control of my transformation. I stopped thinking about the past and started feeling into the possibilities that were present in my life, not in the future or the past. I had fun with my transformation to greater self-awareness, without seeking to stab myself over and over for mistakes I had made.

Your heart will take you on the journey of transformation and self-awareness if you just give it the freedom to do so.

7.3.4: Knowing yourself

Have you ever sat quietly and just listened to the life force inside you. You might even hear it buzzing like a switched-on light globe. This is the 'wattage' I referred to earlier.

We think of ourselves as physical objects, flesh and blood with a brain. But we really are like the light globe – we are full of life-force and electricity. This life force knows what you want out of life. It knows what makes you happy, what you actually desire. It doesn't care what others think you should be. It knows who you are. It has not been polluted by the conditioning of society and is the real you wanting to live the life that your true self desires. It is there to light you up, if you just allow it.

The beautiful song about self-love entitled 'The Greatest Love of All' so rightly points out that the greatest love of all can only be found inside of yourself and comes from living the life you believe is right for you.

After my soul searching, I understand the power of these words. If you don't already, you will after you spend more energy on knowing yourself. It will make your heart sing.

When you feel this force of love coursing through your body, and its powerful presence in your heart, it is unmistakable.

But it can be denied or suppressed, and normally is. Most people feel the life force within them telling them something, but their minds are quick to override it. Logic overrides the fire in their belly or gut feeling.

But our gut feeling is always right if we listen to it closely. It is not conditioned like the man-made mind. The mind has the agenda of helping us fit into the norm and meet the expectations of others. It wants control at all costs and fights your heart for ascendancy. The heart wants freedom, adventure, and love. It wants but does not need anything for validation. It is the real you.

With your heart in command, you need nothing other than the things your physicality needs to survive, but you can still get everything you want once you know what that is.

My life has seen a litany of bad decisions that caused me pain and suffering. Why? Because I kept ignoring my heart or my truth and kept doing what I thought would make me successful. I now know that happiness and fulfilment are the true measures of success in my life, not importance or money; and thoughts that don't align with love are best ignored.

7.3.5: Taking the journey inward

To take the journey inward, to really know and acknowledge yourself, there are some key learnings to understand.

In centuries past, people sat in caves and monasteries, often for years to find themselves and to become 'enlightened'. They would meditate for days on end to allow their preconditioned minds to release their hold on their thinking and allow their hearts to be in ascendancy. Clearly this would not have been pleasant or practical. However, there are some key mindsets or practices that assisted me on my journey to greater happiness.

The practice of going inward is about listening to your heart. It's your heart, so only you can do it.

Whether you adopt a meditation practice or just sit quietly under a tree, the process is the same. You are removing the chatter of the mind or the ego, for that is where your remaining conditioning will reside.

From my experience, being somewhere quiet and in nature helps because it is simply a natural place to be, and let's not forget you are a part of nature. But you can connect to your-self no matter where you are, for it is simply inside you.

It also helps to use your breath to connect to your heart. The breath is life force, and without it you will die, so there is great benefit in breathing into your heart to find your centre. This gives the heart clarity; you are listening to its wisdom.

Initially it's hard to shut down the mind, for it is so used to being in charge of all you do; but perseverance and patience are key. Eventually, with enough practice, you will master the art of tapping in as it is often called.

Relax, breathe, and simply listen.

You can ask your heart (or soul, as it is commonly referred to) specific questions or general ones, like 'what will you have me know today?'

It's important to trust the answers you hear and the physical sensations that your body sends you, because your body and heart are so closely linked. Your body is your antenna to the feelings that your heart wants you to understand.

The practice of listening to your heart is often referred to as intuition, for it teaches you from within your own form. The practice of feeling inward can be awkward at first; but, once you trust it and become accustomed to it, you can use it for everyday decisions where you feel you would like guidance. Big life decisions are best made after seeking this important guidance from within.

After getting used to this kind of decision making, I found that I pretty much use it now for every decision I make, down to what clothes to wear each day.

It's simple, it's easy, it's always right, although you may not see it at the time, and it's free. Best of all, it's always where you are, so you can use it no matter where you are – on a train, a bus, in bed, it matters not!

The more you clear your conditioning, the clearer will be the 'pipe' from your heart to your body and mind, and the clearer the messages become. It just takes effort and commitment and the wisdom to allow it to take place. It is our natural way to live.

There are things to be mindful of when you go inward:

1.   Feel, then think

Feeling your way through life, *then* thinking everything, is key. Your heart knows what is right for you, and its deep intelligence manifests as feelings then thoughts.

What you feel about yourself is more important than what your mind – and the minds of others – think about your life.

Let how you feel direct how you think, not the other way around.

This can be extremely challenging, and the shift to this place was difficult at times for me. Remember, I had grown up to ignore feelings and emotions. Life taught me to seek knowledge, not knowing.

Your logical mind likes to protect you and have you fit in. Therefore, it will resist your heart-based guidance with gusto. The trick is not to give in to your thoughts. Some decisions originating from the heart may be difficult to implement, because they may be significant, like ending a job or a relationship, but the heart is always right.

Trust your own heart and feel your decisions, don't think them! Then let your mind implement them. This is the art of sensing into your next steps.

2.   Focus on fun

Psychologists talk of our inner child. It's the part of our psyche that wants to play, explore, be creative and have fun, like a child.

When I became an adult, I lost my spontaneity and became serious, full of obligation. This grew more prominent when I had children and felt I had to provide and work hard for a family. Perhaps you can relate to this?

But if you are committed to fun, and anticipate it in your life, you can anchor yourself to a life of joy and still meet your chosen responsibilities.

Children learn and grow through fun, and I have found that the best way for me to grow my self-awareness is to follow my heart and have fun along the way.

What better way to allow your life force to express itself than to anticipate and follow joy. After all, enjoyment is no more than the energy inside you expressing itself.

What I found was that many of my great loves in life, like sports, had been suppressed once I became an adult. By feeling for the excitement in my heart, I was able to rekindle parts of my life that had been lost or never found at all. This effectively turned on the light that had been dimmed by obligation.

Be in your joy to find the truth of who you really are.

Succumbing to obligation is more likely to put you in an early grave than finding your pathway to happiness. Have fun and watch life unfold and delight you.

Feel the light to become enlightened.

3.   *Let go of your need to be important*

The ego wants us all to fit in and be important, for in this place lies safety and recognition.

I once strived to win and be important, and for the most part I was successful at this by society's standards. However, my life was relatively dull and unhappy. I became really good at things I didn't like.

What I found as I went inward was, the more that I sensed what I really wanted out of life, the less I needed to promote the idea of myself. I found a much lower desire to impress others with material possessions or any kind of title.

Fundamentally, when you experience more of yourself and the deepness of the energy that animates you, the less you need of anything else. You start to see that the things that once validated you, can simply give you joy instead. You switch from a place of need to a place of preference. You begin to witness the richness in things and how they can contribute to your happiness, and you no longer care about the external recognition they can draw out of others. Here lies potency, not importance!

4.   *Let go of your story*

We link most things that impair our self-esteem to failure, or an event that served to diminish us in some way. In my case this was primarily the trauma of failed marriage, loss of careers, and the related loss of financial status that followed.

We carry through our lives the pain of these so-called failures, unable to forgive either others and/or ourselves, for what didn't go to plan.

But in the pain of these events, you will find nuggets of gold that can change your life, if you are prepared to hold the mirror up to your true self and feel into the self-awareness sitting in the shadows, waiting to be discovered. Rest assured that, when you open up, your heart will bring forth what you need to know about you.

Then, when you acknowledge what's brought to your attention, you will recognise or know the insights they bring. All you need to do is listen to your intuition.

Failure is a state of mind and does not actually exist. When something goes wrong, there is always an opportunity for growth. Allow yourself the compassion you would most likely give to others for their so-called failures.

Just ask yourself how a less than ideal situation occurred, and how you contributed to it. What do you believe about yourself because of the event? Is it still unresolved and causing you or your relationship with another to suffer unnecessarily?

To do this wisely, you need to be able to drop the blame game, and not simply look for revenge, or an opportunity to free yourself of any responsibility for what occurred. Letting go of the past is the fastest way to letting in a new you and a new life. Sometimes good things have to end so better things can come into our lives. I have certainly found this to be the case, and this process of self-discovery helped me to see this clearly.

If we listen to our intuition, in moments of stillness our hearts will tell us what we could change to be happier. From this place, it is a personal choice. Do I let my ego cling to a self-righteous position from which I won't grow, or do I choose self-awareness and the chance not to repeat the same situations going forward?

When you look at what you perceive has gone wrong in your life with fresh eyes, you will seek opportunities to welcome new energies into your life. A new you is capable of stepping forth and creating a happier, less needy you. And what you will always find is that the condemnation we levelled at ourselves was never fair at all. Sure, we make mistakes, but that's the story, that's not you.

Think of yourself as an actor in a movie that may have had a challenging storyline, but with greater awareness you can direct the remainder of the plot.

Once you give your heart or soul the reins to your journey of self-discovery, your transformation accelerates naturally, and you can give in to the magic that starts to occur.

Everything that happens to us in our lives we invite in, so everything is an opportunity for self-reflection, then positive celebration of the lessons learned. As we lighten up, so our experiences will match our growing radiance.

Once you acknowledge the new awareness that your heart gives you, be prepared to act or it will have limited value.

5. *Replace your needs with preferences*

Need is a curse in our lives and blocks our happiness and success.

When we *need* something, we are basically saying we must have that particular thing in our life to be validated or happy. Usually, once you get that thing, you will see it doesn't make you happy, and never will for more than a brief period.

This, of course, does not apply to the things that keep your body alive, such as food, water or shelter.

The heart has dreams and desires. The egoic mind creates needs. But unless your mind is in-sync with your heart, it will most likely convince you to pursue something that is not part of your dream. The question is: do you know what your dream entails? If not, you will be pursuing something hollow and pointless. Perhaps you can relate to this?

Our minds are powerful and will often block messages from our hearts, ones we might otherwise easily access. But we can train our minds to receive this truth from our hearts and invite the message to be a part of the journey, for they are a part of us. We are the only ones who can access this stream of loving advice. It's yours and yours only, and your mind has an important role to play in interpreting what you hear and keeping you in a place of presence.

If we need nothing, we can receive everything, for we will approach life without fear of failure. The need to worry is lost, replaced by the gift of wonder.

6.   *Don't look for a higher authority than you*

I spent much of my life thinking that other people in a seemingly higher place of authority knew better about my life than I did. This ultimately caused me great pain because, although other people I asked were well intending, they could not know what was right for me. This included my parents. By implementing their advice, rather than my gut feeling, I did not trust my true self, and, in many instances, unhappiness was the outcome.

When you are in full connection with yourself, trust yourself and therefore have no need from another person, you are in a great place of freedom. You choose the life you want.

Your life can never be yours if you always care more about what others think of you than you feel about yourself and your own life.

When you receive the messages by going inward, when you listen to them and interpret their application to your life, you alone gain authority over you.

7.   *Set intentions, not expectations*

It is said that results flow where your energy goes. However, this does not mean setting detailed expectations as you follow this adventure. Expectation is the enemy of fun. I encourage you to transcend your need for certainty and instead invite the energy of possibility into your life.

Therefore, try not to set expectations but rather set high level intentions or dreams. I avoid time limits and parameters, as best I can, because I know that they are constructs of my mind and just cause stress. Time is nothing more than a man-made concept that can often keep us all enslaved, busy, and prone to a sense of never being fully on top of things. What we do with our time is ours to control, not the other way around.

Intentions still give you the motivation to be the best you can be, without setting you up for a self-induced fall. This allows us to enter the realm of wonder, not worry. The universe is a giant song of love. It knows what's best for us and our hearts are connected to the library of tunes on offer to support our singing hearts. Play your own I-tunes!

When you go inward, gently invite the awareness to come forward in its own divine timing. Don't force it, because your heart knows when you are ready to embrace a particular truth or embark on a particular project.

8.   *Find your self-love, not the love of others*

True love can only be found within, and once you find it you can't tolerate anything less.

It is your essence that is pure love and no one else can give that to you. It is unfair to expect it of another. And besides, you already have it!

In this place you will find it intolerable to sell yourself out and live a life that you don't own because you cannot be authentic.

In the same way, love in a relationship with another can only exist if that bond allows both parties to be their true selves. Without love and freedom, happiness cannot be the dominant feeling in any relationship.

So, once you start to know more about yourself, your self-love will undoubtedly grow exponentially. This may change how you relate to others, or in which relationships you want to participate. Your life will change, but only for the better. My advice is: don't resist this change.

9.   Connection is key

To find your inner voice or true self, it's important to shut down the mind so your heart can be heard from within.

Some do this with meditation, some find it when they are undertaking an activity of great joy, and some will find that a deep breath into their heart's centre will provide a doorway to your heart. Sexual orgasm is regarded as providing you with one of the greatest points of connection to your heart. In that moment, it's impossible to think of anything else.

However, you choose to connect, it's about being fully present with yourself and listening to what you feel and hear.

You need to draw yourself into your-self. This takes practice and prioritisation initially, but eventually it becomes a gift you can access anywhere, any time, and in an instant. It's actually quite simple.

If you don't connect, you're unlikely to experience the change needed to self-reflect, for this connection gives you a mirror to your soul.

10.   Express the real you to others

Once you find out who you really are, through the journey of self-awareness, and can acknowledge that truth; you will no doubt want to express your truth externally to the outside world. This is the second part of the formula or code of happiness.

This can be easier said than done. Our minds and the minds of others will often want to take us back into the herd, where we thought we once fitted in.

Being your true self can therefore be a challenge and present you with fears.

I found that most people admired my commitment to happiness and my efforts to reposition my life, because deep in their hearts they recognised this desire inside themselves to do the same. But I am a grown man in my 60s, single, work for myself, and both my parents are now deceased, so I may have experienced less resistance than you might in changing your life. Change can be hard for those attempting to break away from a more rigid set of conditioning and obligations.

Having said that here are a few words of wisdom I can share, which I learned along the way about stepping out as the real you:

i.   Find a new tribe

Once you follow a path that makes your heart sing, you will most likely need to find a group of people who are also interested in that activity or way of life.

This new tribe will appear, if you have the courage to stay the course. You are highly unlikely to be the only person in the world with the passions you have chosen.

Your true tribe will arrive when you need them to, and you can share your journey with them. Trust this!

ii.   Allow, allow, allow

Once you put your stake in the ground, because you know who you are and what you want to do with your life force, life will organise itself around you through synchronicity to make it possible.

Miraculously, the right things, the right people and the right opportunities will manifest around you, so that your positive intentions can be expressed.

This takes presence of mind, to let go of your need to control and to trust in the power of love and your life force.

When we resist our heart's desires, unhappiness will persist. Allowing your desires to take centre stage needs you to trust in the power of your feelings.

iii.   Know you are worthy

When we work out what we want, the most likely blockage to it taking shape is our own fears and sense of unworthiness.

Mark Twain once said:

> "Face your fears and the death of fear is certain."

When I changed my life to meet the wants in my heart, I experienced fears that arose inside me. I had to overcome these fears to be able to move forward.

These fears eventually faded away in the face of the extra joy and happiness I experienced, and rarely did I ever want to turn back. Fear just delayed my progress. I was once told, "when fear is no longer perceived as a barrier, one can easily pass through it"; and this proved to be true.

At the end of the day, I knew that if I turned my back on my heart to satisfy others, I was only going to hurt myself again. It was me or them who would be unhappy, and I am only responsible for my own life. The way forward was simple in the end. I had to be the real me at all costs.

We get what we feel that we are worthy of; but it's not enough to just think we are worthy – we need to *feel* worthy and take steps to make it happen.

The moment we stop blocking the arrival of a new possibility into our lives, our new energy will invite it fully in. This can really work, but it does take a little bit of time to see that your beliefs are the block, and then to change them.

iv.   Be the real you, not an approximation

Once you establish what you really are and who you want to be in life, it's important that you are that not a watered down version of that.

Once your heart takes over, you will find yourself enchanted, most likely by your dreams. Be ready to be more vibrant, happier, more successful, attractive, less fearful, and much, much more. This is because you will have an authenticity about you that others will notice. Happiness equates to lightness, and light is radiant.

It's important to express your new self with limited filters. Of course, you can diminish it for periods of time, if you think it is the best course of action; but the more you are the truth of who you are, the more likely you will experience your full presence in life and create the adventure of spontaneity that your heart desires, and so desperately wants you to experience.

This is likely to involve being more honest, more emotional, more direct, and less prone to people pleasing and self-sacrificing.

These will all add up to a happier and more loving you, because it's the authentic you, taking stage, perhaps for the first time, in a very long time.

v.   Give and receive in equal measure

When we discover our real selves, it is important that we don't just give this to the world without being prepared to receive in equal measure.

Once you attain the radiance of being in your heart, people will want to experience more of you and interact with you. Happiness is infectious and becomes a habit, so others will seek to be in your presence.

Give and receive this love and care in equal measure. If all you do is give, the balance in your life will be disrupted and you will stop the flow of positivity from coming into your life.

We all tend to give more than we receive, as we see this as virtuous. However, when you give without receiving you will block the natural balance in your life that nourishes you and helps you to feel worthy.

vi. Action is critical

Once you align with your heart and know in which direction you want to take life, action is needed before anything can change.

Just deciding on, or thinking about, a change will rarely be enough. When you take steps to make change, the universe will support you in making your dreams a reality. Consider yourself to be in a relationship with the universe, and that it is ready to co-create with you.

This may sound obvious but it's important to address any resistance to change that you encounter. If we resist a change, unhappiness is most likely to persist.

vii. Seize opportunities that present

As you feel your lightness pouring forth into your life, like the sun appearing over the horizon at dawn, golden opportunities will undoubtedly present themselves.

If you are clear on what you desire, and the doubts you have disappear, you will know when opportunities arise that align with your desires.

These opportunities may be subtle. You may well miss them if you are not in-sync with what your heart wants.

Confusion usually precedes clarity, but once the fog clears you will be off on an adventure that is both wonderful and uniquely yours. Take the time to be clear of your heart's desire and you will be free of the clutches of confusion.

1. *Create from your centre*

When you stare down your limiting beliefs, find yourself and step forth to express that to the world, you will find greater happiness. In this happy place you will have the opportunity to create, for you are aligned with the life force inside you, which wants you to thrive.

We are all part of a universe that has and always will be creating. Once you connect to your heart you will be consciously part of this creative force. Let yourself be a part of this ecosystem of creativity that arises from joy and fulfilment.

You don't need to be in charge of or control the ecosystem. Your level of importance is truly unimportant in the unfolding of this shift, and without your needy ego you can radiate to new heights.

You can be a part of this creative ecosystem and delight in the experience of transformation. It will set your heart on fire, and you will radiate the light you find within yourself but may not yet have set free.

This transformation is totally worth it, but in making the change necessary you will at times feel alone, for this journey is largely about you.

In these times, remember that you are not the first person to apply the Code of Happiness, or to seek enlightenment, and you won't be the last.

There will always be supporters out there who can advise you if you need help. Never hesitate to reach out to others who have gone before you. You will know who they are intuitively, and they will only be too happy to help you.

CHAPTER

8

Our New Wonderful Belief Structures

Imagine if your old negative and fearful beliefs were replaced by new and wonderful ones that changed your life. Where would it lead you, in all walks of life?

Figure 5 below shows how our core beliefs could be, and the sunshine they would bring into our lives once we allow our hearts to have a say.

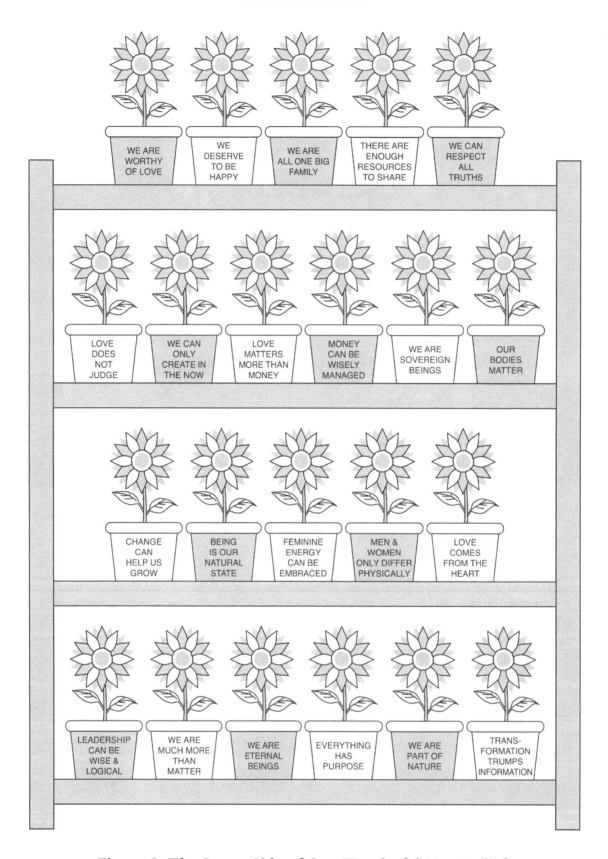

Figure 5: The Sunny Side of Our Wonderful New Beliefs

When we adopt these cornerstone beliefs, we cannot help but transform the world we live in to be a better place.

A new world based on these new beliefs would be a more natural, lighter, and brighter place to be. We could start to know our true selves, because the removal of our contorted conditioned belief structure would give us the freedom to be ourselves.

This transformation starts within individuals, and it can then ripple out into the world, changing all aspects of our world for the better at all levels, from individuals to families, and eventually into a far more united world order. Happiness is infectious!

Why wouldn't we want this to take place?

There are people in this world who, of course, would oppose this type of change, for they are the ones benefitting from the current system of living. These are people with greater proportions of the available money, power, and recognition. They are the externally validated ones, but not necessarily the happy or authentic ones. It could be that their strong sense of self-worth has brought them success in different ways. However, it could also be that they are self-focussed and living in fear of their own insecurities being exposed.

There is nothing wrong with success, if it is measured in units of happiness; but, if we lived a more holistic way of being, more people would be happy and abundant. Greater positivity would breed more inspired lives and this radiance would be infectious.

It would also lead to less judgement, less violence and greater equality, because our world would witness more sharing and care for more people, no matter where they live or who they are. Collaboration could replace competition as our normal way to co-exist.

A world with people working together for a common goal of happiness and unity could not help but be more successful for the collective. Many successful sporting teams attribute their success to all their participants playing for each other and pursuing a common goal. Imagine a whole society based on a shared vision that we can all thrive, not just survive.

In this place of authenticity lies joy, happiness, and wonderful outcomes that only our hearts can inspire us to create.

Imagine how the world could look if we dared to dream and simply changed the belief structures that hold us at bay from our true selves, and the deep knowing that this would unleash.

Many people might call my dream of a better world a fantasy and impossible. However, fantasy is the foundation of 'fantastic' and sometimes it's the only way to truly understand our realities.

Here's how it could look.

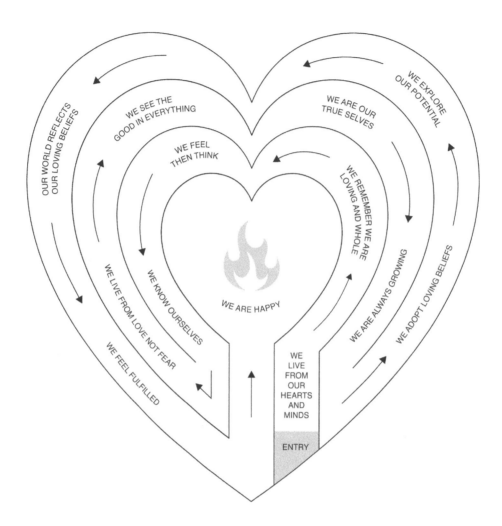

Figure 6: Our Labyrinth of Love

A labyrinth is different to a maze. A labyrinth has a single continuous path that leads to a centre. As long as you keep going forward, you will get to the right place, to the heart of the structure.

A labyrinth is a metaphor for the path to happiness. The path to your joy lies inside you at your heart's centre, and you can go there any time you choose. Your joy may be hidden at first, but you will find it on the journey of discovery. This will take you directly to the life you want.

Yes, you may face some pain as you let go of your old beliefs and past experiences, but this pain is always followed by a lighter, brighter energy entering your life. We need to lose our fear of emotion, as emotions are inside us to guide us and take us to a better life. They are messages from our hearts.

I am sure you will agree the world depicted in Figure 6 looks like a better world for us all to inhabit, a natural ecosystem in line with our hearts. It is yours to claim, even if others don't, because you can create your own reality.

And in this new world we could create the social and economic structures and interactions depicted below:

Figure 7: The Sunny Place Our Hearts Want to Create

In a world lived more from the heart, our new wonderful belief structures would transform society into a field of sunflowers, connecting us with the happiness in our hearts and brightening up our world.

8.1: A natural, wonder-full life

Martin Luther King made a famous speech repeating the words 'I have a dream', in which he passionately spoke of a world with greater equality between people.

Well, I have a dream of the world changing even more than that. The end of racism is part of my dream, but why stop there?

When we change ourselves and release the conditioning that keeps us in an unnatural trance, we can change the world around us. But it starts inside ourselves. Nowhere else. We can't expect others to change if we won't.

When we change our inner world, we ultimately change our outer world too. It's inevitable.

The natural way of being is to feel. We all know it. We just need to let go of our old ways of only thinking, because this leads us to obsess on surviving. Open yourself to a new energy based on thriving in harmony with others. This way we can experience life as it's meant to be lived.

When we get our beliefs clear and in a loving space, our minds will create a world that aligns with this set of beliefs. It cannot be any other way, because beliefs ultimately manifest into the outside world. Our beliefs create our habits, which then create our habitats. Beliefs are everything! Believe and you shall receive!

If enough people transform themselves, we as a society will transform. This transformation can be rapid, but it will require leadership that is creative and has the wisdom needed to make it happen. Not everyone will have the foresight to embrace these possibilities without assistance and direction.

In the following paragraphs, I provide my blueprint for a more natural way of life and describe, to the best of my abilities, how this might feel once achieved. It's my dream on paper, but hopefully it's an understatement of what's possible, and what eventuates. This change will require great courage from us all, but when you access your heart and soul there is no limit to the courage that can come forth. It just takes one pebble dropped on a lake to create a ripple that can be felt across the whole body of water. We need to start, and start soon, in the interests of ourselves, our children and our planet. We can all be the pebble, if only for ourselves.

If you have ever watched the waves on a beach, you will know they seem silent as they approach the shore. Then they break in different places and the associated noise levels grow. But eventually there is enough energy for the entire wave to break and that initial noise becomes a roar. After a series of changes, the entire wave reunites as one. It then finishes its journey, meeting the shore and returning to form part of a new wave.

Collectively, we can be like the waves of the ocean, making a difference together and arriving as one upon the golden sands we shape.

First you need to start with your own pebble, before you cast it into the water.

8.2: Equality for all

A world of judgement creates a world of perceived inequality. Human beings judge one another to elevate their own self-esteem. It's prolific and it's created by insecurity, not strength.

Imagine a world where we all recognised our own sense of self-worth. There would be no value in judging another, no need to place people below you so you can feel more worthy. In this place compassion can replace judgement. Love of others can replace the fear that they are better or more important than you.

When we see that other people are living their lives for their own purpose, not ours, we can have the freedom to let them be (particularly if they do not harm us).

If we all believed in the principle of 'live and let live', rather than thinking other people should behave the way we want them to, the world would be a better place. We can dream this into reality!

Why put people of a different colour, religion or sexual persuasion above or below us? We must, and will, break this ridiculous cycle in all walks of life. All we have to do is recognise its absurdity and change our way of thinking. New structures and ways of interacting will cascade from this fresh perspective.

We should not chastise ourselves for being judgemental in the past. This serves no use or value other than to constantly mire our minds in the memories of past beliefs, and in doing so keeps us in the loop of judgement and the quicksands of time and its many regrets. In effect we continue to judge the judge and the cycle goes on.

We all need to be compassionate to ourselves and others for past judgements, and move forward in acceptance together. The old story can end. In acceptance, inequality can cease to be a part of our lives for it becomes irrelevant and is replaced by our natural state of unity.

We need to be conscious that we will all benefit from this shift. If you are judging others, you can be sure they are judging you back. Every action has an equal and opposite reaction!

Judgement is the great separator in this world. I dream of a world free of perceived inequality! This freedom is just a new belief or thought pattern away. We are all equal. Isn't it time we all got this! It's not that hard!

The 2020 race riots across the world were widely supported for good reason, but they also saw judgement on both sides. The rioters judged people of another colour for the sins of the past. Statues of past leaders were trashed without recognition that those leaders were preconditioned to believe what they believed in their time. Politicians judged the emotions displayed in the marches, giving little back than cursory sympathy that, in some cases, inspired more violence. There appeared to be no concrete calls for change or actions to address the problems.

Riots have been going on for decades and still we have riots. We need real empathy and action to address the problems, not armed police to make riots worse.

This action starts in our hearts, by going inward and knowing that we are all equal. Feel it, not just think it. This is what is currently lacking as our preconditioned minds are still in control. To do anything else will not solve the problem. Belief structures are the core issue and the opportunity, not laws.

My dream sees us dropping the judgement that stifles so many people in our community. We need to stop ranking and judging everyone every time we see or meet them. Ranking can be replaced by acceptance and love. This requires compassion, not analytical thought and comparison.

When I stopped judging others, I felt a huge release of happiness within me. Try it for a few days and see what I mean. This is so critical to all of us and our society. May equality be permanently etched into our way of being.

What if we all dream of equality, like Martin Luther King, not just those who are being discriminated against! I wonder!

8.3: All truths are respected

Imagine a world where all views and opinions are respected. Imagine a shared awareness that there is no such thing as 'the' truth. Truth is a matter of perspective.

There may be facts and evidence that can be proven, but that is different to truth.

When we live from our hearts and minds, we will be able to not just tolerate but rejoice in the fact that there are different perspectives and that, perhaps, just perhaps, we can learn from the perspectives of others.

In this place we can search all human interactions for common ground, for solutions to satisfy all parties. Human beings – in clinging to their individual truths as the only truth and mixing it with their need to be right and win – have used their so-called truth as their justification for judgement, violence, and condemnation. Unhappy people are the ones who start fights.

Imagine negotiations taking place to always find the place of compromise where all views are heard, respected, and considered in the formulation of a solution. Ideologies can differ and that is to be celebrated.

Without different truths, life would be boring. Where would be the challenge in that? Why do we hate being challenged in this way? The simple answer is we feel that we must win and therefore the views of others, if they are contrary to ours, exposes our low sense of self-worth. Does another person's view or ideology make you any lesser? Of course not.

Imagine a world where our leaders respected the views of all around them. Could this help to solve world peace? Could a search for common ground bring communists and capitalists into peaceful harmony? Of course, it could! It's the power of our thoughts that create our world!

Imagine if all our interactions with others were full of empathy and compassion. The search for a collective outcome that satisfies as many people as possible is 'nirvana' in any big decision. Our world does not need to be perfect. Awesome is acceptable. Here trust would exist, and self-protection would not be required. We could use the swords we all carry to cut through our differences, rather than to stab each other in the back.

Many people watch and believe in mainstream media, while others focus on left-field non-core media. Either way, people tend to believe what they see and hear.

Objectivity requires us to respect the views of both. Who knows, our media could be wrong or stretching the facts! Are you shocked by this?

How would our mainstream news media look and feel if it embraced the truths of *all* without criticism or judgement? Probably very different.

In Australia, we live by the concept of freedom of speech. It is a core part of our society, at least in principle. However, the media we listen to or read, whether it's niche or mainstream, usually puts forth whichever truth makes them the most money, twisting it to make it seem more sensational than it is in reality. Of course, they can do what they want, but unfortunately they have so much power to influence public opinion one way or another, they should really be more responsible and careful with their ability to create 'truths'.

Truths can start wars, unless they are properly debated and used to find common ground where all can benefit.

How do you think your life would change if everyone you met respected your views and wanted to listen to them? This, like all improvements in our world, can come once better awareness takes over.

8.4: Emotions for everybody

How often have you seen a man on television get emotionally sad and instantly apologise for this? Why do they feel the need to apologise? Why were they even embarrassed by the fact that they were sad? It's a reflection of our belief structure that feeling *certain* emotions is weak.

How often have you seen a woman on television get emotionally assertive and instantly explain, trying to justify why she might need to be assertive, so others don't judge her negatively? If the situation is appropriate, why apologise? Why do viewers even judge her, calling her 'bossy' or a 'bitch'? It's a reflection of our belief structure that feeling *certain* emotions are inappropriate for certain genders.

Imagine a world where we embrace all kinds of feelings: fun, intuition, empathy and nurturing, as much as we respect aggression, assertiveness and competitiveness – all regardless of gender.

We could make better decisions if we relied as much, if not more, on our hearts as we do our minds. If we listened to our bodies, they could tell us what decisions to make. Our hearts are super-processors that make decisions in an instant, once they know the perspectives at play.

If we could all allow ourselves to feel the full range of emotions spoken by our hearts, our decisions would be more universally kind. It would also enable relationship issues to be resolved more constructively and with love, not the need to be right. Our children would benefit greatly from growing up in a family where *all* emotions were embraced and honoured, regardless of gender.

Imagine if we taught people how to use their gut feelings to direct their lives, both women and men. The teacher within us is waiting to step forth and pour wisdom into our lives. What if we stopped suppressing our full range of feeling, and relied less upon our thinking minds? This may be difficult for people who come from very fear-based conditioning, as to fully feel may seem dangerous or even terrifying. However, when we can pass through this fear and feel the clarity beneath it, we can open to making decisions that lead to joy. When our minds are in charge, it blocks us from receiving the wisdom in our hearts. It's not authentic. It's not who we really are.

Imagine a world where everyone was encouraged to nurture, including caring for children. When we connect to both our masculine and feminine energies, in whatever proportions are natural for our authentic selves, we allow our hearts and minds to become allies not enemies.

A powerful and important aspect of Mother Nature is the powerful ocean upon our planet Earth. Most of us love to admire the ocean and often visit it to experience its beauty. Yet the ocean is calm one day, wild the next. It's colours shift, its currents move, and, without this masterpiece of nature, we would die. The ocean accepts what goes on, in and above it, without judgement.

We admire the ever-changing volatility of the oceans. Can't we accept and embrace the natural side of ourselves? Aren't we emotional beings by definition? As individuals we need to be more like the ocean.

Can you remember an occasion where you fully honoured your emotions without trying to moderate them to satisfy others around you?

8.5: Well-balanced leadership with wisdom

Throughout history, male leaders have dominated the traditional model of leadership in the western world. The fact that leaders have been men is not the issue. The issue is that the nature of that leadership has been dominated by masculine energies. This needs a long hard rethink. The chains of conditioned programming need to be released to allow wise leadership to take over.

The stereotypical vision of a successful person in our society is of one who wins. We then select leaders who are most likely to match this preconditioned mindset of what a leader can give us: a win.

How many men have used their positions of power to feather their own nests and satisfy their egos, rather than work for the collective good of their people? Corrupt incompetent governments have been prevalent for centuries.

Wise leaders would not contemplate these kinds of behaviours.

Our new beliefs would lead to a world full of leaders focussed on being of service to the people they represent, not themselves. We would all be best served in life if our leadership carried a balance of feminine and masculine energies or characteristics. We shouldn't need key performance indicators to make sure we have as many women as men in leadership positions. We should pick those leaders who have the right balance of these energies.

I dream that we will soon have authentic natural leaders, who care about service to their collective, not their own bank balance or a chance to leave their name etched on a wall, statue or recorded in Wikipedia for all to see forever more.

We need leaders who can lead with care, allow all members of the team to be their true selves, have compassion for everyone's struggles yet binds them together with a common direction, have a common purpose yet an unwavering commitment to their team's general welfare, fully present with their team and listens, and not needing to dominate those around them. We need leaders who have strength in just being present, as their power stems from their presence and allows them to be better able to create in the moment at hand. They witness and listen before they act, knowing that they can learn from others around them.

This type of leader will know that life is not perfect and that members of their team will at times not meet their expectations, either at an individual or team level. However, they will be committed to growth and motivating the team to be the best they can be, not winning or losing, because they will know success will come when team harmony is achieved, and energy arising from joy is present.

Current leaders in our society often fail to meet our expectations. This is largely not their fault. Our collective preconditioned tendency to elect smart technical people with a winning background and a propensity for big promises keeps delivering us leaders who disappoint. They are intelligent but may have no heart. They are not whole and, in reality, the jobs they are in are beyond them. They are preconditioned to want the accolades and spoils of leadership without knowing how they need to change to be a true leader. They do not know themselves, so how can they know those they serve?

Leadership is a privilege not a right, yet it is so regularly manipulated for personal gain and egoic validation. This will change when our awareness shifts, and we demand more of our leaders as a society.

8.6: Authentic leadership in all walks of life

When we think of leadership we think of politicians, statesmen and business chief executive officers. But there are leaders in every walk of life. You may be leading yourself in some way, you just haven't thought of it that way – for example, parents in a family, teachers in a classroom, or even captains of a sporting team.

No matter what level of leadership, the principles are the same: more aware and well-balanced leadership is needed to take our world forward.

Organisations, teams, families and even nations have their own soul, and it's the leader that moulds this way of being and allows that soul to come to the fore. People want to follow and copy great leaders. But flawed egoic leaders typically select egoic manipulative leaders to work for them, such that they create a chain of egoic leaders reporting to each other.

The culture of any organisation or team is ultimately set by its leader. People copy the leader above them for they believe the way that that leader behaves is the pathway to success. It may well be, in the short term, and might lead to financial gain; but inauthentic leadership is not sustainable. It eventually falls as team players ultimately reject the culture. They do not trust it. At an intuitive level they reject the lack of care and personal freedom typically imposed on them by the egoic and control-oriented leader.

In truth they live in fear of failure, and it is the leader who imposes this fear on them. It is a very common recipe for low self-esteem in a team and the erosion of positivity with a thousand cuts of inauthenticity.

The greatest attribute a leader can bring to any team is their own sense of self – that they know who they are and what they stand for as a leader. Great leaders tap into the soul of a team, not its egoic need to win. They know how to justify their role as leader, not take the spoils and expect others to lead while they bask in glory.

Once we change our beliefs about what our leaders should be, we will see this mirrored in the nature of our leaders. We will need to drop our own obsession with self-interest to select the right leaders.

Let's look in more detail at what is possible in different types of leadership roles.

8.6.1: Family

The egoic leadership that harms countries, companies and communities also harms the core units in our society: the family.

These days, both parents typically work outside of the home to financially support the family, sharing domestic duties and child-care responsibilities in different ways. Family leadership is therefore shared between the parents, often based on who is better at what task or who does which task more frequently.

However, there is still imbalance in the lack of recognition given to unpaid work inside the home – regardless of who performs it. Thus, if one parent brings in less money than the other but works just as long hours in the unpaid domestic space, they tend to have less power in financial decision-making and less entitlement to self-care time and activities. This can lead to the atrophy of a relationship and ultimately families fall apart. This is inauthentic family leadership.

Children need to be led by parents who both equally value the high importance of child-care work, in order for that value to seep through into the fabric of society. This imbalance can be addressed through a simple shift in our way of thinking.

One solution could be to acknowledge the value of any in-house child-care or domestic duties by allocating a theoretical monetary value to that time, based on how much it would cost to outsource that work to a third party. If we then attribute that theoretical cost to a salary 'earnt' by the parent performing that work – plus tax, plus super – their monetary value increases dramatically, thus the perception of their work.

For example, what is the cost of before and after school care, the cost of holiday care, the cost of paying a child carer to transport children to activities and medical appointments? If such tasks were performed by a third party, hired from outside the family, the costs would all add up to thousands of dollars. Thus, whoever performs these tasks inside the family is saving that family from that spending, and in effect earning that same amount.

By valuing childcare work in this way, families can increase the respect they attribute to child-care work, on an equal level as paid work outside the home, and this will liberate both parents. Both women and men are equally able to perform child-care tasks (even breast-feeding can be shared by pumping milk and bottle-feeding it), so both women and men should be free to choose which tasks they are individually best at and want to perform, regardless of gender. This is the path to true authenticity, and thus authenticity in society.

We can lead our children forward with this equal respect of gender, visible and present through the joint leadership of our families. We all have a right to be who we want to be with the full support of our partners and society.

8.6.2: Corporate leadership

I worked in the corporate world for over 35 years, and the model of corporate leadership I witnessed adopted the egoic-driven model of male leadership as a general rule. There were some wonderful exceptions, but not many.

I dream of the corporate world having a balanced caring and present leadership which has heart, not just mind at its core. It can have great upside with just a change of mindset and a dose of feeling.

The corporate world is not unique in its egoic leadership generating a competitive environment. It is merely a microcosm of society and our current limiting belief structures.

The corporate leadership we need in the future will come from the heart and have the following traits:

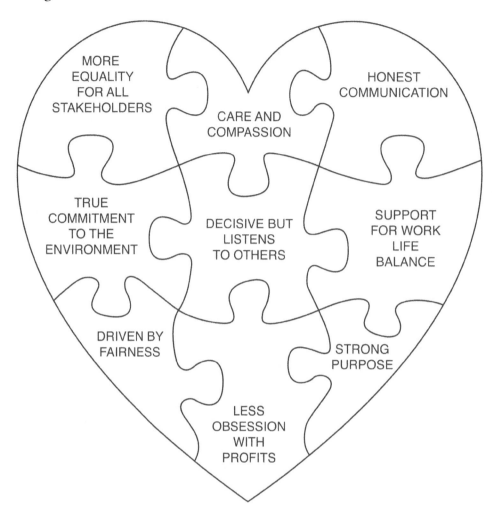

MORE EQUALITY FOR ALL STAKEHOLDERS

CARE AND COMPASSION

HONEST COMMUNICATION

TRUE COMMITMENT TO THE ENVIRONMENT

DECISIVE BUT LISTENS TO OTHERS

SUPPORT FOR WORK LIFE BALANCE

DRIVEN BY FAIRNESS

LESS OBSESSION WITH PROFITS

STRONG PURPOSE

Figure 8: The Characteristics of Wise Leadership

At its core, modern businesses are too obsessed with profits, not people or the planet. When profits drop, they have little compassion for people and become driven by legal contracts and rights. People often cease to matter when profits fall. The share price or bottom line is everything, unfortunately, for its here that the organisation finds its validation and importance, internally and externally.

This is because leaders in businesses are generally trained to think, not feel. They leave their hearts at home. The corporate world is alive with the mindfully self-focussed! Leaders speak of creating businesses with sustainable profits that can sustain the health of the planet, but how much truth lies in this assertion?

Traditional male leadership has focused on results and profits, over health and happiness in businesses. This leads to higher short-term profits and outcomes, but in the long run it will not lead to the results that are possible where an organisation has strong harmony with all its stakeholders. You can only squeeze a lemon so much before it's dry!

But when all participants are in sync, there is loyalty and trust, and when that mixes with purity of purpose, not just an obsession with profits, magical things can happen for a business, and all involved.

I believe we all desire greater fairness in business, not the lopsided legalistic model that has prioritised profit and winning over values and collaboration. This is possible when leaders know themselves and have released the old fashioned beliefs synonymous with our traditional self-focused style of corporate leadership.

The creative people who actually run our businesses need to be paid more. Corporate slavery and resentment need to be replaced by loyalty and care in the corridors. It seems reasonable that our essential workers earn a fair day's pay, given how important they are. What if our profits were sustainable and business operations really were designed to care for the planet? Let's select leaders who know the importance of self-awareness in the workplace, for themselves, their people, and a brighter future for all.

Care is a missing ingredient in many leaders. Care needs to be included in the recipe that makes up our corporate leadership qualities.

I dream of corporate leadership that has a heart because it is conscious of what is possible. This can be reality.

8.6.3: Political leadership

As mentioned previously, leadership at a political level needs transformation. White, rich, aged, male leadership has had its day as the primary model. Our political leaders need to realise that to be loved by their constituents, they need to treat them with the respect they deserve. This means being honest, answering the actual questions asked of them, and acting in the interests of the collective, not their own ego and desire to be remembered as a success. Personal legacy is far too important to leaders, yet means nothing to the collective society.

The reality is that: a *political* leader will never make everyone happy. But leaders can still make wise decisions in the interests of the collective based on their inspired intuition. Leaders can be empowered by their own convictions, and not worry about the views of those standing ready to convict them. They can decide the way forward only after listening to the views of others, not just have a head full of knowledge, a multitude of qualifications and an understanding of what actions will make them popular.

Knowing what others have done, or even what has worked in the past, is a cop out. History may rhyme but doesn't repeat itself, as Mark Twain once said. Fresh ideas are critical to great leadership. Wisdom is creative not repetitive; it has insight and foresight.

All over the world, governments have a well-deserved reputation for being ineffective and inefficient. Let's call them to account, for they have great influence on our way of life.

2020 and 2021 showed us how incompetent governments can be, by the way they under and overreacted to Covid-19, to the detriment of their people. Most leaders seemed incapable of getting the balance right between wealth and health. The concepts of freedom and risk management were largely beyond leaders in many countries, and were drowned out by an obsession with control and 'one-size fits all' rules.

We see too much grandstanding and politics in community and country leadership. Parties of leaders need to recognise that voters have put them in their roles with trust and good faith, and they should not betray that trust. They should also conduct their affairs with integrity and not fight with each other, like children scrapping in a playground.

With so many people conditioned by egoic needs, it's not easy to find wise leaders who are also inspiring and intuitive. But it is possible.

Perhaps the concept of party politics has had its day? Perhaps it diminishes the ability of our elected leaders to think for themselves? I dream of a parliament where all our elected members are independent and form their own view on every issue, rather than voting to stay alive in their party.

8.6.4: World leaders

Imagine a world where world leaders collaborated for the good of all, not compete for recognition. If you consider the varying successes leaders had in dealing with the Covid-19 pandemic, the political structures that were united for the common good achieved the best outcomes.

This is reflective of beliefs. Beliefs are everything!

On a world stage we saw limited collaboration during the pandemic from the respective nations. In the middle of the pandemic, China and America became more confrontational and the repeated reference to Covid-19 as the Kung or China flu by the then US President Trump did nothing but incite aggravation and tension. Where is the collaboration in all this? Of course, it's non-existent.

Collaboration on the creation of an effective vaccine was also difficult to spot during the pandemic. Countries and organisations across the world sensed the massive financial gains to be had from being the first to produce a vaccine. This competition eclipsed the level of collaboration that was possible. Why couldn't leaders see the virtue in one united effort, funded by all nations, to create a common vaccine and distribute it to all!

The answer is clear: this simply is not how the world works. But it should!

Some people aspire to see a world government in place to lead the world. This stems from a desperate desire to see nations united on key issues. Of course, we would all like to see this unity.

However, the structure of governments would not matter so much if belief structures shifted from world competition to world collaboration. Does having world influence really matter? Does it make the population of a nation any happier to be seen as more dominant than another?

In truth, it doesn't. But where a nation as a collective lacks deep fulfilment, it can be led into competition with another as it searches for validation, particularly if it's led by deeply egoic leaders. Like individuals, happy contented nations don't start fights, trade wars, or spy on others. They collaborate and live in peace.

Financial and social structures across the globe will shift for the better once we break the spell of competition haunting the capitals of the world.

I dream of one day seeing collaboration descend upon world leadership to allow global unity to exist, not just be a pretence, particularly among countries that have weapons to destroy life as we know it. This is just a thought away!

8.7: Collaboration replaces competition

Imagine a world where our primary objective is to collaborate and treat each other the way we seek to be treated ourselves. Imagine a world where everything we did had, at its core, care for our fellow man or woman.

At the moment, most things we take part in are unfortunately a competition. Who wants to be a loser? We believe it diminishes us. Self-interest is alive and well in all parts of life. We are programmed to win and, if we don't think we can win, we will think twice about even taking part. Fun is largely irrelevant in our minds.

But when we collaborate, we support each other. We open ourselves up to the possibility that everyone wins. Isn't this fundamentally better than a small minority being the 'haves' and the rest being the 'have-nots'. It doesn't preclude individuals being rich or wealthy. There is nothing wrong with wealth. However, when we genuinely care about others there can be a fairer spread of resources and joy.

I would propose that even the most successful people in society, with all that we aspire to fundamentally carry the wounds of being insufficient in some way. Why did Elvis Presley, Michael Jackson and Whitney Houston have such unfortunate deaths, allegedly at the hands of drugs, yet so many of us aspire to have their talents, fame and fortune?

It is said that competition brings out the best in us as individuals, in our businesses and in our nations. This may have truth, but when winning or losing validates us we lose perspective on what life is all about. Life is to be enjoyed, not endured. It should not be a fight or a struggle.

I dream of competition being undertaken for the opportunity to test yourself, and for enjoyment; and not just for the sake of recognition, validation, or self-worth. We could even consider enjoying second-place, because in the silver medal lies learning and of course it's nice and shiny too.

Fulfilment needs to be the true meaning of success. At present our success determines our level of fulfilment. It's the wrong way around! I can only dream of a world where fulfilment is the primary reason for living, not money or winning. I have made this transition myself, and I can tell you I feel like a slave that has shaken off the ball and chain and been set free.

Success or failure can dissolve as concepts and be replaced by the concept of fulfilment. This dissolving can take place when we drop our need to be perfect and have power over others. None of us are perfect. We all know this, and we often say it, but each time we look in the mirror we want to see a perfect reflection, even though it's impossible.

As we strive for perfection, real fulfilment becomes impossible. Let's measure our happiness not by the number of trophies on our shelves – our trophies won't matter once we are gone from this life – but rather measure it in the memories of the love and fun we shared, that may even endure in our souls and the souls of those we leave behind.

8.8: Time no longer ticks us off

Time is a great enemy of joy. We are slaves to it, as it ticks away on our wrists, phones, and walls.

Imagine life where we did what we wanted, when we wanted to do it.

Now you will say to yourself that this is impossible in our modern lives. We have to be here and there at certain times, in order just to take part in our lives. There is an element of truth here, but only because we have created this time-based world where we see time as money. Time supports our obsession with success and winning. It's a cancer in our world that keeps us welded to obligation.

We do have to attend to the administration activities of life, and this does take time, but not *all* our time. The more obligations we accept, the more we will feel time poor. These things then dominate our lives and leave little space for creativity to enter.

Our minds have created the concept of time. But did man survive before the ancient Egyptians introduced the concept of time? Well, clearly the answer is 'yes'.

When we change our mindset and do what we enjoy and what interests us, time is far less intrusive in our lives.

The great thing about holidays in our lives is that they often dissolve the concept of time from our lives, at least for a short time. We feel free, liberated, and happy – until the holiday ends and we again become slaves to our schedules. What if life felt like one big holiday every day?

I believe we need to follow the energy in our life more than the time on our wrists, like we do on holidays. Imagine living our lives like this. Imagine if our lives were less scripted and were more driven by feeling and our desire. I have done it and, let me tell you, I have much more fun.

But can you see how all these concepts are interrelated? If we need money and recognition to feel validated, then we must create processes and structures that give us the opportunity to compete and get things done. Who is going to pay you for doing nothing of perceived value?

If you've ever worked in big businesses, you would have experienced the obsession with meetings. Every hour in every building there are meetings. Many are held for the sake of it. People don't want to trust their intuition and make a decision, not when they could have a meeting to find safety in numbers.

But to do otherwise requires great courage and self-trust, and as a quality this is rare in our world, particularly in the business world.

And all this infrastructure and process wastes time and our precious experience on Earth. In essence, they block our joy.

Emails unfortunately do the same. There are billions of them sent each year to people who probably don't need them. By reading them, we become slaves to the priorities of others.

When we are connected to our own sense of self, we don't want to give away our sovereignty to live the life that others choose for us. In this place, we can control time, it does not control us.

Time is quite frankly a bad idea, other than to guide the activities we actually want to do for joy and love.

I dream of a world where freedom replaces the chains of time, where time is our friend, not our enslaver. Here we can be humans being (happy), not humans doing out of habit and obligation.

If you share this same dream, it can become a reality by just saying 'no' to relationships and activities that over-schedule your time or which you don't enjoy.

Your heart will tell you where to start, if you listen closely.

CHAPTER

9

The Structures and Interactions Possible in a Transformed World

The transformation of core human beliefs can transform the way human beings interact all over the world; first with themselves, then with others. If pursued, this transformation couldn't help but manifest into new structures and ways of interacting for society and ultimately across the globe.

The place to start is with yourself. You can go through this amazing transformation, even if nobody else you know goes through it. In fact, you might be the reason they then decide to change too, as your new inner reality of happiness would reflect in your outside world and inspire them.

Of course, all human beings have their own perspectives, ideologies, and truths, so change has to gather pace as more and more people get in touch with their heart's desires. Conditioning, deep within our conscious and subconscious beliefs, will thus shift at a different pace in different individuals, communities, and countries. Movement will be slow at first but will be rapid once our operating systems align, and the relief of letting go of the past and future, letting in a lighter brighter way of life allows our hearts to glow and our minds to support a happier way of life.

Let's consider how life could look and feel, after we break the trance of our current conditioning.

9.1: Economic

The economic structural changes possible across the world could be profound and arrest our overly complicated and fragile economic structures, currently based on illusions of value.

Our economic structures could instead move to reflect reality. Currencies and the assets they purchase could have a solid foundation, backed by substance, and actually exist, not be figments of our imaginations, as many currently are in our hopeful minds.

Business profits could be earned from sustainable operations linked to human need and purpose, not short-term desires for profit that disregard the relative importance and needs of all stakeholders in an economic framework, including staff and customers, and the Earth.

Fairness for all is the current rhetoric, but deep down everyone knows that profits come first, because they fund executive and staff bonuses and salaries.

When the world moves to a place where human collaboration and a genuine desire for fairness replaces our obsession with competition, we will no longer need to expel energy and emotion so profoundly at protecting ourselves from others constantly. Imagine a world where you can trust that others will not try to exploit you, and not value your money more than they value you.

Imagine a world where we measure fulfilment as our key driver in life, not the size of our bank balances and houses.

Imagine a world where people work together for the good of all, not to be the richest in the street with the biggest house or the fastest car. And if they do have these advantages, imagine a situation where those more fortunate are making money out of providing authentic services and goods to help the masses have a better life.

We would all experience great relief once we can relax and trust more in those around us.

Let's look more closely at the structural outcomes that would be created by a lighter, more heart-based financial system:

9.1.1: Less legal minefields

Our world is currently mired in a swamp of legal process. Everything we buy or sell comes complete with a detailed form to accept or sign, which contains fine print that only fully functioning, intelligent eyes can see or comprehend.

Imagine a world where legal contracts either weren't needed or were written in a place of two-way trust where fairness was at the centre of the agreements reached. Contracts could be used to record the transaction agreed, but not come with mind-based or fear-driven small print, or terms and conditions that baffle the reader and create a platform for war – and more legal fees – if things go wrong.

Unfortunately, we have allowed lawyers to create a world that is highly lucrative for lawyers.

What would an inherently fair collaborative economy mean for government regulation? Consumer protection legislation and oversight currently in place – to stop people and businesses grabbing what they want – is a huge drag on our economic wellbeing. I can't even imagine how many pages of legislation exist across the globe and need to be administered to protect people from others, more so acting out their preconditioned need to win to feel complete. I dream of a world where this is streamlined, simple and respected by all. Can you feel the relief in your body from this shift?

Our law courts are full of disputes between buyers and sellers, debating how contracts should be applied to unforeseen circumstances. Who are the only real winners? Yes, you guessed right, the lawyers!

All the legal costs in our society ultimately feed into prices for goods and services. We are all paying for the world's lawyers to enjoy views of the harbour from their daytime offices or wealthy mansions on the beach. We have no choice but to use these people when things go wrong, otherwise we get smacked by legality.

How would it feel to know that you have paid your last ever legal bill? Liberating I suspect.

Prices would fall along with tensions, if we learned to find common ground in transactions, because fairness is in our hearts.

The modern governments of the world are also expensive legal machines driven largely by lawyers or ex-lawyers, making laws that generally suit them. Decisions are generally enshrined in legislation drafted by lawyers and supported by law courts and bureaucratic offices. It's hard to understand.

The Australian taxation legislation is 6000 pages long. Imagine if this was 500 pages or less, and anyone could understand it without needing to pay an expensive taxation lawyer or accountant to interpret the complex sections and paragraphs of text.

The legal mind-field we live in exists because of how our core win-at-all-costs belief structure manifests it into reality. It's needed because we are all grabbing for whatever we can get. This includes governments. We can stop this! Only the lawyers are really winning.

9.1.2: Far less haves and have-nots

Our current materialistic world creates a landscape of haves and have-nots.

Some people are deemed to be more important than others and they get the economic spoils, while others get paid far less, even when providing critical services. How can we allow so few to thrive, when so many fight to survive?

Can you imagine a world where there is greater financial equality for all those who contribute? Essential workers have become more obvious during the Covid-19 pandemic.

Our teachers, nurses, cleaners, supermarket workers, bank tellers, petrol station attendees and aged care workers have rightfully been elevated to the status of heroes. Their pay packets need to be elevated to match this.

These people may not create instant financial gain in our bank accounts, like stockbrokers or financiers, but without them we would seize up as a society and our future would be bleak.

Next time you go through the checkout in your local supermarket, give the checkout person a smile and thank them for their valuable assistance. We are all equal and these people have been looked down upon for far too long.

In our organisations, the salaries of leaders and creative workers could be more comparable. It's the creative workers at the frontline, or running the computer systems, who create the bulk of the profits, not the executives sitting in their ivory towers getting all the perks and recognition.

I dream of a society where our leaders embrace a world of greater equality in financial rewards. This is going to take wise leadership, because some of them have the most to lose from this shift. Most likely we will need new leaders to make this happen.

If we change our beliefs, we can have a united society that shares more evenly, recognising that it takes different skills and roles to make it work. We all have different talents and, if fully expressed, our society benefits from the totality of this combined collaboration.

Our society is currently based on pyramid structures, particularly in businesses and other organisations. However, it takes all the stones in a pyramid for it to stand so tall and strong. The stones at the top are only able to point to the sun because the stones at the bottom are carrying their weight.

Can you imagine the feelings of relief and joy you would experience if you felt fully valued in your job and were paid accordingly?

9.1.3: Assets will be more real

The world has been inventing assets for many years. Lawyers and corporate bankers have created masses of complicated documents to support arguable fictitious assets that exist in illusions, created by our minds.

Many of these assets are backed by emotion alone and could quickly vanish once their value and existence were to be questioned by the herd. Many cannot be touched or are not backed by assets that can be physically sighted. Take cryptocurrencies. Turn off the power and some of them may be no more.

Debt can be constructive, but when it becomes excessive it simply creates great unhappiness as we constantly worry about paying it back. What we are borrowing are the profits we hope raise in the future. What if they don't?

The ability for governments and central banks to print money and manipulate markets to hold them up will one day be exposed for what it is: short-term thinking that is just not facing reality. The truth is, our lifestyles are not sustainable, and simplicity needs to find its way back into our lives.

There will come a point where the weight of fake money will be too much to support, and its real value will be exposed. Assets that are illusions will perish.

When the dust settles, we will be left with simpler financial structures that are easier to understand and less based on pure emotion. This was the case after the Great Depression in the 1930s.

It has become fashionable for businesses to list on world stock exchanges so owners can cash-out and realise a financial valuation. Do we really need so many companies listed on the quasi-casino called the stock exchange? How many economic collapses have been kicked off by stock exchanges correcting after becoming wildly overpriced and then succumbing to a dose of reality or worse, an excessively pessimistic fear of falling prices that becomes a self-fulfilling prophecy.

The volatility of our financial markets is unnecessary and makes little sense. They occur quickly because human euphoria suddenly turns to fear. Investors in the herd find safety in numbers and are conditioned to follow others around them. They find this safety in numbers rather than following their own intuition or logic about real asset values.

To some extent values have become nebulous as momentum and herd mentality overrides logic. The mindset is: I may as well pay more because everyone else is. Some call it the fear of missing out or 'FOMO'.

If those transacting seek to do so at a fair price, and not rip off the person they are trading with, we will enter a world of financial trust, not one dominated by fear and the need for constant self-protection.

We could think more about sustainability in our economic landscapes. Boom and busts come from herd mentality and a lust for money. Greed and fear combine to create them in sequence. We need our financial returns and incomes to be more sustainable, and not fickle or illusory.

Why do we insist on companies we invest in making double-digit returns when the underlying growth rate possible is much lower? Greed is the answer.

Why do we create fake currencies and assets, and will them to go higher, when all that sustains their value is a common delusion?

The Covid-19 pandemic showed us that there are many products we can live without. It is now clear to us what we need, and the value of assets in our environment has shifted accordingly.

In the days of the gold standard, currencies were largely linked to the gold stores of a country. Without this kind of reference point, governments can artificially create money; and, off the back of this fake money, markets become un-supportably high. Eventually crashes come along to take them out of their fairyland.

Once people realise the truth about money, we should see a reversal in emotion, and fear will replace euphoria across certain markets. We may well learn the hard way, with the stick not the carrot at play. Unreal assets will eventually lose value. Assets that can be substantiated physically, or are linked to the real needs of people, will endure. The others may well be banished to the history books.

Objects like property, minerals, gold, silver, and so on, will stand the test of time as will incomes associated with the goods and services we need to survive. Once human beings see the unsustainable nature of the financial structures currently in place, and their beliefs change, there will be a restatement to a sustainable level.

Can you feel a pressure in your life to keep earning money to sustain a lifestyle for you and others around you? You may have a big mortgage and never-ending bills. Do you ever crave simplicity and wish all this could go away? I made this change and it felt liberating to say the least.

I dream of a world where *all* assets are backed by some semblance of reality, where currencies are backed by true assets, where financial instruments are not constructs of lawyers and wealthy merchant bankers, and our stock markets are not quasi-casinos. The blueprint for this return to reality lies in our beliefs. It's alright to be rich, but not by exploiting or hurting others in the process.

We should not borrow and consume at the expense of future generations who will pay for our excess lifestyles and delusions down the track. This already looks likely. A reset of expectation, as painful as it may be, is needed before we do too much harm to each other, to future generations or the planet.

You can move your life to a sustainable point by getting rid of excess debt. You don't have to wait for others to lead you there. Be in joy, not excess debt. You will be happier in this place and release the chains that keep you on that treadmill of obligation.

9.1.4: Better financial literacy

In this more simplistic economic structure, there would be far higher financial literacy across the population. This would stop the 'us' and 'them' outcome that keeps those less educated or fortunate in a never-ending cycle of financial despair. After all, what is a government really – a collective of (elected) people who receive the funds from the people to create and maintain the infrastructure of society *for* the people?

We need our schools (and parents for that matter) to teach children about the financial world, about investing, and collaborating financially for collective development, about how money works in society, and about trade. Don't our children deserve to understand money and what it can be used for, not just other cerebral things like mathematics? We all need money, but who needs to understand trigonometry or algebra?

Do you wish you had been taught more about how to manage money when you were growing up? Perhaps you, like me, would have more money today if only you had had more advice?

9.1.5: A more understood government

Understanding needs to set in around government in our economies. Many people seem to believe that governments can just create money out of thin air and that this has no consequence if too much money is printed or digitised.

Governments, for the most part, don't create wealth. In western economies, this is primarily the role of the private sector. Governments collect taxes and spend them for the good of the community. They can legitimately spend more in times of financial difficulty, to temporarily prop-up our economies. However, this cannot be overdone without consequences. The truth is that you and I are the ones borrowing, not the so-called governments. And guess who has to pay it back? Yes, you and I.

We as a community need to get our minds around the fact that governments largely spend the money we give them, and historically they have had limited profit motive to do this efficiently. They can print or borrow money, but if they do this to excess, just like us with our individual budgets, they can directly influence the financial viability of a nation.

With many economies broken by the Covid-19 pandemic, and unemployment rising, growth in money supply across the world has reached problematic proportions. We may see excess money creation as the thing that made our economies sick in the end, not the virus itself. Different nations have done different things, but an inability to find a sensible middle ground, based on unity and care for each other, may led us down a hole.

The truth is that we need everyone in the world to be healthy and financially well. Disunity disrupts all of us. If human beings were truly in it together, rather than focussed on maintaining our individual lifestyles, we could share more and care more about each other, rather than turning purely to the government with our hands out, expecting them to keep us in the lifestyle to which we have become accustomed.

As well as understanding, I also dream of a more responsible and realistic government, which can make sensible decisions in the bad times, not just the easy popular decisions that come from giving to everyone. Sharing is caring and it does not diminish us, just because our individual bank balances fall, even temporarily.

This can all change, but it can only do so when we have understanding and seek fairness from our governments.

9.1.6: Theft and cybercrime no longer exists

Human beings have long tried to steal from each other, first for survival and of course just to get rich fast. Who wants to work when you can get rich fast? Cyber-crime has come along in recent decades as a better way of criminals to grab money from us. They can sit in a foreign land and take money in huge quantities from unsuspecting victims.

I dream of a world where theft and cyber-crime are rare, because we are united and sharing resources far better.

Our wealth is diminished by what it costs to protect it from others. Why do we tolerate this? I dream of a world where this is not needed. If you have ever been to a country town, you will witness much less effort is made to lock cars and houses because trust exists between the locals. Imagine our cities being like this. Many readers will say that my head is in the clouds by even suggesting this is possible. However, if we all live from our hearts and drop our traditional conditioning, based on life being a competition where self-interest rules, a massive shift here is possible.

Again, it will take greater unity and sharing between us. You never know until you try! Your heart knows that this is right, if you listen closely enough. Am I correct?

9.1.7: Health services are fair for all

The Covid-19 pandemic has shown that we do not invest enough in our own health. Most people, if asked, will tell you that their health is more important than their wealth; but most of us live the other way around.

In a new world, where wellbeing trumps wealth, we would all have better health systems across the world, not just for the rich.

I dream of a more heart-based world, which would look to ensure health services for all human beings, prioritised and invested in properly. At the end of the day, how good is life when you are always chronically ill? It's not a great place to be. I can attest to that!

Can you imagine a world where genuine care and support was available, and you were not seen as weak because you are sick?

9.1.8: Workers are not slaves

I dream of a world where workers are valued as people, and not seen as expendable slaves or a means to an end.

Our leadership is weak when it comes to people management. The care factor that is spoken of is a fair-weather care. Leadership needs the guts to say 'no' to the analysts and stock markets that mark down its share price in tough times and support the people who really make their business run. Our leaders need to take a longer term and fairer attitude to the people who work for them, beyond the next profit announcement. Of course, if a rebound in business health is not possible over the long run, staff levels will require adjustment, but this can be done humanely, and not with a ruthless conversation and people escorted from the business with their belongings in a box.

The care and love of loyal staff needs to be respected, and any leader who can't do this and lead from their heart and mind, needs to be replaced or re-educated.

Staff matter as much as leaders, for without hard-working staff there are no roles for leaders.

How do you feel when you think of the organisation you work for, having a deep care and love for your welfare and valuing that on equal terms with money? Awesome, I suspect.

9.2: Social

Human beings are social beings, as well as individuals. We crave and need connection to be fulfilled. The Covid-19 pandemic has shown us how much we do need to interact with others. We cannot exist in isolation. Unity is the natural way to live.

The idea of being home on our own, or with our families, has been too hard for many to endure; and has ultimately helped the virus to prosper and spread, as they attempt to escape their isolation.

We need each other to be happy, yet our conditioned focus on self-interest is in direct contravention with this, and the collision between these two forces causes a battlefield of despair.

This can all be changed for the better. It's just a thought away.

9.2.1: People know themselves deeply

Self-awareness is the greatest gift you can give yourself, and thus your community. Those who truly know themselves and are able to take responsibility for their own lives, rather than blame others, can find greater joy in life and express that openly and directly. This then spreads into your community, into wider communities, and eventually the planet.

Anyone who sees you getting out of life what you put in, can then start making similar changes to their lives that align with what they want to experience. If every action has an equal and opposite reaction, then the way we treat others will be directly reflected in the way we are treated. If we live from love, we will be loved back. Can you expect others to love you and treat you with respect, if you don't love and respect yourself or others? As a rule the answer is 'no', unless all your friends are like Mother Theresa.

If we compete with others, fail to share, don't listen, separate ourselves from others, judge, and rate others constantly – guess what we will experience? The same in return. And for many in the world, this is currently life as they know it. Bitterness is a common emotion, because our lives have not turned out the way we had dreamt they would or should.

Imagine if we all woke up every day with a desire to be loving, follow our purpose, and experience joy? What if we all measured our life on our degree of fulfilment? What if we all saw our less-than-ideal outcomes as nothing more than learning opportunities and a chance for change? What if we all allowed ourselves to be our authentic selves, not manufactured versions of what we think society would like us to be? What a community that would be to live in and enjoy!

When we finally love ourselves, and give ourselves the chance for freedom of self-expression to descend upon our lives, we will see that the notions of success and failure vanish into the ether and are replaced by satisfaction and fun – for ourselves and everyone around us. Can you feel in your body the desire for this?

Imagine a whole community that lives this way, content and free of the constant need to have their egos stroked with praise, money, or compliments. Here we would discover a society living from a different operating system to the current mind-based model. This new society would live from the heart. It would feel as well as think, it would be intuitive, based on equality, recognise and understand the many different views and truths that make a society rich in contrast and fascination. Being humble would be easy, because we would all be equal and one big, potentially, happy family.

When we are *all* secure in who we are, unity becomes possible, not alienation and separation. Truth is born out of the lack of need to be right. Love can spring from the well of genuine care for ourselves, then each other. Happiness swings between love and freedom, as we all feel the balance of both – so true bliss can pervade our lives every day, as we each express to the outside world who we really are, while feeling safe and accepted as a whole.

Imagine always being in the moment where we are. Inauthenticity comes from being in a place we don't want to be in, doing something we don't want to do to please others. We all sense it. You can't hide it. Imagine if everyone in the office loved their work and had fun each and every moment, because the life force within them was inspired to experience the joy of the day's adventures, and the privilege of interacting with other human beings. Imagine our self-aware leaders becoming teachers above all else and showing others how self-awareness is gained and applied. Imagine self-awareness being encouraged in business, in our schools and in our homes, because its power is understood.

We will see great changes collectively once we allow our lives to lead us forward through wiser thinking and fresh belief structures. Love supported by logic is the answer, and to make this possible we can switch operating systems within ourselves, then show that to the world.

At present, generosity is often only expressed once we feel secure and safe. But is this real love? Many only give to others once they think they have enough to be safe and valid. Imagine when giving is just as common as receiving in our society.

Many of us currently see love as a way to safety. We need it to fill us up, for without it we are lost and lonely. Society says we must be in a relationship to be complete. Imagine a world where relationships are driven by want and desire, not neediness, checklists, or expectations.

When everyone knows themselves, this is where we will be. Can you picture your life in this wonderful place?

9.2.2: No need for excessive substances

Many people hide from life and find escape in drugs and alcohol. Drugs and alcohol can give you a brief high, but the height of the high is usually matched with an equivalent low.

I'm not saying any one thing should or shouldn't be banned. Like everything, if it's consumed in moderation, it has its place. If it's consumed for fun and not because you need it, that is a good way to be. For example, imagine a world where alcohol was not the basis of most adult social interactions. We encourage it in others, because many of us need it to have fun. Peer pressure to use alcohol is so destructive. It can ruin families and relationships. This peer pressure is another word for conditioning.

Imagine this conditioning replaced by self-security and a willingness to be real when we interact with others. This authenticity is the key to our society becoming more natural.

9.2.3: The return of extended families

I dream of more united families, born together and bonded together, not fragmented so life is easier and more efficient. How does the idea of that make you feel?

Many modern families struggle to balance work and family life, along with the desire to provide safe environments to care for our children while we are away working – yet there is an easy resource for this in our own retired parents.

Equally, the Covid-19 pandemic has shown how dangerous it can be to put our ageing relatives into aged care homes, whereas they could add greater love to family homes. Many parents, having struggled to raise their children without family support, see their own ageing parents as a burden in a time when they may be tired of care responsibilities. We may love them, but see them as a limiter, not a liberator, housing them in nursing homes, like unwanted possessions put in storage and visited on weekends, till they die.

But when families live from a place of collective love, they will give greater love to their ageing family members and include them more in their lives. They can both give and received to families.

Of course, there may eventually be a need for in-home support – for instance by nurses and the like – but this is likely to be cheaper than full time care by strangers in a money-making institution.

Where people need full time care because home care is not practical, then of course nursing homes are the best option. But apathy and a lack of respect – on both sides – are not valid reasons to export the value and love that active and involved grandparents can bring to a family. Open and authentic relationships can form the basis for this possibility.

9.2.4: Honest open media

At present people watch the media that they most trust or can afford. Our opinions often reflect the media that we subscribe to, however, most media sources are a microcosm of society. They want to win, as do their executives. They want the best ratings, the biggest profits, and salaries to match.

Imagine our media authentically in search of objective facts and opinions and respecting the myriad of perspectives or truths that circle our world. The polarity of opinion could be a source of compassion and compromise. But at present we see it as a source of anger: 'My media told me this, therefore it is the truth, and your media is wrong!'

I dream of news broadcasts full of balanced opinions and good news. It's possible, if we strive to live from a place of joy and do not need to see the pain of others to feel better about our own lives.

A happier world would see the media scratching around to find ugly stories to report, or better yet covering the happiness that abounds. Would you be more inclined to watch the news if it left you more joyous and not in fear of leaving your house?

9.2.5: Love is greater than money

I dream of a world where we put our love and health ahead of our finances. This doesn't mean money is not important. It just isn't love.

In this place we would put the love and health of our friends, family and children above our need to be successful. What good is money if we are lonely and miserable, sick and unhealthy, or don't know our own children? What kind of life do we create where we spend every waking hour trying to impress others with our perfection, houses, cars and holidays?

Our children and partners love us. They are not in love with our money, and therefore life is vastly improved when we give love to others, not cash.

I learned this through bitter experience, but I turned it around with no more than: fresh ideas!

Assumption is a killer of happiness. Imagine the regular sharing of honest desires and dreams in families. This is a good way to break the conditioning and brainwashing that currently exist within. I have learned to have authentic conversations with my children and it's incredibly positive. We all need to stop assuming that our kids want money more than our time, that our partners want a new kitchen more than emotional support or help with their dreams. If we all do that, perhaps more relationships will endure the test of time and be happy?

Money can help us to be fulfilled and happy, but it will only do so when we are authentic in our love and relationships, with ourselves and others.

Which do you prioritise most in your life: love or money?

9.2.6: Healthy relationships abound

Imagine a world where unconditional love is not only widely understood but is present. Imagine it being taught to our children and role-modelled by parents. Imagine a world where self-esteem was so high that we entered relationships to simply add to our joy, not to be a necessary ingredient of it. Imagine relationships that are built on want, not on need; with love based on acceptance, not judgement. Imagine total trust in relationships because both partners understand there is no love in control. Conversations could be based on true feelings. Priorities could focus on love not money. Fulfilment could be derived from the feelings in our hearts, not from our egoic measurements of success or failure.

Imagine if people knew that love could not be created from a checklist assessed by the mind or displayed on a website; and that looks and incomes do not define who you were capable of loving or being loved by. Imagine people realising love did come from their souls, and it cannot be manufactured; it just is, and we can't create it. Imagine a world where sexual pleasure was one of the greatest journeys available to a human being, and therefore not worthy of guilt even if the church has a negative or prudish view on that. Can you imagine lovemaking in your relationship that never fades or dies, in fact it just keeps getting stronger. This is possible. Remember, energy flows where your attention goes.

Society can get to the point where both men and women can give and receive equally in sexual experiences, without feeling judged. Imagine a world where orgasms did not need to be faked. Imagine a world where sexual partners can give and receive in equal measure and lovemaking can be an experience that lasts for hours, with orgasms experienced across your entire body. Tantric sex, if you wish to explore it, teaches how this can be mastered by lovers.

Imagine greater compassion, collaboration, and care in our relationships, for all genders and sexualities. Our children would be the great benefactors from healthier more loving relationships.

Domestic violence and sexual abuse have reached alarming heights in our society, normally perpetrated by men against women. Welfare organisations designed to help women would be in less demand.

Our children need better role models, to teach them how to love without fear, need and turmoil.

We owe it to them, but initially we as adults owe it to ourselves.

9.2.7: Crime, greed, and punishment

As I mentioned earlier, a change in beliefs to a society based less on competition and more on care and collaboration would see more sharing for each other. In such a place, crime, activities of greed (such as gambling), and the resulting law and order issues could abate. Happy people don't steal (unless they need to, to survive). Our courtrooms are full of people being tried each day, and our jails are full of people found guilty. Our communities are similarly full of people whose lives have been shattered by criminals.

When we reach a place of greater self-love and self-esteem, we will change our perspectives on punishment. When compassion replaces our need for revenge in the courts, we can move to a place of greater forgiveness. This doesn't mean offenders won't be punished. Accountability in society is important, and when we behave badly, we all need to face the consequences. The difference is, we will be more capable of forgiving an offender, and this will help them to be properly rehabilitated in love, not hate or fear.

Once a person does their time in jail, we need to give them a fresh start in life. We tag them with a criminal record and treat them with low or disrespect. No wonder so many ex-prisoners reoffend and end up back in jail multiple times. Our tendency to judge them harshly forever does not help matters.

9.2.8: Better use of technology in our lives

Our lives have become more and more based on technology for many things, from communication, to banking to entertainment. The days of communicating with merely our voices are long gone, replaced by texts, emails, and social media sites. We have become obsessed with information and knowledge about things outside ourselves.

Can you imagine knowing more about yourself, than people you've never actually met?

Entertainment is now so accessible on our devices: gaming, movies, television shows, gambling sights, Facebook, and Instagram are just a fingerprint or swipe away. We no longer need to live in the real world, because in seconds we can live inside the worlds of others or show them what we are doing. It's live, it's addictive, and it's often meaningless.

People are embracing technology for so many positive reasons. It gives us the ability to connect more widely with others and to communicate instantly. It gives us access to untold levels of information through the internet, which can be a wonderful timesaver.

When human beings begin to come home and live from their hearts, they will see many of the media outlets they are tuned into are mere distractions from their own lives; and they will see the joy that can be gained from looking into their own reality, not someone else's. Is watching someone else cook a meal, go on a date or renovate a building really that exciting? I am here to live my life, not live someone else's life through my television set. Do you feel a need to escape your own life by living someone else's? If you do, it may be time to go inward and do some self-discovery. Who you are may very well be covered up? It may be time to take that cover off.

Life is not a spectator sport, and we are wasting our valuable money and life-force watching others live, not being in our own reality. We need to replace the information age with the transformation age, and get to know ourselves. Why not replace YouTube with the reality of you?

Imagine if we used the time that technology saves us, to get out in nature, be with our families, listen to our own feelings or speak with another human being?

When we communicate person-to-person there is so much more that is possible in the communication, because our senses detect so much more than can be transmitted in text. Here we can feel the loving connection of another.

I dream of technology making our lives better, giving us more time for the things our hearts aspire to, as was promised 40 years ago when computers first appeared. But we have become slaves to them, rather than the other way around. We need to break our chains and be set free.

9.2.9: We will return to nature

When we drop our competitive obsession with winning and our need to make money, we will crave a return to a more natural way of living.

During the Covid-19 pandemic, there were signs of this starting to take place. If you can work remotely and don't need to live in a crammed expensive city to make money, why not live in a quiet, pretty rural or beach town where the air is fresh, the grass is green and there are less crowds? Sure, there may be less concerts and stadiums, but this can be offset with much lower travel time and a lifestyle close to nature. During the pandemic, concerts and stadiums have been closed to us anyway. But the beach rarely shuts down. Nature does not care about the state of the economy, it simply is.

When we see that we are a part of nature, it will become more common to extract ourselves from the crowded concrete-worlds we have inhabited. Are we about to see a re-birth of country towns, where you can become part of a community, grow your own food, and live in greater peace and safety further away from pandemics, traffic and crime?

Many country towns that have atrophied in the last 30 years could spring back to life, as we are called back to nature and a more relaxed and real way of life.

Can you see yourself living close to nature, but still able to work for your employer in the city? If so, how does it feel in your heart?

9.2.10: Holistic medicine will be more accepted

As human beings start to see the link between their subconscious pain and their cellular structures, they will turn more to holistic medicines to heal themselves.

We are yet to understand how many afflictions that impact on our bodies are self-imposed and have their resonance in our fears and regrets. After all, they are called diseases because they often stem from the unease in our minds.

When we are not being our true selves, our bodies effectively attack themselves. Any negative energies or fears we hold, in our conscious or subconscious minds, are directly reflected in our cellular structures. If we go inward and listen to our hearts and bodies, we may well be told what belief we are holding that is causing our pain.

As we release our fears, we can then move to a place of freedom from many (not all) forms of illness. I know this is hard to comprehend, but my experience has shown this to be true. As people start to live from their hearts and understand the potency of the energy of joy within them, they will take a more open mind to alternative types of medicines, and shy away from the drug-based, pill-popping culture readily pedalled by western medicine.

From my experience, the happier I have become, the less sickness I have had to endure. It's amazing! Why not come along on this journey?

9.2.11: Greater religious tolerance

Commensurate with a move away from judgement and the need to be right, I dream of a world free of religious tensions.

Google says there are 995 different names for 'God' in this world. How can this be? We are no clearer about divine knowledge than the ancient Greeks or Romans who worshipped multiple gods in ancient times!

But when we live from our hearts, we will come to terms with who we are as a race and discover that we are all one family from the same source. Until that day comes, I dream of a world that accepts everyone's right to practice whatever religious teachings they choose. Most religions carry positive messages that only do good. There is no reason why religions, if they need to exist, can't co-exist in harmony.

One day, human beings will see that the fastest way to access and take joy from universal energy, is through their hearts and not the church door. In this place, churches can play a more benevolent role, and not the role of wealthy businesses disguised as benevolent hope-givers and charities.

The ego of man has tapered with the wonderful intentions with which religious organisations were established. Of course, much good is done by churches; but, once humans see the light within their own hearts, they will become less reliant on the preaching of their local church. In its place, teachings will come from their own hearts.

9.2.12: Change is needed for transformation

When we go to our hearts as our operating system of choice, we will find that fear is cast aside and replaced by inspiration. In this place, a love of life takes over.

To advance as a world – and move towards a better loving and happy place – change will be necessary. We will need to let go or drop our excess baggage and pick up the new suitcases we will need in a more loving world. It's time we started packing our bags for this new destination – in our hearts and minds.

Money and material items will be replaced in many cases by wisdom and self-awareness, as our key assets in life. When we no longer need the things, we once relied upon, they will cease to have the value or importance we once placed upon them. Here we will need to be resilient and strong, and look to the horizon for a lighter, brighter future.

When one goes out to sea and is surrounded by water, or climbs a mountain to witness a new land, we must be prepared to live with few of our old reference points. We don't know what our future holds and this is the adventure our hearts revel in. Our minds may create fear of the change that's possible, but our hearts will allow us to forge into new places without fear, for this is their very essence. The only way to achieve this will be to approach the change with faith and unity. Life is an adventure, and we are here to challenge ourselves and be bold as much as possible. We are here to be on the field of play, not in the stands watching.

Would you prefer a life that is full of adventures and fun, or one where the ending is already known and dull?

9.3: Environmental

I am not a scientist or a qualified environmentalist, but like everyone I can see the big changes we can make to the way we treat our planet, when our beliefs shift for the better.

I dream that once we open our hearts to see that we are simply part of nature, and not separate from it, we will act differently towards the planet and its many inhabitants.

We may be different to some other beings because of our higher intelligence, but it makes us no better, just different. In fact, we probably have more chance to do harm to our planet than any other species, which act purely out of natural instinct.

When we see that we are just as reliant on this planet and all it provides to us, just like other flora and fauna, we will begin to show our home more respect and care.

Everything we own or use is made from materials derived from the Earth. Even the bodies we live in are made from natural substances found here on Earth, even metals. It is said that our bodies are made up substantially of water. We are influenced by the seasons, breath in the air around us, sunlight influences our sleep patterns, and everything we eat or drink is ultimately supplied by Mother Nature. We breathe in the purified air that trees breathe out. The list goes on. Once we get that we are just a part of the ecosystem of the Earth, we will treat it with the respect it deserves.

We can learn a lot from observing nature. The plants and animals around us follow their instincts. They don't carry grudges, they don't try and beat each other up unless it's necessary for survival, and they are in the flow of life with no regard for time. A tree does not compare itself to the tree next to it and lament its situation or try desperately to stop its leaves from falling. Even if the weather knocks it down, the tree moves on to its next role and becomes compost, or the light in a fire. It accepts its natural place.

Animals are the same. If you have ever owned a dog, you will witness their ability to love unconditionally. Even if you leave them alone for days on end, they will still wag their tails and love you upon your return. They don't resent you for days because you were busy elsewhere. They live for now!

The Earth is there to support us and has incredible resources for us to use into perpetuity, if we don't get greedy and overstep our mark. We need to look upon the

Earth as our home, not something that's available for exploitation. Would we treat our individual houses the way we do the Earth? Our disrespect for the Earth stems from our belief structures. Everything follows from our beliefs – everything!

I dream of a world where energy sources are sustainable and consistent with the long-term future of our planet. Greater investment in solar energy is a great example that could gather pace. Electric cars, less use of aircraft when other forms of communication are available, can assist us with preserving our home. But this transition needs to be made sensibly and from a place of unity, not self-interest.

As we come to grips with what we really need to be happy, our lower demand for luxuries and products designed to validate our very existence will allow us to reduce the natural resources we waste on unnecessary items. Simplicity follows from a different belief structure in which we seek fulfilment in happiness, not material possessions.

I dream of our society having changed beliefs, which will allow us to respect the animals and plants on the planet much more. We can take and use what we need, but we go much further than that at present.

I dream of a world where animals are not killed or abused just for sports, entertainment or out of ignorance. We are part of the cycle of life, just like the flora and fauna. They rely on each other for food, but they only eat what they need. We go way beyond this and eat other animals to satisfy our wants and pleasures. This is uncaring and will change once we see the arrogant and selfish belief structures that this entails.

I dream of a world where we know we are natural beings, and not some kind of aliens distinct from it. We are a part of nature. We need the Earth to survive, but it doesn't need us. When we become natural, we will know we are part of nature.

What if we became what nature intended, and care for our home as much as it cares for us? We are not landholders, because Mother Nature is holding us.

Is our modern world really modern? It will be when we live in harmony with nature and each other.

9.4: World order

The world order has been unstable for centuries. Wars, trade wars and the egoic separation of nations have plagued the world. This reflects our obsession with competition and winning, even at an international level.

We talk of developed and developing countries like they are unrelated and in competition, like everything else we rank them. But each nation should have the right to follow its own heart.

At the same time, when we see that we are all one big family – despite our different cultures, languages, and colours – the way we interact will change.

Wars will never be fought again. They need to be erased from the minds of man as ever being an option. The ego creates wars, not the heart. There is never a reason to kill another just to gain control of resources or land. We seem to believe it is acceptable to take lives for principle. Nothing justifies taking another person's life; nothing! I dream of the world being led by world leaders who care about human life, including in countries they don't even govern. It is ultimately up to us to put in power the people who are able to love other people and have collective interests in their hearts. Our leaders have been a microcosm of our belief structures. Our sense of separation, insecurity and acceptance of judgement and violence have manifested into leaders who fit this mould.

Many nations invest billions of dollars into what they call their defence budgets. For some countries this should be called their attack budgets, because their military hardware is there to ultimately provide the world power and influence their minds think they deserve. A nation living from its heart and mind would never think this way.

Meaningful sharing of resources across the globe is another activity that I dream will eventuate once we believe in unity and not separation.

The have and have not concept is alive and well, but is even starker on a worldwide level, because rich countries give lip service to helping those less fortunate. I dream of a world where genuine care and co-operation exists between nations, not competition for resources and wealth. Why should a child born in Africa receive inadequate education or food and water, while a child born in Australia has a mobile phone and iPad by the age of four?

I dream that this will change, once we see that we are all one big family. Would you allow your cousin or sister to die while you live in luxury? The sharing of resources and technologies needs to lift, and this will only do so when we really live from our hearts, and not from the egos that keep us trapped in our low level, dense desire, for money and importance. When will we see that we are all equal and have equal rights to the resources of the world?

The world structure is fragmented and variable with different countries exhibiting different laws, cultures, ideologies, and languages. This is acceptable because sovereignty is important at all levels. However, we do need a common belief structure based on love, compassion, unity and genuine care to bring the world together. Add to this: wise loving leaders – and you have the recipe for real happiness, peace and unity.

If all our belief structures were aligned, and world bodies had the unwavering support of world leaders and their populations, this would quickly manifest into a more equal world, where all nations were supported in the areas that matter. Currently, 400 million children live in war-torn countries and regions. Surely we need to stop this, both within nations and between them.

What I am advocating may seem unrealistic and far too hard to even consider. It's probably easier for us all to cross our fingers and focus on our own lives. But everything is just a belief or thought change away, and change can be rapid even across the world.

Did you come to Earth to be bold and give you and your children a better life? Or did you come here to bury your head in the sand, pretend that you are all that matters and fit in till you die?

This is what most of us subconsciously seem to believe.

CHAPTER

10

Concluding Remarks for Your Reflection

I have lived a relatively privileged life because of where I was born. Australia has been an amazing country in which to grow up. And yet in my life I have felt great personal suffering and unhappiness. Why?

The answer is very clear to me now. I fitted into a world that, deep in my heart, I did not want to fit into. By all definitions I was a success: tall, educated, well-credentialed, married (for long periods) with wonderful children, and a financially rich career.

But my success came from me achieving what my mind felt I needed to do and be to impress others, and therefore find security in life. My life was one of hard work, an obsession with time, and a focus on being a provider. I had deep disguised insecurities, invisible to those who were following the same path. I was truly in chains, not a world of happiness. My very being was inauthentic and out of step with the true me. I didn't really want half of the things I managed to attain; I simply got them to impress the rest of the world, but mainly those I loved, because this made me feel more loveable. I did not really like, let alone love myself, which is why I needed to feel loved and important in the eyes of others.

Little did I know, along the way, that I was out of alignment with what my heart wanted me to be and experience. This, I am still discovering each and every day and it's a great adventure. The last five years of listening has shown me that within my heart lies the wisdom for me to experience love, purpose, and a great sense of fulfilment, each and every day regardless of the circumstances.

I finally let go of what I thought I was and found my way back to my heart. This is where I am truly at home.

To know myself, and not the artificial Mark I thought I was, was possible once I dropped many of my old, conditioned beliefs.

Some say that this process of self-discovery is painful and brave. To me it was full of wonder, and I would not have missed it for the world, despite the occasional tears.

With the wisdom of my heart, and the wisdom of others who went ahead of me, I have got to the point where I am at peace with myself. I am now what nature intended, but in some ways, I am far from normal. I probably don't fit in to the norm easily anymore, but that's alright. I am finding my own herd of like-minded souls and speaking openly about myself whenever the right moments arise.

I never want to go back to what I once was, even if that person had admirers, more money, and seemingly fitted in. He was a dull perfectionist with a heavy heart, focussed on surviving not thriving, but he was very, very good at acting out the script written by others.

I am actually truly happy now, and loving life every day, even if life is more simplistic and I have no fancy title or fancy home.

I have written this book to share my journey of transformation, knowing that it will resonate with some people, and may help them to find a platform from which to investigate their own lives.

Some readers, on understanding my experiences and what I have learned, may have a light bulb moment, and recognise why they are not totally happy in their lives. They may see themselves following a similar pattern of self-destruction. After all, I think I was a typical person walking through life in a conditioned trance for many years. Perhaps after some self-reflection, these readers will work out what they want out of life and go out and get it!

There are many different paths you can take to find your mojo, and there are many people only too willing to help you find yourself.

But remember this: you are the only person who can ever know who you were intended to be or want to become. So, go inward and listen to your gut feelings and your heart, for they are fully versed in the answers, and you are the only person who can hear the music they are playing. Others can advise you, but never know the truth of you.

Our own individual worlds and that of our collective societies can shift once we find greater joy and happiness. This shift is exciting to contemplate. Be the change you want to see in the world and watch your outer world change for the better around you. We can all do this, and we must – for the sake of our own happiness and for the sake of the children who will follow us. It's time we created a natural world, not the so-called normal world we currently endure. The first step is for every one of us to become more natural.

I hope this book has shown you how critical it is to find the real you, and to express that in this world with no fear. You are here to have fun, be bold and be happy, not to worry or do what the forces of time and obligation impose upon you. You have options to choose from!

As I discovered, if you enter the code of happiness into your new operating system (i.e. your heart) and have the bravery to take steps forward, the ingredients for your happiness are waiting to be discovered. Your heart is desperate to tell you who and what you really are so you can transform your life and then the world around you. It's knocking on your internal doors, waiting for you to listen. I suggest you answer, as you alone have the key. Your heart has always known what makes you happy, so you will actually just be acknowledging what part of you already knows.

Happiness is no more than a habit and a choice, and our feelings and thoughts are the gateway to a lighter, brighter you. Be happy and inhabit a better habitat with just a change of mindset and a better understanding of who you were truly meant to be, not what others hoped you could be.

Consider whether any of my twenty-two preconditioned belief structures have held your life in states of fear. Then go inward to find your joy. Know yourself, then express that to the world around you with pride. In truth, your heart is the only place you will find this true joy. Turn over the rock that your happiness has been hiding under, and let your light radiate out for the world to see.

The ancient Egyptians, and other races, built pyramids partially to protect valuable golden artefacts and the wisdom that sat in the heart of the pyramid. This gold was encased in giant stones to protect them from the elements. When we as a race take away the heavy stones encasing our hearts, we will expose – for all the world to see – our true golden hearts full of light and love. It will be beautiful to behold and will be well worth the pilgrimage to our true selves, as I have described in this book and lived for myself.

Modern society is the culmination of humanity's history on Earth. Recent history is not really as wonderful as it could be. Our story needs to have a far more positive plot, based on collaboration and fulfilment, not competition and obligation. Our future as a race is arriving in every present moment. We need to be present, and not living in the future or the past so we can feel it and enjoy it. Be your happy loving self, for it is why you are here.

As a race, we can be comforted by the fact that forgiveness and compassion can heal all the wounds we may have inflicted on each other. Love can remove the scars if we allow it to flourish.

Greater self-awareness is the key to help us create a more pleasant story for all, as our futures unfold. Know yourself, and happiness is well within your grasp.

As you know, you grow, and like a flower in the soil, you can only grow where you are in any given moment. So forget the need to be somewhere else to be happy, and just be present where you are now.

The messages I provide in this book are closely aligned with many thoughts made famous by the English rock band, the Beatles. When we go inward to find the love, we already have for ourselves, we will see that: 'All You Need Is Love'. Once we find the glow in our hearts and 'Let It Be', we will be able to say, 'Here Comes The Sun'.

We can strive to achieve all we like in life, but it's not what will truly make us happy. I challenge you to feel this, not think it. We need nothing in life other than simple essentials and our own love and the happiness it gives us. From this magical place you will see that anything and everything is possible because fulfilment becomes our key goal in life. Here we care less about what we become, because it doesn't define us.

Miracles do happen, but the path of love and truth is the only way to the light that is our birthright.

The irony of life is that, when we need nothing, we get everything because we stop setting expectations that only act as the enemy of fun. It's time we transcended our need to be certain and lived in the mystery of life.

The views in this book are not a fantasy. They are the basis of a fantastic change we can all enjoy.

Once you find where your happiness hides, you can take the journey that it alone guides. It's ready to shine a light on the path you truly desire to follow. Be brave and open the gate to find the adventure that awaits you.

It's time to live in wonder, not worry. It's wonder-ful.

APPENDIX I

A Checklist to Guide Readers' who want to Do More SELF-Investigation

If you have read this book, perhaps it has sparked your interest in investigating ways to make your life happier.

I am walking proof that giving up is not an option! Happiness is within you already, if you take the steps to discover it.

Set out below is a framework of ideas and questions you can begin to consider on your journey to better self-awareness and finding the happiness that to date may have eluded you. Feel your way into your responses, rather than think them.

Conditioning

- Consider the environments you have grown through in your life, including your family:

  - Who were the key influencers of your life, such as a parent or teacher?
  - In what ways were you encouraged or forced to fit into a certain way of living?
  - What did you adopt in your life that you copied from your family or societal culture?
  - Were you ever punished for not being like those around you or meeting their expectations?
  - Which of the twenty-two core limiting beliefs in this book, and/or the associate conditioned beliefs, resonated with you and/or made you feel emotional?
  - Do you have the opportunity to discuss these with a partner, colleague, friend or family member? If so, go ahead and instigate that conversation. Now, how did their reactions to your thoughts make you feel?
  - Can you see how the conditioning that applies to your life caused you to direct your life in a less than ideal way?
  - What parts of your life do you feel have been less happy or joyful than you would have hoped? What do you think these less-than-ideal moments have taught you about yourself, and what you could do differently in the future?

- Can you observe how your conditioned beliefs are mirrored in others around you, and what impact do you think and feel this has had on the various parts of your life, your job or the society in which you inhabit?
- What are the major fears in your life, and have you ever tried to overcome them?

- Which of the following factors in your life are linked to your feelings of unhappiness:

  - Your sense of self-worth
  - Your propensity to self-sacrifice your life to make others happy
  - A lack of money or resources
  - Your need to always be right
  - Your perfectionism
  - Your inability to build the kind of relationships you desire
  - Your lack of time
  - Your obsession with making money or providing for others
  - Your lack of sovereignty or independence
  - Your sense of being judged or needing to judge others
  - Your exposure to inequality or sexual impropriety
  - Your struggles with your romantic relationships or family
  - Your interactions with bad leaders
  - Your lack of access to nature
  - Your fear of death
  - Your addiction or compulsion with technology and the information it offers

Are any of these areas calling for you to face pain from the past, or to release your expectations of the future?

Knowing yourself

- How much effort have you made in your life to get to know your deepest wants and desires?
- Have you suppressed or ignored dreams because you thought they were not practical, or you thought others would criticise them?
- Do you generally honour your feelings and emotions, or do you try and suppress them, and listen to your logical mind in making decisions?
- How impulsive are you in life, or do you live with a checklist or plan with which you must comply?
- What parts of your life would you consider boring or scary, and hence you would like to change them?
- Do you still carry regrets or scars from your perceived failures in life?
- Do you have a need to be important rather than potent and happy?

- When you were a child, what did you like to do and/or gave you great passion in your life? Have you ever felt a desire to return these to your life?
- What hobbies or activities excite you when you think about getting involved with them?
- Do you believe you are worthy of being the real you, and who do you think would oppose you changing your life to become the real you?
- What benefits do or would you receive from becoming your true self?
- Have you ever experienced the power of meditation?

Expression of your truth

- What barriers do you think stand in the way of you becoming the real you?
- What key aspects of your life would need to shift to enable you move to become the real you?
- How do you think you would feel, after you have taken steps to express your truth in the world?
- What does your true tribe of like-minded people feel and look like?

ACKNOWLEDGEMENTS

Firstly, I would like to thank you, the reader. I am honoured that you have spent your valuable time (and perhaps money) considering the ideas I have put forward in this book, and I hope that you have found them valuable.

My special thanks go to the dedicated people who have helped to make this book a reality. As a first-time author, I am humbled by the trust that has been shown in my work.

Zena Shapter, my wonderful editor, has applied her amazing gifts to bring further light and sparks of love to the words, to enhance the experience of my readers. From the beginning she was passionate about the purpose of the book and its content and added enthusiasm and professionalism to the process of the book's creation.

Andrea Gussy, my producer and coordinator, has gone above and beyond, to type and prepare this entire book from my handwritten notes and added all the illustrations and diagrams as they came forth. By doing what she does best, making things happen, she has allowed my original manuscript to be manifested into this book.

Bill Shapter, a gifted graphic artist, and my internal diagram creator did a wonderful job turning the visions in my head into real pictures. This has added much to the messages and stories in the book. His creativity and efficiency brought great gifts to the process.

Azari Da Roza, my illustrator extraordinaire, created the book cover and brought light to its contents with the fun illustrations at the start of each chapter. She did this with grace, patience, and intuitive creativity. Her work has done much to align the book with the personal journey I took, and the happiness this book seeks to create.

Sue Thompson provided great insights and wisdom to guide the awareness put forward in this book, and also assisted me by providing an extra layer of review prior to the book's publication. She is truly a remarkable woman, and her abilities deserve greater prominence in this world. I have been blessed to work with her on the project and on my own awareness.

I also thank my family for their encouragement and support during the compilation and creation of the book. My five children watched me change careers, conduct my research, and spend hours writing this book when, at times, they must have thought I had lost my mind. In some ways, they were right because I had finally found my heart. I hope my actions have taught them the importance of being true to their hopes and dreams in their own lives.

Finally, I thank all the souls who have interacted with me during my life. By being with me to experience the many steppingstones of love and life, they have given me the opportunity to grow and glow, then convert this understanding and joy into 'Where Your Happiness Hides'.

Thank you all from my whole heart and mind.

ABOUT MARK WORTHINGTON (AUTHOR)

Mark Worthington

Mark Worthington, the author of this book, has lived most of his life in Sydney, Australia.

Up until the age of 57, he followed a traditional and unspectacular path as an accountant and auditor, working first in professional practice, then in a series of large financial services organisations. A safe existence you might say.

At 57, he embarked on a journey of personal discovery, because the pain he felt, from feeling imperfect in life, because of various perceived failures, was too much to endure any longer. By facing, rather than running from this pain, he found the truth that would change his life forever.

His limiting beliefs were the architect of his own unhappiness. They made him sick, sad and led him to deny himself the fun and happiness that was truly his birthright as a human being. He was out of alignment with his true self.

Today he is a lighter, brighter version of Mark. Knowing who he truly is, and the self-awareness that brought, has freed him up to live with joy and wonder, not worry.

This book will show you what's possible when you transcend the need for certainty and security and see life as the adventure it can be.